D1511561

solo verdura

also by Anne Bianchi

From the Tables of Tuscan Women: Recipes and Traditions
Zuppa! Soups from the Italian Countryside

solo verdura

The Complete Guide to Cooking Tuscan Vegetables

Anne Bianchi

Photographs by
Douglas Hatschek

THE ECCO PRESS

Copyright © 1997 by Anne Bianchi
Photographs © 1997 by Douglas Hatschek
All rights reserved

THE ECCO PRESS
100 West Broad Street
Hopewell, New Jersey 08525

Published simultaneously in Canada by
Penguin Books Canada Ltd., Ontario
Printed in the United States of America

Library of Congress Cataloging-in-Publication Data
Bianchi, Anne, 1948-
        Solo verdura : the complete guide to cooking Tuscan vegetables / Anne Bianchi ;
    photographs by Douglas Hatschek. —1st ed.
            p. cm.
        Includes index.
        ISBN 0-88001-543-8
        1. Cookery (Vegetables). 2. Cookery, Italian—Tuscan style.
    I. Title.
    TX801.B53   1997
    641.6'5'0945—dc21   97-9344

Designed by Susanna Gilbert, The Typeworks
The text of this book is set in Diotima

9   8   7   6   5   4   3   2   1

FIRST EDITION 1997

Contents

In memory of John,
my friend and
longtime guardian angel

Acknowledgments

There are times when I feel I must thank all of the Lucchesía for help in compiling material. Certainly, it is the spirit of the area, its generosity, its very essence that serves as my continuing muse. But there are also certain key people who give the muse an extra little jolt and to these, I offer my deepest *ringraziamenti*.

First, the usuals: Douglas Hatschek, not only for the photographic images that bring my stories to life, but for his patient readiness whenever I announce at 6:30 A.M. on a Wednesday morning that, by 8, we have to be in Barghecchia to photograph a *vendemmia*; to my mother, whose lifelong love affair with vegetables imprinted on me at an early age; to Amerina Castiglia for her continuing efficiency in spotting every Italian word where I've added an extra "r" or forgotten the accent mark (*grazie mille*); to Tom Gelinne for bringing his Minnesota-bred powers of scrutiny to the thankless task of checking my recipes (thank you thank you thank you); to Sandra Lotti, co-owner of *The Toscana Saporita Cooking School*, writer/researcher extraordinaire and one of only two people I know who has, at her fingertips, the answers to every conceivable question.

I also want to thank my cousins (Ombretta, Paolo, Alessio, Reno, Alfredo, Tina, Morena, Serenella, Mauro, Renza, Daniela, Adriana, and, of course, Loredana), my friends (Allesandra, Roberto, Assunta, Tiziano, Lucy, Diane, Doris, Micky, and most especially, Marco—*il tempo cambia; l'amici, mai*), everyone connected with Camporomano and *Toscana Saporita* where I do much of my recipe testing—especially Ugo, Elena, Gianfranco, Mariano, and Teresa; and all the wonderful people at The Ecco Press—Judy Capodanno, Mary Jane Cratty, Allegra D'Adamo, Jacqui Brownstein, Gail Feinberg, Martha Davis, and, of course, Daniel Halpern.

To all of you, *un grande abbraccio*.

Introduction

It has been said that the character of Tuscans is most evident in their food; that only by carefully observing the nature of what they bring to the table can we gain insight into their notorious penchant for perfectionism and parsimony. Sample the simple elegance of new spring onions basted with olive oil and grilled to perfection and you will undoubtedly agree. The dish is, without question, as close to perfect as food can get. And yet the ingredients and preparation are simple in a way that elevates parsimony to the apex of virtue.

Tuscans are not shy about lauding their cuisine. "The best in the world," you will be told again and again if you spend any time at all in this fair region. While few people have ever expressed any doubt (especially following a plate of *tagliatelle* with fresh *porcini* mushrooms), those claims have now gained the support of the health industry which recently declared Mediterranean cooking to be "among the world's healthiest." A report issued by the National Institute of Health cited Italy's "heavy dependence on fresh fruits, vegetables, grains and olive oil" and its "minimal use of red meat and almost total exclusion of saturated fats and prepared foods" as prime reasons for the healthful nature of its cuisine.

Although that description can certainly be applied to many of the country's regional cuisines, the concept of healthy eating reaches its gastronomic peak in Tuscany where cooks are blessed with both an abundance of fresh seasonal ingredients and a philosophy that venerates the excellence of honest, traditional food—often humble, rarely elaborate. The Medicis may have dined opulently, but today's Tuscans are known throughout Italy as *mangiafagioli*—"bean eaters," a reference not only to a love for all kinds of beans and bean dishes but to a culinary dependence on the simplicity of vegetables.

It is easy to be a vegetarian in Tuscany, although few people would identify themselves as such. Walk into any restaurant or trattoria and the menu literally brims with *contorni*—freshly prepared vegetable dishes ranging from radicchio sautéed in olive oil and garlic to artichokes stuffed with parsley pesto to asparagus drizzled with a mustard vinaigrette. *Contorni* means contours, which is how

Tuscans see the role of vegetables: as establishing the parameters for the remainder of the meal's ingredients.

And yet no one will actually ever say, "I am a vegetarian." I suspect the reason has more to do with the Tuscan aversion to limits of all kinds than to any great appetite for meat. The fact is that when included at all, meat is either served in small, thin slices surrounded by vegetables or used as a flavoring agent in soups and stews. In my house, my mother ate only vegetables, and as a result, so did I until food became a career and my diet expanded to include a little bit of everything. Vegetables are still my culinary passion, however, which is why I decided to make this a book solely about vegetables.

When I first began testing recipes, I scribbled copious notes under columns headed "Color," "Texture," "Fragrance," "Appearance," and "Flavor." One day, I saw my friend Alba inspecting my workbook with great consternation. "Who cares about color and appearance?" she asked after quite some time. "All that really matters is flavor!"

No, *cara*. Flavor is not the be-all and end-all when it comes to vegetables. Certainly, it is of major importance whether a dish tastes good or not. But when I sit down at the table I like to feed my other senses as well. I like to gaze upon a palette of colors pleasing to my eye, to delight in a food's aromatic essence before even placing anything between my lips, to feel on my tongue a satisfying array of textures.

Vegetables lend themselves especially well to this holistic approach. As a matter of fact, I suspect that one of the reasons I favor them above all other foods is precisely their amazing diversity. Brilliant purple peppers. Virgin white eggplant. Crisp green beans. Creamy roasted garlic. Bitter broccoli rabe. Sweet caramelized onions. Pungent white truffles. There is simply no limit to the colors and flavors and textures and smells.

When my cooking school is in session, the students and I spend a great many mornings at local markets evaluating the various vegetables for possible inclusion into that day's meal. "Just look at these squash blossoms," one might be moved to gush. "The colors and the crispness!" "How about these mushrooms," another will counter, his nose pressed against an earthy golden cap. "They smell as if they were just plucked from the forest floor!" *Obviously,* that day we are going to prepare risotto with *porcini* mushrooms and squash blossoms stuffed with herbed shallots and whatever else we find that entrances us beyond our ability to just walk on by.

These almost-daily forays into local markets simulates perfectly the Tuscan way of living which is largely focused around what one will eat that day. Tuscan markets pulse with activity, day in and day out. There is no such thing as buying a week's worth of produce and storing it in the refrigerator. If Signora Velia Angeli serves braised red cabbage for lunch on Tuesday, you can safely assume she purchased that cabbage earlier the same day. If there is any left over . . . well, it might be fed to the dog, but I'm not sure even dogs in Tuscany eat leftovers.

The Tuscan way with vegetables was born of poverty and thrift, and, as a result, many of the recipes in this book are simple and straightforward. Others were influenced by Italy's *nuova cucina* movement which has taken classic Tuscan preparations and given them a lustrous new identity. While the comparisons to France's *nouvelle cuisine* are many, I must insist on one great differentiation: *nuova cucina* still delivers enough food to constitute a satisfying meal. Tuscans *love* to eat, and no movement that espouses artistic minimalism as a culinary goal would ever pass muster. As the old proverb states so beautifully: Gluttons demand quantity. Epicures quality. Tuscans both.

As with my other books, I have attempted to give you the flavor of a people as well as of a food. All recipes are, in a sense, journeys, and what journey would be complete without getting to know the area's inhabitants? Certainly, Americans' enduring love affair with Tuscan food has to do with more than the ingredients and preparations employed. Is it not a grand panoply of factors including climate, landscape, attitude, and, yes, people?

By way of hammering home this point, allow me to recount the story of Lucullus, the great Roman general who spent the latter part of his life ensconced in a sumptuous Tuscan villa. Lucullus, it seems, loved to host grandly, and every one of his dinner parties cost what would now amount to about $1,200 per person. One night, however, he informed the chef of his plans to dine alone, and that unfortunate man presented a dinner that cost only about $500. Severely scolded for his decision, the chef defended himself as best he could. "But you were alone," he reasoned. To which Lucullus replied, "Take special pains at those moments, for then Lucullus is host to Lucullus."

Now then, does that story not color your preparation of the recipe on page 93? Does it not make you more likely to infuse the food with a certain care and dignity? I rest my case.

But more than just introducing you to Tuscans at large, I have, in this book, made a special attempt to introduce you to a great many members of my immediate family—to my cousin Adriana and her desire to open a health spa, to cousin Mauro and his absurd feelings about Pellegrino Artusi, to my mother and her daily trips to the cemetery to clean and polish the marble. It is my way of enhancing the very intimate process of sharing recipes, my way of including you in one of our huge dinner parties where you will sit with me and my family around a long wooden table hoisting our glasses in one grandly clamorous *cin cin*.

I look forward to sitting next to you.

Some Notes on this Book's Organization

The vegetables I have chosen to include in this book are only those one would find in Tuscan markets. There are no sweet potatoes, for example, nor is there corn (except in the form of polenta). On the other hand, I have also not included typically Tuscan greens such as *braschette* which is a wonderful cabbage-like leaf not available in U.S. markets. When shopping, I have repeatedly stressed, you should think like a Tuscan and demand only the freshest, most perfect of vegetable specimens. The quality of produce throughout Tuscany is without parallel and remains the all-important key to successfully reproducing any of the recipes that follow.

After every recipe, I have included some information on the amount of time each will take to prepare and the level of difficulty:

EASY: Involving a minimal number of directions and simple
   preparations
MODERATE: Involving a number of directions but no difficult
   techniques or preparations
ADVANCED: Involving one or more techniques or preparations that
   require prior knowledge or experience

I've also offered variations that can be employed and indicated which steps can be done ahead of time. In no way should you limit yourself to my suggested variations. Tuscan cooking is nothing if not open to infinite experimentation. Take many liberties and remember to guide yourself not only by taste, but by smell, feel, look, and attitude.

Beginning every recipe chapter is a list of the vegetables included in that section and some botanical history as well as practical information on buying and preparing. The first actual recipe page is called Quick and Easy and lists basic yet delicious ways to prepare individual vegetables. Instead of devoting entire pages to exquisitely simple recipes such as baby green beans drizzled with extra-virgin oil, for example, I have presented it along with a number of other very basic cooking techniques (generally my favorites) on one narrative page. The vegetables themselves are grouped according to type (pods, seeds, tubers, roots) and include many that, while mainstays of the Tuscan kitchen, are just beginning to gain popularity with Americans (salsify, cardoons, fava beans, fennel). All the vegetables featured in this book are available in the United States.

The first two chapters are devoted to basics. Chapter 1, "Essentials," operates on the theory that it is hard to get started if you do not have the proper equipment and ingredients—the pots and pans and knives and herbs and oils and cheeses required to do justice to Tuscan vegetable cuisine. Chapter 2, "Techniques," is devoted to explaining the various methods for cooking vegetables in the hope of fostering a certain amount of culinary autonomy. It is one thing to perfectly recreate a recipe for braised red cabbage with apples and chestnuts; how much better to so thoroughly understand the mechanics of braising as to decide to substitute artichokes for cabbage and eliminate the apples in favor of shallots.

The last chapter is a collection of basic preparations used throughout the book: sauces, broths, pastas, pizza dough, and pestos. In addition to serving as the essential element in specific recipes, these techniques can be adapted in infinite variations limited only by your imagination.

I intended this book to serve as a complete source for Tuscan vegetable cookery, from what to purchase to how to prepare it and why. My hope is that you will become very Tuscan in your love and respect for the most wondrous of the earth's bounty.

solo verdura

CHAPTER ONE

Essentials

This chapter deals with what you must have on hand in order to get started: the cooking equipment, the pantry staples, the herbs and spices, the knowledge about when to buy and how to store. *"Prima ti fornisci,"* an old woman I know used to say. *"Dopo fai."* First you equip yourself, then you do. Unfortunately, there seems to be a divergence of opinion among Tuscan cooks as to what exactly is meant by "equipping oneself." Many are those who pride themselves on having one knife, one pot, one skillet, and—maybe—a cutting board. Truth be told, the food they produce is just as marvelous as that emanating from designer kitchens—sometimes more so.

My very first group of cooking school students can speak with great eloquence on the pros and cons of a bare-bones kitchen. Initially, the cooking school was to be up and running in the spring of 1995. But the previous October, a small group of women made us an offer we couldn't refuse. Let us be your "test" group, they said. Charge us less, and we'll serve as a sounding board whenever something needs fine-tuning.

The problem was, our kitchen had not yet been completed. Hence, the lessons would have to be conducted in the kitchen belonging to Contessa Elena Pecchioli, who owns the estate that houses the school. On first inspection, the kitchen seemed large, lovely, and possessed what looked like all the necessary equipment. "Fine," we said, and a few weeks later the women were on our doorstep.

It turns out there were severe shortages in the equipment department. What knives there were had not been sharpened since the days when the Contessa's ancestors ruled Lucca. The cutting boards were warped, the sauce pans had no lids, and vegetable peelers were a nonexistent entity. "We'll cook like the average

Tuscan," said my Tuscan partner, Sandra, with a perfect market-savvy smile. And, in fact, that's exactly what we did, holding the vegetables in our left hands and dicing them with small knives held in our right. ("Reminds me of my Russian grandmother," said one of the students. "That's the way Babba always cut everything.") It all worked, and the food turned out better than anyone could have imagined.

Make no mistake about it, however. It is far easier to cut carrots when you have a vegetable peeler, a cutting board, and a good, sharp, 8-inch chopping knife. And so, with that in mind, the following pages contain a bare-bones listing of items and informational gems that I consider as essential as Parmigiano on pasta. Don't run out and buy everything at once. You can do without a mandoline until you learn to slice with a simple cook's knife.

Kitchen Equipment

Knives

A knife is one of the most important tools, and you should make sure it is well constructed. The extension of the blade seated in the handle of the knife is called a tang. It may go the full length of the handle or only half way. The best-quality, most durable knives have a full tang, which means that the tang runs the full length of the handle. In good knives, the tang is also held in the handle by rivets; this is the most durable construction. Some less expensive knives have a short "rattail" tang secured by friction or cement to the handle. These tend to work loose quite quickly.

A full tang puts weight into the handle and helps to balance the blade. The point of balance should be on the blade, just in front of the handle. To test whether your knife is properly weighted, balance the knife on your finger, using the point where the blade meets the handle as your fulcrum. The knife should neither tilt towards the blade nor the handle.

Two kinds of steel are used in knife blades: carbon steel and stainless steel. Either kind must be of high quality to take a sharp edge. Carbon steel is easier to sharpen but rusts and stains easily. To remove stains, rub the blade of a carbon steel knife with a soft cloth dipped in scouring powder; then wash the blade in warm water and dry.

Stainless steel knives are shinier than carbon steel and, as the name suggests, resistant to most stains. High-carbon stainless steel is a relatively new alloy that combines the best aspects of carbon steel and stainless steel. It takes an edge almost as well as carbon steel, holds the edge longer, and will not rust, corrode, or discolor. Knives made of this material are highly prized and relatively expensive.

There are a few general rules for taking care of knives. Use a knife only on a wooden cutting surface (refer to the cutting board section for a discussion on plastic cutting boards) and only for the proper job. Do not use a good kitchen knife for cutting string or paper or for prying off lids. Do not let the blade enter a direct flame, as this ruins the temper of the steel. Knives should be washed and dried after using but not in a dishwasher. Store knives separately, either on a magnetized knife rack or in slotted holders which sheathe the blade. Never leave them loose in a drawer.

For maximum efficiency, sharpen your knives periodically. You can take them to a professional knife sharpener or grind them yourself using an electric sharpener, a stone, or a sharpening steel. An electric sharpener is easiest and efficient but wears away too much of your expensive knife and does not make as good an edge. A stone gives the sharpest edge, but, in most cases, what you generally need is either to *true* the edge—perfect it or smooth out irregularities—or to *maintain* the edge—keep it sharp as it is used. Both require the use of a sharpening steel which, when used often, minimizes the need to sharpen your knives on a stone.

THE KNIVES YOU NEED

Your skill at handling a knife should determine what knives you use. A skilled cook can make the 10-inch wide-bladed cook's knife do almost any kitchen job; an old Tuscan grandmother can do the same with a 4-inch parer. But for most people, a better all-purpose knife is the 8-inch cook's knife which is small enough for most jobs and easy to handle.

Here are some suggestions for a basic knife collection:

Paring knife: 3 to 3½ inches; for light jobs—peeling, paring, and cutting small fruits and vegetables.

Utility knife: 5 to 7 inches; for heavier jobs—peeling, paring, and chopping large fruits and vegetables, and meat trimming.

Chopping knife: wide, 8 to 10 inches; for chopping, mincing, and dicing fruits, vegetables, and meats.

Narrow slicer: 8 to 10 inches; for slicing cheese, cold meat, and poultry.

Bread knife: 10 inches, serrated edge.

SLICING VEGETABLES

While it is easily possible to roll along through life with mediocre knife skills and still be considered an excellent cook, proper slicing and dicing techniques make the job easier and more successful (in that uniformly cut foods cook more evenly). And furthermore, you look better when you cut with a fast, steady rhythm.

The first rule with respect to proper cutting technique is to hold your knife correctly. Thumb and forefinger should be placed on opposite sides of the blade just in front of the guard when cutting something that needs pressure as well as degree of precision—cubing carrots or making equal strips of pasta, for example. Holding the knife this way may feel awkward at first, but practice will make it seem natural.

To make a basic cut, hold the vegetable with one hand, thumb tucked behind and fingers in a claw-like position. Hold the knife in the other hand, at a sharp angle, with the tip on the cutting board. The blade should then slide up and down against the middle joints of your first two fingers as the edge cuts into the vegetable. Move your vegetable-holding hand back with each slice and follow it with the knife, keeping as close as possible.

BASIC CUTTING TECHNIQUES

1. *Cubing:* Cut slices into strips ½ inch or more wide, gather them together, and cut them across into neat little cubes.

2. *Dicing:* Cut the food into strips ⅛ to ¼ inch across. Line up and stack strips; cut crosswise to form pieces.

3. *Chopping:* Cut the food into irregularly shaped pieces.

4. *Julienning:* Cut food into slices about 2 inches long and ⅛ to ¼ inch thick. Stack the slices and then cut lengthwise again to make thin, matchlike sticks.

5. *Mincing:* Cut into tiny, irregular pieces. Use the largest, heaviest cook's knife available. With one hand lightly holding the handle and the other counterbalancing it across the back of the blade near the tip, rock the knife rapidly up and down over the food to be minced. Gather the bits together from time to time with the flat of the blade and repeat cutting until all is finely minced.

Other Cutters and Choppers

There are many efficient small tools and machines to help you in cutting and chopping. Here are some of the most useful:

Peeler: The swivel action pares vegetables very thinly and also follows the contours of the bumpiest potatoes quite closely. The best have carbon steel blades.

Mandoline: A mechanical slicing machine that enables you to slice firm vegetables very rapidly. The best ones have supporting struts to hold at an angle and extra blades for various cuts as well as corrugated blades for making such things as latticed potato chips. To use, you place the mandoline in front of you facing forwards, hold the vegetable firmly, and pass rhythmically across the blade using the heel of your hand to push. Mandolines are easy to use, clean, cheaper than food processors, and have the advantage of being able to slice the food rather than crush it.

Mezzaluna: These half-moon-shaped two-handled cutters have large blades that you manually roll from side to side over vegetables on a board. Mezzalunas take a bit of getting used to, but once you have mastered the technique you'll be very pleased with your ability to chop quickly and to various degrees of fineness. Double-bladed mezzalunas chop twice as fast as single blade ones; they also come with three blades.

Food mill: A food mill is a simple machine with a handle, a large perforated bowl, and a blade-like paddle attached to a central hand crank. On many models, the paddle is connected by a central screw fitted with a wire spring on the underside that turns close to the bowl. The wire spring scrapes off the puree as the paddle presses it through the bowl's straining plate. Some inexpensive models have one permanent plate, but the better ones have three interchangeable plates with holes in graduated sizes. Most food mills have hooks that allow the machine to rest on the bowl or pot that will catch the puree, but some are freestanding with suction pads on the base. Food mills come apart for easy cleaning and are simple to reassemble.

A food mill simultaneously purees and removes fibers without incorporating air, as food processors and blenders do. While food processors are ideal for making mayonnaise, vinaigrette, and other emulsions, vegetable sauces and purees become unpleasantly foamy when blended in this manner.

Food processor: These have their pros and cons. The two biggest cons are that food processors are often used for pureeing things that should be passed through a food mill, and that, by doing so, they not only create less than tasty food, but compromise the intimacy that would otherwise signal the very best part of the cooking process (an intimacy without which it is virtually impossible to become a truly great cook). The pros are that it enables you to do many *nuova cucina*-type things that bring a certain elegance to your preparations and would otherwise be too tedious to contemplate. Thickening a soup or a stew, for example, has traditionally been done with flour and butter, but with a food processor you can puree vegetables and use the mash as a thickening agent.

The best food processors have very quiet, strong, constant-speed induction motors. But these are significantly more expensive than the popular brand types which rely on a series of far noisier motors that tend to vibrate and slow down when confronted with resistance of any kind.

Pots and Pans

METALS AND CONDUCTIVITY

A good cooking utensil should distribute heat evenly and uniformly. If it does not, it will develop hot spots that are likely to burn or scorch the food being cooked. Two factors affect a pan's ability to cook evenly. First, the *thickness* of the metal. A heavy-gauge pot cooks more evenly than one made of thin metal. Thickness is most important on the bottom. Second, the *kind* of metal. Different metals have different conductivity which refers to the speed at which they transfer heat. The following materials are used for pots and pans:

1. *Aluminum* is the most-used metal. It is a very good conductor, and its light weight makes pots and pans easy to handle. Because it is a very soft metal, it should not be banged around or abused. Aluminum should never be used for storage or for long cooking of strong acids, because it reacts chemically with many foods. Also, it tends to discolor light-colored foods such as sauces, especially if they are stirred or beaten with a metal spoon or whisk.

Pans made of anodized aluminum, sold under brand names such as Calphalon, have harder surfaces that are more resistant to corrosion than regular aluminum pans. Although not strictly a no-stick finish, anodized aluminum is less porous than untreated aluminum, so foods are less likely to stick. Also, it is more resistant to acids than regular aluminum and will not discolor light-colored foods. However it is much more expensive and not quite as durable as standard aluminum.

2. *Stainless steel* is a poor heat conductor, and pots and pans made of it tend to scorch food easily. Stainless is ideal for storage containers, however, because it will not react with foods, as aluminum does. It is also useful in low-temperature

cooking, such as steaming, where scorching or hot spots are not a problem.

Stainless steel pots and pans are also available with a heavy layer of copper or aluminum bonded to the bottom. This feature gives you the advantages of stainless steel (its hardness, durability, and the fact that it does not react with acid foods or discolor light sauces) as well as the heat-conducting qualities of copper or aluminum. These pans are usually expensive.

3. *Copper* is the best heat conductor of all and was once widely used for cooking utensils. However, it is extremely expensive and requires a great deal of care. Also, it is very heavy and, today, used mostly for show. Copper reacts chemically with many foods to create poisonous compounds, so copper pans must be lined with another metal such as tin or stainless steel.

4. *Cast iron* is a favorite metal with many chefs (myself included) because of its ability to distribute heat evenly and to maintain high temperatures for long periods. It is used in a large variety of griddles and heavy skillets. Cast iron cracks easily if dropped and rusts very quickly unless kept properly conditioned and dry.

5. *Teflon* (no-stick plastic coated) provides a very slippery finish but one that requires a lot of care because it is easily scratched. Do not use metal spoons or spatulas with this cookware. A good idea is to have one no-stick pan to use for cooking eggs.

TYPES OF POTS AND PANS

Saucepan: The best are made of metals that conduct heat well and have both firmly attached, comfortable handles and close-fitting lids. Saucepans should be heavy and disperse heat evenly so that you can braise or stew with a minimum of liquid. You also want to be able to sauté without sticking or burning before adding liquid. The base should be thick (thin will buckle with high heat and cook unevenly) as well as smooth; some are slightly concave, especially those made of two metals sandwiched together to allow for different rates of expansion over heat. Straight sides are best for general purposes.

The classic saucepan is round and almost twice as wide as deep with straight sides. Handles should be attached with rivets—not screws or welding—and placed some distance below the rim so that lifting and pouring is comfortable. Saucepans that are very large or those made of cast iron should have two handles or one handle and a little rim. The best have handles made of a metal that conducts heat to a lesser degree than the pan itself.

Sauté pan, slope-sided: Heavy-gauge pans used for general sautéing and frying (also called frying pans), the sauté pan's sloping sides allow you to flip and toss without using a spatula (sauté—or, in Italian, *saltare*—means "to leap"). They also make it easier to get at the food when a spatula is used. Because frying requires that heat be transmitted rapidly and evenly, frying pans should be made of heavy gauge and of good heat-conducting metals. They should also have long, strong handles to make lifting and maneuvering easy. Frying pans are generally 6 to 14 inches in top diameter and have no lids, as the retention of moisture would make the food soggy. They are excellent for making frittatas.

Sauté pan, straight-sided: These are used for browning, sautéing, and frying as well as for cooking sauces and other liquids, especially when reduction is needed (the broad surface area makes for very rapid reduction). They generally come with lids for braising or other moist-cooking purposes and are 6 to 16 inches in top diameter.

Stock and sauce pot: Large, deep, straight-sided pots for preparing stocks and broths as well as for simmering large quantities of liquid. Stock pots are larger than sauce pots and often come with spigots that allow liquid to be drained off without disturbing the solid contents or lifting the pot. Sauce pots are somewhat more shallow and are also used for sauces and soups. Both should be of fairly heavy gauge and come with tight-fitting lids. Make sure the diameter of the bottom does not exceed the size of your burners.

Various and Sundry

Chopping board: These should be thick (2 inches at least) one-piece constructions made of a type of wood that does not absorb stains—teak, iroko, beech, elm, ash, or sycamore. Despite some cities' restaurant laws, cutting boards should *always* be wood, never plastic which has been shown to harbor bacteria and, certainly, never glass or marble which blunt knife edges. New boards should be allowed to absorb a liberal dose of flavorless cooking oil on both sides—2 days per side—before being used. They should be covered with aluminum foil while seasoning and, after both sides have been treated, wiped with absorbent paper, sponged with soap and water, and dried thoroughly. Never soak cutting boards in water for any length of time; they will swell, warp, or split on drying.

Cutting boards should always be dried quickly in open air; their surface softens if wet for a long period and moisture seeps down through the grain. If this happens, you can try restoring a degree of hardness by sprinkling salt thickly over the board, rubbing the salt crystals into the surface with a halved lemon, and leaving it overnight to absorb moisture. Salt has a slightly abrasive cleaning action and can also be used to take away onion or fish-related smells. Lemon juice can be used to bleach out light stains.

Rolling pin: There are many kinds of rolling pins, but the best are made of plain, unpolished hardwood, sanded and rubbed as smooth as possible. Get one without handles so you can feel the food more closely and vary the degree of pressure applied. A good weight is 1¼ pounds; remember that the larger the diameter, the less you will have to roll. Italians have special pasta rolling pins called *matarellos* which, at 24 inches in length, are perfect for working with large sheets of dough. Whatever the type, all rolling pins should be lightly floured before using to prevent sticking, and all should be cleaned immediately after use with a slightly damp cloth. Always air-dry before stowing.

Wooden spoon: Strong, inflexible, and irreplaceable precisely because they are such poor conductors of heat. The best are made of hardwood—beech, ash, sycamore, hornbeam, or olive. Softwoods exude resin whenever heat is applied.

Gratin pan: Used whenever food is meant to be served in the same dish in which it is cooked. They are made of good heat-resisting and heat-conducting materials—copper, porcelain, earthenware, or cast iron—and used in the oven as well as under the broiler. Most are shallow to give each portion a generous amount of crust and also to fit under the broiler. All have small rims or handles projected to the sides rather than on top in order to give a better crust. The sides are either straight or sloping; sloping sides are good for increasing surface area, but straight sides are necessary for cooking vegetables that need to stand up.

Steamer: An expanding basket made of interleaved panels, all perforated. They can be used inside pans and pots of any size from 5½ to 9½ inches. Steamer baskets have central stems for lifting that can be removed if you want to steam large foods. They are efficient, very inexpensive, and take very little storage space.

Pasta machine: Some cooks I know look upon any discussion of pasta machines as evidence of a certain lack of cooking expertise. To which I respond with a very hearty "pooh!" While I have certainly made my share of hand-rolled pasta—and will continue to do so—I also know the joy of feeding that lumpy ball of pasta through the rollers of a manual machine and having it come out the other side a long golden sheet of perfectly even dough. In fact, one of my favorite things about cooking school is to watch the faces of students who have never before made pasta marveling at the sheet of perfection they are able to attain by just cranking the handle of those venerable old machines.

Nowadays, of course, it is also imperative, in any discussion of pasta machines, to include mention of the all-in-one electric machines that have finally reached a certain technical perfection that makes them worthy of consideration for the beginner cook. Not that the early ones did not produce somewhat acceptable pasta, just that you were afterwards relegated to an hour or more of cleanup duty. The new ones have handily solved that problem by making it just as easy to clean the machines as it is to make the pasta in the first place. Essentially, you place the flour and liquid in the mixing chamber, and less than five minutes later you have fresh pasta. The only problem—in addition to being offered a wealth of attachments, many of which are completely ridiculous (there's a reason why you never see pasta stores selling fresh penne)—is the cost. Pasta machines are not cheap. Nevertheless, if you decide the cost is worth it, you will undoubtedly find yourself experimenting with all kinds of "flavored" pastas (in spite of my advice to stick with the basic semolina-and-water recipe), and you will also find yourself reluctant to go back to the hand-cranked version.

This would be a mistake. For, while speed is the password with the electric pasta machines, perfection is the defining characteristic of the completely manual or motorized manual models. For starters, you have 8 or more thickness options with a manual and only one with the electric. But equally important is that the manual allows—in fact, requires—you to knead the dough until all ingredients are thoroughly blended. Kneading is what creates the gluten that makes the dough stretch without overworking it. With an all-in-one electric model, there is no kneading and the resulting pasta is granular and porous. (See page 312 for more information on making fresh pasta.)

I have worked with many different manual pasta machines and cannot, in good conscience, recommend one over another. They are all very simple machines and, when properly cleaned and cared for, provide a lifetime's worth of good pasta results.

Pantry Staples

This section contains a list of essential food staples and, as such, serves to describe what I see when I open the door to my pantry: those beautiful bottles of extra-virgin oil, an eclectic collection of glass jars and bottles housing dried herbs, my always-growing collection of vinegars (I am *addicted* to good vinegar and can never quite make it through a new specialty store without pausing to buy at least one new variety), various containers of salt, a half shelf devoted exclusively to peppers, another half shelf containing flour jars, five or six cans of peeled plum tomatoes, and on and on and on.

    La buona cucina comincia nella dispensa. The success of a dish begins in the pantry, says the old Tuscan adage. And so, because this book is dedicated to making *all* your dishes successful, I offer the following list of necessary items to have on hand before you begin.

Olive Oil

There can be no discussion of a Tuscan kitchen without first and foremost understanding what is meant by "olive oil," or, more appropriately, what is not meant by "olive oil." What is not meant is anything having to do with "light" or "pomace" or "blended with canola" or any of the other terminological frauds perpetrated on a public increasingly interested in the health and flavor benefits of olive oil. When buying olive oil, the only descriptive term you want to see on the label is "extra-virgin." Anything else signifies the oil has been processed in some way.

    Olive oil is a very low-tech product. The harvest season begins in late fall and continues through early spring. Nylon nets are spread under the trees to catch the olives as they fall. Although mechanical methods of harvesting have recently been developed (chief among them, hydraulic tree-shakers that clutch the tree and shake the olives loose), most crops are still picked by hand either from the tree itself or from the nets. Crushing takes place as soon as possible after harvesting, because even a few hours of storage can make a difference in quality. While many of the giant consortiums now use more sophisticated grinding mechanisms to crush the olives, the truly great (a.k.a. small) producers continue to use the same old behemoth granite millstones that have been used for centuries. No longer powered by mules, the crushers are now turned by modern machinery. Weighing several tons each, these giant stones can crush olives into paste in as little as 40 minutes.

Olive oil—the most important ingredient!

The pressing process starts by spreading the crushed paste on circular hemp mats which are then piled one on top of the other around a central guide. Pressing plays a major factor in the quality of olive oil; limited pressure releases only the better quality extra-virgin oil. Stronger pressure, applied later, extracts harsher oils which are often blended with others to create lower grades of extra-virgin. Olive oil quality is determined by its amount of oleic acid (the best are significantly lower than 1%) and its organoleptic rating (used to rate the oil through the senses of taste, feel, odor, and color; a good rating is over 6.5 as determined by panels of experts).

EXTRA-VIRGIN OR NOT EXTRA-VIRGIN?

As mentioned above, the lesser quality extra-virgin oils are blends of two or three olives and rarely identify their acidity levels (which, nonetheless, still hover around the 1% mark). "Virgin" is a term reserved for oils resulting from greater pressure being applied to the extracting mechanism. It is not the first oil given up by the olives; in most cases, it is not even the third or fourth. It has higher acidic levels (between 1 and 2%) and an organoleptic rating between 5.5 and 6.5. The taste is harsher and sharper than extra-virgin but no chemicals are used during extraction. Those labeled simply "olive oil" are oils resulting from chemical heat pressing and to which some virgin oil has been added to raise the grade to marketable quality.

Price is a good determinant; very good extra-virgin oils cost anywhere from $15 to $60 per liter. If you are paying $8 or $9, you may be getting extra-virgin, but it's most likely a blend and certainly not a very good grade. Is it worth it to spend more? Unquestionably, yes. In my mind, there is no factor more crucial to the eventual outcome of your dish than a good-quality oil. What I generally do is reserve my best oils for moments when they will really make the most difference: making salad dressings, drizzling over soups or a plate of freshly cooked beans, freshening up a finished dish with a final tablespoon or two right before serving.

For cooking, I use lesser quality extra-virgin or, more often, high quality extra-virgin that was pressed the previous year so that it is still wonderful but not quite as wonderful as my bottles of *olio novello*. Do I ever use anything other than extra-virgin? No. First of all, the taste is simply not there. The beauty of Tuscan vegetable cooking lies in its simplicity; there are no complicated procedures or heavy muddy flavors. The goal is to present the vegetables in a way that features their intrinsic tang. Any flavor I add must be equal to that of the vegetables in terms of purity, cleanness, and excellence.

Also, there is the question of health considerations. High-grade extra-virgin oil is simply crushed olives—nothing more. Olives are not treated with pesticides, nor is the ground from which they grow. To buy a grade of oil that compromises that wholeness is not only silly but self-defeating.

STORAGE

I have to laugh when including this section, since, in my house, olive oil storage is an oxymoron. Rarely does a bottle last long enough to even court the odor of staleness. Nevertheless, if you are a less-than-frequent user, keep in mind that—unlike wine which improves with age—olive oil deteriorates rapidly. Store in a cool, dark place and make sure to cap it tightly, since, like wine, air exposure hastens its decline. If you are going to be away for any length of time, you may store the oil in the refrigerator, although the change in temperature will affect the flavor. Always use olive oil within one year of purchase, and if you detect any hint of rancidity or oldness, throw it out.

THE PROPER AMOUNT TO USE

A running joke permeates the climate of every class at my cooking school, one that comes into play during the very first lesson and involves a basic difference in culinary tendencies between me and my partner, who lives less than a mile away from the school. Simply put, she—Sandra—uses at least twice as much oil as I do. The joke arises when students who have watched her doing an initial sauté on Monday watch me do the same sauté on Tuesday. "Sandra uses a lot more oil," they'll say. And by Friday, just the mention of "oil" will get a big laugh, since she and I will have openly argued about it all week.

How much oil you use is a matter of personal taste. Naturally, you don't want your food to be floating in a pool of it. But—and here I risk my reputation as a health-conscious minimalist—one thing I have learned from working with Sandra is that the ideal amount is somewhere beyond the consideration of most Americans.

I am remembering a ten-day period last winter when two of my cousins came to New York to visit and wound up cooking dinner for my friends on a snowy December night. The three of us had come home too late to consider anything elaborate, so my cousins decided to make pasta with a simple tomato sauce. By the end of the meal, my friends—all of whom are as into food as I—swore they had never before had a tomato sauce as good. Upon questioning, my cousins revealed the ingredients to be much the same as everyone expected. With one exception: they had used my best oil (the one I had just brought back from Tuscany and which had just been pressed two weeks earlier), and they had used plenty of it.

Oil is an ingredient, not merely a fat in which to sauté foods. Since most people in this country are used to cooking with relatively flavorless oils such as vegetable, corn, or canola, cooking with a highly flavored oil takes getting used to. Also, coming at a time when the mere mention of the word "fat" is enough to send shivers up most people's spines, the concept of liberally using any oil seems almost untenable. Except when one considers the following two things:

1. Research has shown that the best form of weight control is to eat foods that are satisfying enough to quell the desire to either overeat or snack. In this view, a little extra oil goes a long way; not only does the food taste better, but it takes on a certain richness that subverts the tendency to feel deprived.

2. Olive oil is good for you. It is monounsaturated (which not only means it is free of harmful LDL but it is also able to boost the body's beneficial HDL), has absolutely no cholesterol, and contains no more calories than any other oil but, with much more flavor, gives the feeling of being complex and rich.

As you experiment with the recipes in this book, also experiment with using very good oil (look on the label for some variation of the words *olio di frantoio* which means "oil from the mill," distinguishing it from that produced by the large industrial refineries) and use a little more of it than you might otherwise consider. You will be very surprised with the results.

Vinegar

I'm not sure whether or not I have convinced you to spend more money on olive oil, but now I am going to try to do the same with vinegar which, used correctly, should be one of your most trusted staples. You may have noticed a few paragraphs earlier that I have freely identified myself as "addicted" to vinegar. By that I mean vinegar of all types, although I am particularly partial to very good balsamic, so let me start with that.

Balsamic vinegar is the ultimate contradiction of the old adage that says "vinegar is wine gone bad." For starters, good balsamic vinegar costs as much as a very good Brunello wine. Also, it takes much longer to "make"; consider that, in the old days, vinegar barrels were bequeathed to descendants as part of one's estate. Let me explain the process:

After the grapes have been pressed, the unfermented must is boiled in copper cauldrons over an open flame for hours until it is reduced by 30 to 50%. This sweet, concentrated grape juice is left to settle and clarify until the following spring, when it is placed in wood barrels whose bung holes are covered with pieces of white linen. Because the must is so concentrated, fermentation and acetification proceed slowly and occur more or less simultaneously.

Balsamic vinegar is made in a series of graduated wood barrels (these can include oak, chestnut, cherry, mulberry, ash, or juniper) over a long period during which the bacteria works its alchemy. Initially, must is placed in the largest of the barrels in each series. Each year, as more liquid evaporates, a small amount (perhaps a liter) is drawn off from the smallest (generally this is reserved for the private use of the owners). Then all the barrels in each series are replenished with vinegar from the next largest ones, except for the largest which are once again filled with fresh must. Each series, or *batterie*, is comprised of 3 to 10 barrels, but may stretch to 24. As the vinegar progresses through the series, the barrels become smaller and smaller until, at the 20-year mark, the total amount of vinegar produced might fit in a small vase.

It is now possible to buy balsamic vinegar for $2.99 a bottle in just about any specialty food store. The difference between this and "real" balsamic, however, is like the difference between fresh string beans and those that have been canned. The popular variety is nothing more than boiled-down grape must mixed with regular vinegar, darkened with caramel, and aged as little as one year in barrels that once held the real thing. Real balsamic vinegar, on the other hand, is thick, syrupy, and complexly flavored with vestiges of the various woods.

Do you need a $50 bottle of balsamic vinegar in your pantry? Let me be diplomatic and restrict my answer to this: taste a few drops of real balsamic drizzled over roasted vegetables or chips of freshly shaved Parmesan or perfectly grilled *porcini* mushrooms, and then decide for yourself.

In the meantime, let's talk about non-balsamic types, and, here too, let me take a moment to explain something about how vinegar is made. When I was a little girl, every Tuscan winery also made vinegar, which is simply a process of exposing fermented grape juice to air long enough for bacteria to form on top and turn the wine sour. But because winemakers fight against bacteria and the making of vinegar encourages its growth, Italian law eventually regulated vinegar-making to such a degree that most wineries stopped making it. Today, in fact, it is very difficult for wineries to be granted the necessary licenses to resume production.

But a few have successfully negotiated the bureaucratic obstacles. And from them we learn that vinegar-making is a process as complex as making wine. Essentially, to make good vinegar, you must start with fine wine. The best vinegar goes through a series of percolations during which the wine is allowed to slowly oxidize and develop the necessary bacterial supports—a process that takes all of two weeks but that completely preserves the aroma and flavor of the wine. Compare this with industrially produced vinegar which can be made in one day but smells and tastes mostly of acetic acid.

Good vinegar is then aged up to a year in wood casks (generally chestnut) and removed for another year or two to small oak barrels which ultimately confer great body to its structure and refine the taste. Whether white or red, there is no substitute. But, as always, you pay dearly for things that have no substitute.

When purchasing good vinegar, look for dates testifying to how long the liquid has been casked. Also, check the acidity level (it should be about 6%) and look for as much information about the origin of the grapes as possible.

Broth

Throughout this book, you will notice many recipes calling for a basic broth of one type or another, and I want to make clear that when I say broth I do not mean stock. The difference lies in the degree to which the flavor is condensed. Stocks are thicker, darker, and more concentrated; broths are lighter in both color and taste—a fact that works especially well with the more delicate flavor of vegetables.

Pages 307 to 310 detail a few basic broth recipes. Make more than called for and freeze in an ice cube tray. Empty the tray into a plastic container, seal, and when needed, simply use a cube.

Cheese

Throughout the following recipes, you will often see me calling for either Parmigiano-Reggiano (which I will sometimes refer to as Parmesan in the interest of simplicity, although every time I do so, I feel a shiver of fear that my readers will misunderstand and rush off to the store to purchase grated Parmesan in containers with perforated tops) or *pecorino*. Actually, the same fear paralyzes me with respect to *pecorino*, a wonderful cheese whose misfortune is to be allied in this country with salty, grated Pecorino Romano which is also sold in pre-packaged shaker-top containers.

My intent in stipulating either Parmesan or *pecorino*, however, is that you should go to a good cheese store or counter and buy only the real thing, preferably sliced just that moment from a large, moist wheel.

There is only one Parmigiano-Reggiano, and it comes from a production zone in Emilia-Romagna whose boundaries are fixed by Italian law, as are the ingredients utilized (only milk and rennet) and the period of aging (at least eighteen months). *Pecorino*, on the other hand, is a catch-all name for a wide variety of wonderful sheep's milk cheeses (*pecora* means "sheep") whose texture, color, and flavor differ depending on the sweetness of the sheep's pasture and the cheese-maker's technique. *Marzolino*, for example, is a particularly wonderful cheese whose name, Little March, originates from the fact that what sheep eat— grass and herbage—is at its freshest and most green in March.

There are times when I am in New York, sitting at my desk and staring out at the concrete streets, and suddenly I'll find myself dreaming of being in Massarosa on a Tuesday morning—Market Day—and going up to Giulio's—the local cheesemaker's—counter and asking for a wedge of new *marzolino*, and he slices it from a form that is less than a month old and starts to wrap it, and I say, "*Non ti disturbare, la mangio ora*"—Don't bother, I'll eat it right now—and he hands it over, and I feel its softness and smell its delicacy and break off a tiny piece and put it in my mouth and . . . *o Dio, che bonta!*

When choosing a *pecorino* for grating, specify that you want one of the harder varieties; otherwise, try either the aforementioned *marzolino* or *caciotte* which is firm and somewhat peppery. Remember that, like fine wine, Parmigiano-Reggiano and *pecorino* deteriorate when exposed to air for long periods. Their moisture evaporates and they begin to taste old and bland.

When purchasing cheese in conjunction with the recipes in this book, buy more than is called for and treat yourself to the experience of eating cheese as an entity unto itself rather than as a recipe ingredient. Parmigiano-Reggiano is wonderful eaten in chunks with ripe comice pears or fresh purple figs; *pecorino* hits its true stride when eaten with freshly shelled new spring fava beans. Also, save the rinds and throw them into soups to create a thicker, creamier consistency.

Canned Tomatoes

Most Tuscans swear by one brand of canned tomatoes or another. My mother, for example, uses only Primetta. Sandra, my partner, recommends either De Rica or Valfrutta. My friend Adriana would prefer not to use canned tomatoes at all rather than use anything other than Cirio. No question but that all these culinarians are correct in their own ways. When in Tuscany, however, I am far less cautious about choosing a brand of canned tomatoes than I am in this country. The reason is simply that while, in Tuscany, one brand may be somewhat better than another, they are all basically quite good. All use only the very ripest plum tomatoes (plum tomatoes are sweeter than the round varieties), and all pack plenty of them in cans filled with thick, syrupy tomato liquid.

Contrast that with any but the very best canned tomatoes available in American markets (the very best, by the way, all come from Italy and generally say "San Marzano" somewhere on the container): the tomatoes are often of the round variety and—even worse—small and underdeveloped. In many cases, they were green when canned and have now turned yellow. The liquid is basically water and there is more of it than tomatoes.

When you use canned tomatoes you should squeeze them into the recipe. Squeezing produces a shredded consistency that blends instantly with other ingredients; it also gives you that intimate tactile connection relished by all true cooks. But you cannot squeeze tomatoes that are not ripe. For one thing, you're in danger of winding up with tomato juice spritzed all over your chest. Ultimately, you wind up with a handful of hard, rubbery chunks and a sense that you should definitely have purchased the more expensive variety.

Salt

In the last few years, Americans have been confronted with a wealth of research suggesting that we have gone overboard in limiting our salt intake. Suddenly, salt is not the villain it was once thought to be. In fact, as we have once again realized, salt is essential—as essential as other taste components such as sweet, sour, and bitter. Used as a seasoning—pulling flavors together and accenting them—salt is not only not harmful, but can actually be beneficial since, together with calcium, magnesium, and potassium, it helps regulate the body's metabolism.

The problem comes when people indiscriminately use salt as a topping, shaking it over their food before even tasting. The palate, which may already be dulled by prepared foods (most high in salt additives), is further dulled to the point where it becomes impossible to taste anything *but* salt. As every good cook will tell you, the first taste of a dish should never be salt.

Tuscans do not salt their food at the table (in fact, it is very rare to find anyone who even *owns* a salt shaker). The food is properly salted when prepared and almost never will you find anyone desiring additional seasoning. Such a request would be construed as a serious affront to the cook, evidence of your gastronomic inferiority, or both.

Like professional cooks everywhere, Tuscans keep an open crock near the stove and salt with their fingers. The amount they use is more a reflex action than an active judgment, an intuitively perfect pinch developed through a lifetime of experimentation. Used this way, salt becomes not an overpowering assault to the palate but a miracle crystal enhancing both the texture and taste of food. In general, Tuscan cooks use a coarse-grain salt that is very similar to what we call kosher salt.

TYPES OF SALT

When travelling, I almost always include salt in my pantheon of food purchases and am continually amazed to find how much different salts vary in flavor. All salts come (or came) from the sea, but they are all processed in different ways. Today, the majority of the world's salt is obtained by pumping water into the generous supply of underground deposits left by the oceans that once covered the earth. Machines are used to pump up the brine which is then concentrated by evaporation and further purified.

What we call common table salt is really finely ground crystals mixed with starch and phosphate of lime to keep it free-flowing. The consequence is a generally flat and metallic taste. Iodized salt goes through a heavy refinement process that strips it of its natural iodine and then replaces it in the form of sodium iodide; the result is a muddy, acrid flavor. Kosher salt, which has no additives, got its name because its large grains were once used to draw blood from meat in accordance with Jewish dietary laws. Of all the commercially available salts, it is the cleanest-tasting, and its coarse grains make it very easy to use.

Sea salt is generally obtained by evaporating sea water in protected areas. This purification process leaves it with a high percentage of sodium chloride and many trace elements including magnesium, zinc, calcium, iron, and potassium. Now available in both fine and coarse grains, sea salt has a much fuller flavor which, of course, means that less goes farther.

For general purposes, I either bring my sea salt back from a certain distributor in Tuscany (who, by labeling it a "sea" product, has managed to avoid the scrutiny of the state which controls the production, distribution, and sale of salt) or use La Baleine which is routinely available in American markets in both coarse and fine crystals. La Baleine comes from the Mediterranean, has a fresh, bright flavor which works especially well with vegetables, and is sold for about $2.70 for a 1-pound, 10-ounce container.

Recently, I have begun using salt from Brittany whose cold, active North Sea currents combine with large tides and other marine and climatic conditions to offer a unique and flavorful mix of minerals. The salt is harvested from ocean water channeled into pristine ponds edged with natural waterways, wild grasses, and other green plants. The wind and sun evaporate the ocean water, leaving a mineral-rich brine from which salt crystals form. This highly flavorful salt is raked by hand from special beds lined with a natural layer of clay and sand (refinery salt is harvested from concrete beds which pollute the salt).

I would highly recommend either of the following two brands: Natural Celtic Sea Salt which carries Natural ($8 per pound), Light Gray ($10 per pound), Fine Ground ($22 per pound), and Flower of the Ocean ($56 per pound). All can be ordered through The Grain and Salt Society (800/867-7258). Fleur de Sel costs about $25 a pound and can be purchased at high-end specialty stores (Dean & De Luca: 800/221-7714 or Zingermans: 313/769-1625).

When determining which salt to use, you should first and foremost consider the method of processing. At its purest, salt is 40% sodium and 60% chloride. But different processing methods can alter that balance and, hence, the taste. My personal preference for sea salt has to do with the very definite character imparted by minerals like magnesium and copper that are left in minimally refined brands. Another factor to be considered is the size of the crystals, which not only affects the taste but ease of handling. One good way to find out which you prefer is to conduct an informal salt tasting; try shaking a few crystals on a slice of boiled potato. Limit your experiment to four at a time—any more becomes overwhelming.

Whatever salt you use, to avoid too salty a taste, don't season at the end of cooking. Instead salt food judiciously while it is still cooking. Allow a few minutes for the flavors to blend before deciding whether to add more. If additional salt is needed, add only a few crystals at a time.

Pepper

Pepper is one of the most underutilized of spices; even those who use it regularly admit to rarely going beyond the standard black peppercorn. But the pepper world is a palette of flavors and colors that, in addition to basic black, also includes green, pink, and white.

Green, black, and white peppercorns all start out the same way—as the fruit of a perennial shrub called *piper nigrum*. The green, unripe variety always comes either pickled or freeze-dried; its flavor is so mild that the pickled peppercorns must be rinsed before using or the brine will overwhelm the taste of the spice. Since their fruity flavor fades almost immediately, they are always added to a dish as close to serving time as possible.

Black peppercorns also start out as underripe green berries, but are then sun-dried and fermented to the point of withering. Their flavor, which lasts somewhat longer than that of green peppercorns, is smokier and more pungent.

White pepper berries are the only ones allowed to ripen and redden on the vine; their outer skins are then buffed free of color and, when ground, used mainly in light-colored foods that would otherwise look dirty if speckled with flecks of black. Of the three, white pepper is my least favorite; its flavor always seems clawing and bitter.

Pink peppercorns are not, botanically speaking, part of the peppercorn family. Used mainly for their appearance appeal, their oh-so-faint hint of fruit and pine fades too quickly for any use other than immediate consumption.

Pepper should always be ground at the moment of using; its flavor fades too quickly to let stand.

Herbs, dried

While many people presume that all herbs are better in their fresh, natural state, the reality is that dried herbs serve just as valuable a function, albeit a different one. Of the green herbs, chervil, parsley, and chives have little value in their dry state. Better are those that grow on woody stems, like thyme, rosemary, sage, marjoram, winter savory, and oregano. Dried basil falls in the category of personal preference. Some cooks claim that drying dissipates basil's essential oils, leaving nothing but a bitter grassy flavor. Others (myself included) feel that, while not as warm or fresh as the living variety, dried basil lends a zesty spice to long-simmering sauces, soups, and stews.

Dried herbs release their flavor over a long period of time and are thus most suitable for slow-cooking dishes such as root vegetable stew or oven-roasted potatoes or even a hearty vegetable minestrone. Since their flavor is concentrated, you need to use far less than if they were fresh—a pinch is usually sufficient.

Store dried herbs in airtight containers (such as glass jars) in cool, dry places. Do not place on spice racks located near the stove as cooking heat dissipates flavor. Dried herbs should keep their scents and flavors for at least six months. Should they develop a musty smell or change color—signs that they have lost their flavor—throw them away. Before using, always test their potency by crumbling a few leaves between your fingers. To ensure the freshest flavor, consider drying your own by tying the herbs at the base with kitchen string or twine and then hanging the bunches upside down in a dry location with temperatures ranging from 60 to 100 degrees. The warmer the temperature, the faster they will dry, and more oils will be retained.

Dried herbs should be used with greater discretion than fresh because drying tends to concentrate as well as alter their flavors. Once you are familiar with their individual characteristics, however, you can be as adventurous with dried herbs as you are with their fresh forms. Here are some particularly good marriages between dried herbs and vegetables:

Bay leaf: This aromatic herb is used to flavor cooking liquids for beans, rice, and soups. Whole leaves are often threaded onto skewers to be used for broiling vegetables.

Marjoram: Sweet marjoram and its stronger sister, pot marjoram, have a sweet, spicy flavor that blends with almost any vegetable.

Oregano: This pungent herb is an important component in many marinades and goes especially well with tomatoes.

Rosemary: Very intense and resinous, rosemary is wonderful sprinkled on vegetables before grilling or added to the water for boiling them.

Sage: Use this musky herb in lentil soups or with oven-roasted potatoes.

Savory: Winter and summer savory both have a piquancy that makes them possible substitutes for salt; winter savory is stronger and should be used more discreetly. Often referred to as the bean herb, savory also complements cabbages, squashes, or onions.

Thyme: Common thyme, which has the strongest flavor of any member of the thyme family, appears most frequently in bouquets garnis and braises.

Herbs, fresh

While fresh herbs are not exactly what one might consider a "pantry" item, you might have the real thing growing on your windowsill or in your garden or—the next best thing—stored in the vegetable compartment of your refrigerator. With greenmarkets now widely available in major cities, most people are reassuringly close to a stable and varied supply of fresh herbs, and their use has become so commonplace as to make us forget that, just a few years ago, it was impossible to find anything more exotic than fresh parsley. The next best thing to totally fresh, however, is to have individual leaves fossilized in your freezer compartment or marinating in oil in your refrigerator.

If you have not yet succumbed to the romance of growing your own herbs, I highly recommend you start, even if you have only one pot of fresh thyme tucked away in a sunny corner of your kitchen. There are few things in life as satisfying as the aroma of fresh herbs—the scent on your hands after handling, the fragrance that greets you when you walk in the room, the bouquet that wafts from the pan when you stir a handful of freshly chopped fennel into a bowl of warm shell beans.

With their widely varying tastes, vegetables offer a generous scope for the use of fresh herbs. In general, they should be used in more substantial quantity than their highly concentrated dried counterparts. Because they release their flavor immediately, fresh herbs should be sprinkled onto cooked or raw vegetables, used in sautés, grills, stir-fries, and other quick-cooked dishes. Woodier varieties, such as thyme and tarragon, can also be layered into a slow-cooked dish, with one amount added early enough to thoroughly blend into the basic flavor, and a second portion sprinkled into the dish just before serving for freshness and appearance. And, of course, any combination of minced herbs works wonderfully stirred into a salad vinaigrette. Try also blending fresh herb minces with olive oil, lemon zest, and/or crushed garlic for a wonderful sauce that can either be stirred into hot soups or used as a topping on pizzas, pastas, and steamed vegetables.

While there are no cast-iron rules for which herbs to use with which vegetables, the following suggestions are generally accepted as reliable guidelines:

Basil: This herb's clovelike aroma is perfect with tomatoes but also good with squashes, beans, potatoes, and most leafy greens. A Tuscan classic consists of sliced tomatoes, leaves of basil, sliced *bufala* mozzarella, extra-virgin oil, and a faint drizzle of balsamic vinegar.

In Tuscany, rosemary grows in every available nook and cranny.

Chervil: A cousin of parsley, chervil has a delicate lemon-licorice taste that goes with almost any vegetable but especially with asparagus, artichokes, and carrots. Add it at the last minute as cooking kills its fresh flavor. Or toss sprigs of chervil into your salads.

Chives: Finely snipped, these mild relatives of onions can complement any vegetable from potatoes to eggplant. Use both leaves and flowers but only add during the absolute last minutes of cooking.

Dill: In addition to its traditional alliance with cucumber, leafy (or baby) dill enhances potatoes, cabbages, carrots, squashes, and peas. Its mature seeds are typically used in pickling brines.

Fennel: Anise-tasting fennel fronds go well with mild-flavored vegetables such as potatoes or carrots.

Lovage: Long cooking brings out the sweet, celery-like taste of this herb. It is good in braises, with potatoes, and roughly chopped into salads.

Mint: For a cool, aromatic aftertaste, add mint to carrots, cucumbers, and tomatoes as well as peas.

Nasturtium: Young, tender nasturtium leaves make peppery additions to soups or salads. Also use the blossoms, either whole or minced as a beautiful addition to your salads or in making nasturtium butter.

Nepeta: This cross between mint and marjoram is a must with mushrooms.

Parsley: Its taste is so mild that parsley may be used in quantity with any vegetable—or be a vegetable on its own. Only the Italian flat-leaf variety, however; the curly-leafed type has basically no flavor and should only be used as garnish.

Purslane: This slightly sour, slightly lemony herb is very juicy and succulent. An excellent addition to salads, soups, and stews.

Rosemary: A powerful herb with a pronounced musky taste. Use with oven-roasted vegetables or sprinkle onto *focaccia* dough before baking. Immerse in olive oil for a wonderfully-scented condiment.

Sage: The slightly musky taste of this plant can dominate; use it sparingly and only with strong-tasting vegetables. Excellent when sautéed in butter and used as a sauce. It also can be fried and served as a vegetable on its own.

Tarragon: A strong herb with a sweet anise taste, tarragon goes well with artichokes or asparagus. Tarragon mayonnaise and tarragon butter are wonderful toppings for steamed vegetables; snippets of tarragon are also a novel addition to tomato and bean salads.

Thyme: The many varieties of this herb include lemon thyme, whose faint citrus flavor is delicious with braised vegetables, and leaf thyme, a mild version of common thyme which is especially excellent in marinades.

Wild Plants

Tuscans have always used a savvy blend of both cultivated greens and wild plants in their cooking. I remember, in fact, being young and journeying into the fields with my cousins to pick leaves of this and that to bring home for the salad or a vegetable sauté. "Is *this* good?" I would ask whichever adult was chaperoning my group. "How about this one?"

The following is a list of wild plants I use for cooking. Depending on where you live, you may or may not have access to these particular greens. But I heartily suggest buying yourself a book on foraging and getting out there. If you're not a country dweller, be wary and use your judgment about where you pick from. There is really nothing quite like a salad made entirely of wild plants—both in terms of taste and the sheer indulgence of being so closely connected to the earth.

Chicory: Wild chicory is more angular and more sparsely leafed than the cultivated version, but it is just as deliciously piquant. The plants, which grow to 4 feet and can be found along roadsides and in vacant lots, bloom continuously in the Northeast from mid-June through September, with occasional—and beautiful blue—flowers even later. Look for dark green leaves sprouting from a rosette at the base. Use young leaves in salads; sauté older ones in olive oil and spritz with lemon juice.

Daisy: Every part of the daisy is edible, from its familiar daisy flower head with its yellow center and white petals to the small, oblong, irregularly toothed leaves. The flavor is buttery and somewhat peppery although it changes drastically depending on the age of the plant. Like its hybrid cousins, the wild daisy grows about 1 or 2 feet tall and blooms most prolifically in May and June. Look for the wild varieties on road embankments, vacant lots, and sunny open areas. For salads, use only very young leaves (older ones can be somewhat bitter) as well as the white petals. Place older leaves and flowers in soups and stews, or use as part of a vegetable sauté.

Dandelion: Like its cultivated cousin, wild dandelion is good to eat (the two flavors are almost identical) and highly nutritious, with great quantities of Vitamins A and C. Look for it anywhere a patch of green can grow—even in the cracks of roads and sidewalks—and use in all the same ways you might use the hybrid version.

Burdock: Burdock is a large plant (2 to 4 feet tall) with equally large, heart-shaped leaves that are extravagantly ruffled in a way that brings to mind the plays of Tennessee Williams. Its tenacious taproot frequently grows straight down through the soil to a depth of 4 feet or more. For the first few years after I bought a country home and began serious gardening, I referred to it as the "nuisance plant" because it was so hard to get rid of. But that was before I realized how good it was to eat. My favorite preparation is to peel the thick, bitter rind, dice the peeled stems, and plunge them into boiling water for 8 to 10 minutes. Drain, add fresh boiling water and cook for 5 minutes until the stems are tender but crisp. When cool, toss the stems with a light vinaigrette and enjoy. The flavor is somewhat like that of cardoons. Alternately, sauté the cooked stems in butter for about 5 minutes and season with salt and freshly ground white pepper. Cooked burdock can also be baked in a cream sauce or coated with bread crumbs and fried. The Japanese also make frequent culinary use of the root, which is dark brown and resembles a long carrot.

Lamb's Quarters: There is nothing quite like the tips and young leaves of lamb's quarters to spice up an early-season salad. One of our best wild pot-herbs, this delicious, easy-to-find plant is closely related to beets, chard, and spinach, both in genus and taste. From early spring to late fall, it can be gathered practically at your doorstep; look for erect stems, many branched and frequently tinged with red. The leaves are oval or triangular in shape, with toothed edges and are dark green above with mealy white undersides. Minute green flowers are produced continually from June until November. Lamb's quarters is very good sautéed with garlic, oil, and lemon but pick twice as much as you think you'll need since it cooks down to about half.

Wild Mustard: Anyone who has ever driven past a field in mid-spring knows what wild mustard looks like. In California, it is often called "Yellow Carpet" because of its tendency to take over entire meadows with its wispy yellow flowers. Similar in taste to cultivated mustard, it can be used in all the same ways—sautéed, steamed, in salads, in pestos, as a pasta or pizza topping, and, in the case of older leaves, for soups.

Plantains: The ubiquitous plantain is a low-growing plant that is found virtually everywhere—from sidewalks to meadows, from mountains to shores. It almost seems as though, the worse the conditions, the more it thrives. Look for a flat rosette of dark green, oval or spade-shaped leaves and only bother gathering from early April to late May. Older leaves are stringy and unpalatable, but young ones can be used in anything from salads to pestos to fish marinades.

CHAPTER TWO

Techniques

There are as many ways to cook vegetables as there are the proverbial pebbles on the beach. Well, almost. Suffice to say that there is more opportunity for innovation and imagination than with meats, fish, grains, and soups. In fact, the sheer number of vegetables alone requires a book just to enumerate and describe.

On the following pages, I have attempted to group the most popular cooking and preparation techniques and to suggest how they can be applied to individual vegetables. At the risk of shortchanging my recipes, I have to say that this is probably the most important part of the book. Once you have understood such things as how a braise is different from a sauté and why peanut oil is better than olive oil for deep frying, you will be on your way to viewing recipes not as intractable directives but as creative stimulants.

Vegetables Change As They Cook

The cooking process changes four things about vegetables: their texture, color, flavor, and nutrient structure. These changes can be minimal or great—the degree is determined by you. Unfortunately, you do not always have total control; in many cases, you will have to settle for straddling a thin line between the pros and cons of many different approaches. For example, boiling chard in an uncovered pot in plenty of water will give you a bright green, sweet-tasting vegetable. But many of its nutrients will either leach into the water or float out of the pot on the steam. On the other hand, if you use less water and cover the pot (as in steaming), the chard will be grayish and have an overly strong taste.

Texture

A vegetable's texture is determined by its fiber structure, the amount of starch it contains, and the degree to which it is cooked. Fiber structure gives vegetables shape and firmness; the job of cooking is to take that shape and firmness away. Vegetables differ in the amount of fiber they contain. Spinach and tomatoes have less than carrots and turnips, for example, and older, tougher carrots have more than young, fresh ones.

Fiber is softened by heat (in general, longer cooking means softer vegetables) and by alkalis, which is why you should never add baking soda to green, leafy vegetables. Not only does it destroy vitamins, but it turns them into a mushy heap. Conversely, acids strengthen fiber. Lemon juice, vinegar, and tomato products added to vegetables strengthen fiber and, hence, extend their cooking time. Sugar also strengthens fiber or cell structure, which is why poached fruit always simmers in heavy syrup.

Starch is another textural strengthener. Dry, starchy foods like dried beans, peas, and lentils must be pre-soaked to replace lost moisture and then cooked in enough water so that the starch granules can absorb even more moisture and soften to the point of digestibility. Moist, starchy vegetables like potatoes have enough moisture of their own but must still be cooked until the starch granules soften.

A vegetable is considered done when it has reached the right degree of tenderness. Winter squash, eggplant, and celery are generally said to be done when quite tender. Most vegetables, however, are best cooked very briefly, until they are crisp or *al dente* (firm to the bite). At this stage of tenderness, they not only have the most pleasing texture, but they also have maximum flavor, color, and nutrients.

For uniform doneness, vegetables should be cut into uniform sizes before cooking. Those with both tough and tender parts need special treatment so that the tender parts are not overcooked by the time the tougher parts are done. For this reason, it is always a good idea to peel both broccoli stems and the woody stalks of asparagus. In general, different vegetables should be cooked separately, since each requires its own individual cooking time.

Flavor

Many flavors are lost during cooking both by dissolving into the cooking liquid and by evaporation. The longer a vegetable is cooked, the more flavor it loses. Hence, vegetables should be cooked for as short a time as possible in boiling salted water. Placing vegetables in already boiling water shortens cooking time and the addition of salt helps reduce flavor loss. Also, add a small amount of oil to the cooking water; oil absorbs some of the lost flavors and then clings to the vegetables when they are drained, carrying some of the flavors with it.

Young, freshly harvested vegetables have a relatively high sugar content that makes them taste sweet. As they mature, or as they sit in storage, the sugar gradually changes to starch. This is especially noticeable in corn, peas, carrots, turnips, and beets. To serve sweet-tasting vegetables, either serve them young or add a small amount of sugar to the cooking water to replace lost sweetness.

Color

Pigments are compounds that give vegetables their color. Different pigments react in different ways to heat, acids, and other elements that may be present during cooking.

White pigments, called *flavones,* are the primary coloring compounds in potatoes, onions, cauliflower, white cabbage, and the white parts of such vegetables as celery, cucumbers, and zucchini. White pigments stay white in acid and turn yellow in alkaline water. To keep white vegetables white, add a little lemon juice or cream of tartar to the cooking water. Be careful not to add too much or you will toughen the vegetable. Covering the pot also helps keep acids in. Cooking for a short time, such as in a steamer, also helps maintain color (and flavor and nutrients as well). Overcooking turns white vegetables dull yellow or gray.

Red pigments, called *anthocyanins,* are found in only a few vegetables, mainly red cabbage and beets. Red pigments react very strongly to acids and alkalis—acids turn them a brighter red; alkalis turn them blue or blue-green. Beets and red cabbage, therefore, have their best color when cooked with a very small amount of acid (red cabbage is often cooked with tart apples for this very reason). Again, be careful how much you use; too much will toughen the vegetable. Red pigments dissolve easily in water. This means you should use a short cooking time, as little water as possible, and whenever possible, serve the reduced cooking liquid as a sauce. Beets should also always be cooked in their skins to prevent bleeding.

Green coloring, or *chlorophyll,* is present in all green plants. Both acids and long cooking destroy chlorophyll and turn green vegetables a drab olive green. To protect chlorophyll, cook uncovered to allow plant acids to escape and cook for the shortest time possible. Moreover, steam whenever possible. Do not use baking soda to maintain color; soda destroys vitamins and results in a mushy, slippery texture.

Yellow and orange pigments, called *carotenoids,* are found in carrots, corn, winter squashes, rutabagas, sweet potatoes, tomatoes, and red peppers. These pigments are very stable and little affected by acids or alkalis, although long cooking can dull the color.

Nutrients

Vegetables are our major sources of vitamins A and C and are rich in many other essential nutrients. Unfortunately, many of these nutrients are easily lost due to cooking at high temperatures, long cooking, leaching, and alkalis. Some nutrient loss is inevitable because it is rarely possible to control all these conditions at the same time. For example, pressure steaming shortens cooking time, but the high temperature destroys some vitamins; braising uses low heat, but the cooking time is longer; baking eliminates leaching, but long cooking and high temperatures cause nutrient loss; boiling is faster than simmering, but the higher temperature can be harmful, and the rapid activity can break up delicate vegetables and increase loss through leaching; and cutting vegetables into small pieces decreases cooking time but increases leaching by creating more exposed surfaces.

The most important thing is to remember that the best cooking methods are ones that produce the most attractive, flavorful vegetables, and that attractive, flavorful vegetables are more likely to be eaten. Vegetables left on the plate benefit no one, no matter how nutritious they are.

Cooking Techniques

At my cooking school, Toscana Saporita, we strive to teach students to understand the theory as well as the method behind what they're doing. Why, for example, does red cabbage look even redder when cooked with a hint of lemon juice? Why is oven steaming a better method for cooking beets than boiling? That is really the purpose behind this chapter—to get you to the point where you can create your own recipes and use the ones in this book merely as fillers.

With that in mind, I have divided the cooking of vegetables into five distinct methods: Boiling and Steaming, Frying and Sautéing, Braising and Stewing, Baking and Roasting, and Broiling and Grilling. Each has its own arsenal of basic in-

formation, its own set of dos and don'ts, and its own special strategies which, when employed, greatly enhance the finished product.

Boiling and Steaming

Boiling and steaming are both the bane and the blessing of vegetable-cooking techniques. When done properly, you get crisp, firm, tender vegetables with all their flavor and nutritional value retained. When not, the result is a dull, mushy mash. Boiling is actually an inaccurate term, since, in most cases, vegetables should be simmered rather than boiled. The agitation and high temperatures of boiling break up delicate vegetables and destroy nutrients.

Vegetables may be either completely boiled/steamed or parboiled which means cooking the vegetable *partially* as a preliminary to other preparations (e.g. softening the leaves of cabbages to prepare them for stuffing). Parboiling differs from blanching only in the amount of time the vegetable remains in the water. Vegetables to be puréed are almost always boiled first.

A MAXIMUM OF WATER OR A MINIMUM?

Hot water affects the chemical composition of vegetables in very different ways. It can leach out water-soluble nutrients, release compounds that dull the color of green vegetables, rob sweet ones of their sugar, and produce a sulfurous taste in cabbage. No one method can prevent all these things from happening. The best way to preserve natural color, flavor, and texture, for example, is to immerse green and strong-flavored vegetables in a large quantity of boiling water and cook them uncovered. But then, according to nutritionists, you lose a great deal of the nutritional value. On the other hand, if you use a minimum amount of water and a covered pan, greens will be somewhat duller, and strong-tasting vegetables like cabbage, broccoli, and cauliflower will taste even stronger.

When green vegetables—leaves, most stalks, some seeds, some pods, and all members of the cabbage family—are immersed in water, they release natural acids that dull their color. Large quantities of water and cooking without a cover allow the acids to disperse in the air and water, but this method also leaches out some of the nutrients. The best middle-of-the-road approach is to cook with a small amount of water and disperse the acids by leaving the pan uncovered for only the first few minutes of cooking. Although the color and flavor will not be as good as with the open-pan, deep-water method, it will be good enough, with the added benefit of maintaining maximum nutritional value.

One technique that works well with highly nutritious, strong-tasting members of the cabbage family—broccoli, cauliflower, brussels sprouts, and cabbage—is to decrease cooking time by cutting them into small pieces that can be cooked, covered, in small quantities of water before either their colors or flavors change.

In cases where color and strong taste are not problems—with carrots, potatoes, rutabagas, turnips, and parsnips, for example—the maximum-water, covered-pan and the minimum-water, uncovered method work equally well.

THE BENEFITS OF STEAMING

Vegetables can be steamed over plain boiling water or water to which a flavoring agent, such as garlic or herbs, has been added. Steaming takes longer than boiling, but it does a better job of preserving nutrients because you use a covered pan and the vegetables sit in a bamboo or metal basket and never actually touch the water. Whichever type of steamer you use, make sure the water does not touch the bottom.

With quick-cooking, small vegetables such as young peas or green beans, try steaming in wet lettuce leaves which, when heated, release moisture that steams the enclosed vegetables. Rinse two or three large leaves and arrange so that they cover the bottom of a saucepan and extend partway up the sides. Place the peas or beans in the center, leaving a margin so that they do not spill out when the lettuce leaves shrink as a result of cooking. Add a few more leaves, cover the pot, and place over low heat. When the lettuce is completely wilted after about 7 minutes, the enclosed vegetables will be steamed.

PARBOILING/BLANCHING

Parboiling, as I said earlier, means boiling the vegetables in water or stock until they are partially cooked. This technique is used to soften dense vegetables that will then be cooked using another preparation (e.g. parboiling potatoes before they are roasted or parboiling peppers in order to stuff them). Blanching means plunging food into boiling water for a very short period in order to soften it slightly (as in green beans that will then be used in a salad) or to facilitate the removal of skins or shells (as in tomatoes or fava beans).

HOW TO BOIL OR STEAM ANY VEGETABLE

The following list gives boiling and steaming times for all the vegetables profiled in this book. Because a vegetable's boiling or steaming time varies with its size, age, and tenderness, the list offers both minimum and maximum times. Note that the term "cut up" refers to vegetables that have been cut into equal-sized 1-inch-thick pieces. Cooking times are the same whether using the open-pan, maximum-water (at least 2 quarts for every pound of vegetables) or the covered-pan, minimum-water (1 cup for every pound) technique. In either case, place the vegetables in the water when it has come to a boil and begin timing when the water returns to boiling. Note that some vegetables require acidulated water which consists of 1 teaspoon lemon juice to 1 quart water.

Artichokes: Boil whole in acidulated water for 10–25 minutes, 5–15 minutes if cut up. Use a nonreactive pan. Do not steam.

Arugula: Boil whole leaves for 1–2 minutes, steam whole leaves for 5–7 minutes.

Asparagus: Boil whole for 5–8 minutes, 3–4 minutes if cut up. Steam whole for 10–15 minutes, 5–7 minutes if cut up. Use a nonreactive pan.

Beans, Fava: Blanch freshly shelled beans in skins for 3 minutes. Peel and boil for 10–15 minutes. Steam for 15–25 minutes.

Beans, Green: Boil whole for 5–10 minutes, 4–7 minutes if cut up. Steam whole for 15–20 minutes, 10–15 minutes if cut up.

Beets: Boil whole and unpeeled for 40 minutes to 2 hours. Do not steam.

Broccoli: Boil whole stalks for 5–10 minutes, 3–7 minutes if cut up. Steam stalks for 15–20 minutes, 10–15 minutes if cut up.

Brussels Sprouts: Boil whole for 5–7 minutes. Steam whole for 15–20 minutes.

Cabbage: Boil quarters for 10–15 minutes, 5–7 minutes if shredded. Steam quarters for 25–35 minutes, 10–15 minutes if shredded. For red cabbage, use a nonreactive pan and acidulated water.

Cardoons: Boil quartered ribs for 25–35 minutes. Do not steam. Use acidulated water.

Carrots: Boil whole for 15–20 minutes, 5–15 minutes if cut up. Steam whole for 25–40 minutes, 15–35 minutes if cut up.

Cauliflower: Boil whole for 15–20 minutes, 5–8 minutes if cut up. Steam whole for 45–50 minutes, 20–30 minutes if cut up.

Celeriac: Boil cut up for 10–15 minutes. Do not steam.

Celery: Boil whole ribs for 12–15 minutes, 10–15 minutes if cut up. Steam whole ribs for 20–25 minutes, 15–20 minutes if cut up.

Cucumbers: Boil peeled, seasoned halves for 7–10 minutes, quarters for 5–6 minutes, cut-up pieces for 3–5 minutes. Steam halves for 15–20 minutes, quarters for 10–15 minutes, pieces for 10–15 minutes.

Eggplant: Boil whole and unpeeled for 15–20 minutes, 5–10 minutes if peeled and cut up. Steam peeled and cut up for 20 minutes.

Fennel: Boil whole for 30–35 minutes, 10–15 minutes if quartered. Steam quartered for 20–25 minutes.

Greens: Boil whole beet, collard, mustard, or turnip leaves for 5–7 minutes. Steam whole leaves for 10–15 minutes.

Kale: Boil whole leaves for 10–15 minutes. Steam whole leaves for 15 minutes.

Kohlrabi: Boil whole for 30–40 minutes, 20 minutes if quartered. Do not steam.

Leeks or Scallions: Boil whole for 10–15 minutes, 2–3 minutes if cut up. Steam whole for 30 minutes, 7–10 minutes if cut up.

Lettuce: Boil separated romaine leaves and whole butterhead for 2–3 minutes, whole romaine for 5–10 minutes. Steam separated romaine leaves and whole butterhead for 10–15 minutes, whole romaine for 20–25 minutes.

Mushrooms: Do not boil. Steam whole for 3–8 minutes.

Onions: Boil small yellow or white onions for 15–30 minutes. Steam for 25–40 minutes. Do not steam or boil large onions.

Parsnips: Boil whole for 10–15 minutes, 5–10 minutes if cut up. Steam whole for 25–35 minutes, 20–30 minutes if cut up.

Peas: Boil large mature peas for 4–10 minutes, small young peas for 2 minutes. Steam large peas for 15–20 minutes, small peas for 5–7 minutes.

Peppers: Boil halves for 6–7 minutes, 4–5 minutes if cut up. Steam halves for 15 minutes, 8–10 minutes if cut up.

Potatoes: Boil whole and unpeeled for 25–30 minutes, 10–15 minutes if cut up. Steam cut up for 35–40 minutes.

Potatoes, New: Boil whole and unpeeled for 7–15 minutes, 10 minutes if quartered. Steam whole and unpeeled 25–35 minutes.

Rutabagas: Boil whole for 30–40 minutes, 15–20 minutes if cut up. Steam cut up for 30 minutes.

Salsify: Boil whole for 25–35 minutes, 20–30 minutes if cut up. Steam whole for 30–40 minutes, 25–35 minutes if cut up. Use aciduated water.

Sorrel: Do not boil or steam. Parboil whole leaves for 1 minute using a nonreactive pan.

Spinach: Boil whole leaves for 1–2 minutes. Steam whole leaves for 5–10 minutes.

Squashes, Summer: Boil whole and unpeeled for 5–20 minutes, 7–10 minutes if cut up. Steam whole and unpeeled for 10–20 minutes, 10–15 minutes if cut up.

Squashes, Winter: Boil cut up for 10–15 minutes. Steam cut up for 25–35 minutes.

Swiss Chard: Boil leaves for 1–2 minutes, ribs for 10–12 minutes. Steam leaves for 5–7 minutes, ribs for 5–20 minutes.

Tomatoes: Do not boil or steam. Blanch for 1 minute to remove skins.

Turnips: Boil whole for 10–15 minutes, 5–10 minutes if quartered. Steam whole for 25–30 minutes, 15–20 minutes if quartered.

Frying and Sautéing

There are two basic ways to fry vegetables: sautéing (also called pan frying) which means cooking in a minimum of hot oil or fat; and deep frying which means cooking in a large amount of very hot oil or fat. Either way, your vegetables come out crisp, since they are cooked only briefly without coming into contact with water, and delicious due to the coating of oil, fat, or batter that adds flavor while sealing in the vegetables' own juices.

When frying, vegetables must be cut into small, even-sized pieces that will cook quickly and in the same amount of time. Shredded vegetables may be bound with a batter and fried as *crespelle* (pancakes) or blended with thicker ingredients and fried as croquettes.

Moisture-retaining vegetables such as tomatoes must be coated with bread crumbs or flour batter to seal in their juices and protect their delicate flesh from the heat of the fat and the pan. Dense vegetables that require a long time to cook—cauliflower, cardoons, carrots—must be parboiled before frying to minimize the amount of time spent in the frying oil. In the case of deep frying, most vegetables (save potatoes whose high starch content acts as a moisture sealant) require a protective coat of batter to keep them from burning and drying in the sizzling oil.

BEFORE SAUTÉING

Quick-cooking vegetables such as baby green beans and mushrooms need no preparation before sautéing other than to be cut into small, even-sized pieces. A simple, all-purpose method for sautéing one or more vegetables is to place a shallow skillet containing a thin layer of butter or oil over moderate heat, add garlic or onion and cook until golden, add the vegetables, and cook 3–4 minutes, shaking the pan constantly. For single vegetables, you can add bread crumbs and cook for a minute more, until the crumbs have browned, before serving. For vegetable combinations, you can add a final squeeze of lemon and/or a dusting of freshly chopped herbs.

Fragile vegetables such as tomatoes, summer squashes, or sliced cucumbers should be coated to protect their flesh from high heat and to seal in moisture. Preparations for coating are simple: cut the rinsed, unpeeled, raw vegetables into thin (½-inch) slices that will cook quickly. The cut surfaces will be moist enough to make the coating adhere, so the coating can be simple: flour, dried bread crumbs, cornmeal, or cracker crumbs. Season the coating with salt, pepper, and, if you like, dried crushed herbs.

Coated vegetables should be turned only once to brown the coating on both sides, while those that are uncoated should be flipped constantly with a spatula—or shake the pan—to keep them moving briskly in the oil and to avoid overcooking.

In the majority of cases, Tuscan-style vegetables are sautéed in olive oil. Butter can also be used, but since it burns easily, the vegetables must either be very quick-cooking or the butter must be clarified or used as part of a butter-oil mix.

CHOOSING THE RIGHT OIL OR FAT FOR DEEP FRYING

Two factors must be weighed in choosing the proper fat or oil for deep frying: heat tolerance and flavor. First and most important, it must not smoke or burn when heated to temperatures of 375 degrees. It must also impart a complimentary flavor or, at the very least, refrain from imparting an uncomplimentary one.

Extra-virgin olive oil has the most flavor, but its smoking point is too low for most deep frying. Other vegetables oils—corn, soy, sunflower, and peanut—stand up well to high temperatures and impart various degrees of subtle flavoring. Avoid anything labeled "salad oil"; the smoking point is very low and heat makes it quickly turn rancid. Most animal fats—especially butter, chicken fat, and goose fat—have very low burning points. The exceptions are suet (beef kidney fat) and lard (pork fat) which also store well and have distinctive flavors, albeit ones that do not suit every palate. My personal favorite is peanut oil with a smoking point of 425 degrees and a faint flavor that does not mask that of the vegetables. It is also fairly inexpensive and stores well.

To keep the fats and oils fresh, store them in an airtight container in a cool, dark place. If refrigerating, allow them to return to room temperature before using. Never use any fat or oil whose smell or taste has changed, usually a sign of rancidity.

To use, pour in enough so that you can completely immerse the food, but to prevent dangerous spattering, never fill the pan more than half full. Use a heavy pan and preferably one that is deeper than it is wide or as close to that standard as possible; the more surface area exposed to air, the more quickly the oil or fat reaches its smoking point.

Oil and fat can be reused after frying, although its smoking point will be lower each time. Let the oil cook, then strain it into a container that has been lined with a double thickness of cheesecloth. Straining removes food particles that would burn when the fat is reheated. Food particles also speed spoilage.

COATING WITH A BATTER

Vegetables other than potatoes will dry out rapidly in the hot oil required by deep frying. You can, however, protect the integrity of the vegetable by sealing it within some kind of starchy batter. Almost any vegetable, from sorrel leaves to mushrooms to string beans, can be fried this way. You may prefer to fry only one type of vegetable at a time—onions are usually done alone because of their strong flavor—or you can combine as many as you like. Each, however, must be prepared in advance, from cutting to pre-cooking to even marinating, which works well with bland or sweet vegetables. A good marinade includes lemon or vinegar (or even wine), extra-virgin olive oil, salt, pepper, and herbs. Allow vegetables to steep in the marinade (turning every so often) for 1 hour before coating in batter and frying.

To ensure that the batter coats vegetable pieces evenly, it should be made well in advance of frying and allowed to rest for an hour at room temperature. In this way, the flour can absorb the liquid and sufficiently thicken the batter. A good all-purpose, Tuscan-style batter contains flour, salt, egg yolks, water or milk, and beaten egg whites. The proportions of the ingredients can be varied to taste. The addition of more liquid will produce a thinner batter that is crisp and light when fried but tends to spread out in the oil. A thicker batter, on the other hand, will cling to the vegetables but have a spongier, more breadlike texture. For a lighter batter, substitute water for the milk; for added flavor, use beer.

To make Tuscan-style batter, sift the dry ingredients into a large bowl. Make a well in the center and add the oil, egg yolks, and liquid. Whisk the ingredients, starting in the well and incorporating flour a little at a time. Continue to whisk until smooth. Cover and let rest at room temperature for 1 hour. Immediately before using, add the beaten egg whites (they should be beaten to the point of forming peaks). Using your hands, gently fold the egg whites into the batter. Coat each vegetable individually just before frying. If you do not have a deep-frying thermometer, drop a little batter into the oil. If it sizzles on contact, the oil is sufficiently hot for frying—375 degrees.

Braising and Stewing

In braising and stewing, vegetables cook slowly in a relatively small amount of liquid. Unlike boiling, where the aim is to cook vegetables as quickly as possible to conserve their individual flavors and textures, braising requires long, slow cooking because the object is to mingle the flavors of the ingredients. The fact that vegetables transfer their flavor to the braising liquid is a plus since that liquid, reduced during cooking to a thick sauce, is as much an essential part of the finished dish as the smooth, soft texture of the braised vegetables.

Braises and stews differ in only one factor: braises consist of a single vegetable cooked with a little added liquid, and stews contain a mixture of many vegetables often cooked in their own juices. The choice of liquid is paramount in creating a braise or a stew. Wine or another acid such as tomato or lemon juice will keep soft vegetables intact while they cook and contribute zest to the finished dish. Vegetable or veal stock provides a mild-tasting complement to any sort of vegetable, while beef stock creates a more robust flavor.

Both braises and stews include seasoning elements—garlic, herbs, or aromatic vegetable sautés (sofrittos)—and sometimes even sugar, added to counterbalance naturally acidic vegetables such as tomatoes or to produce a rich glaze.

Vegetables may also be filled with savory stuffings before being braised. Vegetables braised singly are generally served as an accompaniment; if served as an entrée, they are most often surrounded by a starch such as rice or pasta and/or another vegetable dish such as a salad. Stews, on the other hand, consist of multiple vegetables and are generally thicker, more robust creations; as such, they tend to be served as free-standing entrées.

THE WHYS AND WHEREFORES OF BRAISING

Braising always involves long, slow simmering, but preparations and flavoring ingredients can be added to suit different vegetables or to vary the effect of the finished dish. The braising liquid itself is a critical flavoring element and can include juices, stocks, wine, beer, or just plain water which will create a braise tasting primarily of the individual vegetables. The ideal liquid is one that enriches the flavor without imposing too much of its own character. It should also have so much body that by the end of cooking it will have reduced to a syrupy sauce that needs no thickening (except in cases were thickening agents are added to enhance flavor, as in the case of eggs and cream).

Firm, sweet vegetables such as carrots acquire an extra richness when braised in sugar, butter, and liquid, a process known as glazing. During the cooking period, the liquid evaporates, leaving the vegetables coated with a shiny film of syrup. Onions, parsnips, and beets are also good candidates for glazing. Glazes may be even further reduced so that the sugar caramelizes, coloring the vegetables a rich brown—a treatment particularly appropriate for small white onions. For both clear and caramelized glazes, use a sauté pan or skillet large enough to hold the vegetables in one layer. If the pan is overcrowded, the vegetables will steam in their own juices, preventing the evaporation that forms the glaze.

Vegetables braised in wine taste different from those braised in water or juice or stock, and not just because of the flavor of the wine. Also at play is the wine's acidity which keeps vegetables firm during cooking so that they may be simmered for longer periods than usual. And long simmering means a more thorough blending of flavors.

The type of wine to use depends on the vegetables you are braising. Strong-flavored vegetables—leeks or red cabbage, for example—may be cooked in either red or white wine. But mild-flavored vegetables such as zucchini or eggplant will be overpowered by red wine; braise them in a less assertive white.

Any wine should be tempered with an equal amount of stock or water. As always, the wine should be of good quality. Remember the old adage: "Never cook with a wine you wouldn't drink."

STUFFING VEGETABLES FOR BRAISING

Large onions, peppers, eggplant, and zucchini are all the appropriate size and shape for stuffing; they also keep their shapes during braising. Vegetables vary greatly in the amount of preparation they require before stuffing. While zucchini and eggplant must both be halved and hollowed out, for example, zucchini's flesh can be easily removed with a spoon, while eggplant must first be precooked to soften the firm flesh. Peppers, which should be firm and square-shaped to stand upright, need only have their tops cut off and the seeds and ribs removed. Onions are more difficult; the insides need to be scooped out with a spoon or a small paring knife.

Fillings can range from a mixture of mushrooms, onions, and tomatoes for a lighter dish to one that incorporates rice, bread crumbs, or polenta as bulk-adding binders.

Ripe summer tomatoes make an excellent braising sauce for many stuffed leaf dishes. To make a sauce from fresh tomatoes, chop them coarsely and put them in a stainless steel, enameled, or tin-lined pan. Add salt and herbs—basil, parsley, and thyme—and chopped onions and garlic. Taste the tomatoes before cooking. The ripest ones are naturally sweet, but if others have an acidy taste, add a pinch of sugar.

Simmer the chopped tomatoes gently, stirring occasionally to prevent them from sticking. When the tomatoes have softened—this will take 30 to 40 minutes—pass them through a food mill to remove the skins and seeds. The resulting sauce should have the consistency of heavy cream; if necessary, reduce to the desired level.

STEWING VEGETABLES IN THEIR OWN JUICES

In most mixed vegetable stews, the vegetables themselves render the liquid that serves as the braising medium. In some cases, as in stews containing tomatoes and zucchini, which release a great deal of moisture, the liquid must be significantly reduced before the stew can be served. When attempting to create a sauce reduction, never raise the heat while the vegetables are in the cooking liquid; the agitation caused by fast boiling damages the vegetables. Instead, strain off the liquid, pour it into a shallow saucepan, and boil until it has reduced by half before returning to the stew. When making stews composed mainly of firm, dry vegetables, always include one that renders moisture—like lettuce—and add a little water as well.

Almost any vegetable can form part of a mixed stew, although different vegetables should be added at different times according to the amount of cooking needed. Preliminary preparations are also a consideration; tender young vegetables are usually added raw, for example, but older vegetables require parboiling. Parboiling also minimizes the strong flavors of vegetables such as leeks and fixes the crispness and color of baby string beans which would become limp and gray if braised raw.

TURNING BRAISES INTO RICH, CREAMY SAUCES

Any braising liquid can be turned into a thick sauce by adding either flour or a mixture of egg yolks and cream. If you use flour, add it at the start of cooking so that it will have enough time to "lose itself" in the other flavors. Egg yolks and cream, on the other hand, can stand neither long simmering nor high temperatures and should be added just before serving. But make sure you do not allow the sauce to boil, or the egg yolks will curdle instead of forming a smooth emulsion.

Baking and Roasting

The myriad ways in which vegetables can be oven-baked are limited only by the imagination of the cook. Roasted whole and unadorned, vegetables develop mellow yet concentrated flavors. Sliced and baked in a covered pan, they steam to perfection in their own aromatic juices. Gratins, puddings, and soufflés blend textures as well as flavors. And, of course, there's always stuffed vegetables—elaborate and delicious.

Cooking vegetables whole and in their own skins is the simplest baking technique, ideal for root vegetables as well as for eggplant and winter squashes which all have tough enough skins to protect their flesh from the drying oven heat. Potato skins should, of course, always be pierced to allow for the escape of steam that might otherwise cause an explosion. Beets take three or four times as long as potatoes, but the resulting flavor is so astoundingly sublime as to warrant heating the oven expressly for them. Their skins, however, while thick enough to help retain the beets' juices, are not thick enough for protection against drying. To keep beets moist, wrap each one in foil and roast in a preheated oven set no higher than 325 degrees for 2 to 3 hours.

Bulbs of garlic, baked in their skins, develop a mild, sweet flavor without any trace of harshness. They are also easy to peel and soft enough to puree. When blended with olive oil, the puree can be stored in a jar, refrigerated, and used as a flavoring or added to a vinaigrette. For longer storage (up to 1 month), add enough olive oil to create a layer thick enough protect the purée from the air, and a little bit of some kind of acid, like vinegar or lemon juice, to inhibit bacterial growth.

STUFFING VEGETABLES

Any vegetable that can be stuffed and braised can also be stuffed and baked. But you can also work with vegetables that would not otherwise survive the slow, moist cooking braising demands—vegetables such as mushroom caps which would become rubbery if braised but are crisply tender when baked. Or tomatoes which would disintegrate in a braising liquid but hold their shapes beautifully during baking, provided they are not overly ripe.

When deciding which ingredients to include in a particular stuffing blend, consider the amount of moisture generated by the vegetables during baking. Tomatoes, for example, have a very high water content and require moisture-absorbing starches to soak up rendered tomato juices. Artichokes, on the other hand, exude very little liquid during cooking and, since they require up to 1½ hours of baking, can dry out in the oven. To prevent this, stuff them with a moist mixture that will provide some liquid. A glass of wine or stock added to the baking dish will also provide flavor and serve as a basting liquid.

BAKING VEGETABLE SLICES

When you bake vegetables that have been peeled or cut so that their flesh is no longer protected by their skins, you must ensure that they will stay moist in the dry heat of an oven. One way is to add liquid such as stock, water, or wine. Some vegetables—notably eggplant, tomatoes, sweet peppers, and zucchini—can be cooked without added moisture because they render water during cooking. When cooked in a covered vessel, they will actually cook in the aromatic steam from their own juices.

A few steps should be followed if the vegetables are to steam successfully. They should be tightly packed into their baking dish to conserve moisture and expose as little of their flesh as possible. A little extra-virgin olive oil dribbled over the top at the start of cooking will also keep the vegetables from scorching before they begin to render their own juices. The cover, be it glass, metal, or foil, should also be as tight as possible to keep steam from escaping.

GRATINS

Gratinating vegetables *(gratinare)* means baking or broiling them until the surface layer becomes brown and crispy. Generally, gratin crusts are either dry and crunchy (which means they were created with grated cheese, bread crumbs, or both) or delicate and chewy, in which case the vegetables were coated with cream, *besciamella,* or a cheese custard. Many vegetables are gratinated only as a finishing touch (braised radicchio, for example, can be coated with cream and briefly baked to create a crispy crust), but the making of a crust can also be an integral part of a dish's preparation.

The trick to creating an integral gratin with raw vegetables is to cook the vegetables without burning them, yet still achieve an appetizingly crisp crust. To this end, quick-cooking vegetables are usually arranged in a shallow porcelain baking dish so that a maximum surface area is exposed to the browning heat. Vegetables that render their own water (spinach, chard, tomatoes, zucchini) may be gratinated without adding any other liquid to the baking dish. To heat the dish quickly and speed the baking, the cooking process begins in a very hot oven; then the temperature is reduced to bake the vegetables to tenderness. The crust does not form until the last few minutes of cooking, at which time it may be necessary to raise the heat to fully develop the crust.

Vegetables that render very little moisture, such as artichokes, need added liquid to prevent them from shriveling and drying out in the oven. Sandwiched between layers of moistened bread, for example, only the topmost bread dries out to produce the gratin. Chopped onion, garlic, herbs, and anchovies may be added to the bread.

Slow-cooking vegetables like winter squash need even more consideration to keep them from drying out. One method is to cut them into cubes, toss in olive oil and herbs, pack them in a deep dish, and cook at low heat (325 degrees) for a long period of time (2 to 2½ hours). The slow cooking time and the thickness of the vegetable layer allow the evaporation of just enough moisture to reduce the squash's bulk and intensify its flavor. The cubes at the top brown to a crust without the aid of any further topping.

Cream can also be used to keep vegetables moist during gratinating, and it also provides a sauce when they are done. Furthermore, the cream undergoes a chemical reaction during cooking: its natural sugar forms a browned crust on top of the sauce. Grated cheese or bread crumbs can also be added to provide a crisp contrast to the sauce beneath. Underlying vegetables can be thinly sliced or even grated.

Flour-based *besciamella* and cheese custard sauces can also be used to create a hearty, moist gratin. While the former produces a light but substantial crust, the latter results in an especially airy crust that puffs up like a soufflé.

Broiling and Grilling

Broiling and grilling are both very simple cooking techniques, but when vegetables cook over or under such intense heat, special precautions are needed to retain their juiciness. In most cases, vegetables are thinly sliced to expose a maximum of surface area; this method insures that vegetables cook quickly with minimal drying. Another way to cook them rapidly is to cut them into small pieces and skewer them.

Soft vegetables such as eggplant, zucchini, and tomatoes should be oiled or marinated before cooking to keep them moist. Dense or fibrous vegetables such as celery, fennel, potatoes, or carrots must not only be coated with oil, but repeatedly basted to keep the surfaces from drying out before the interiors cook.

When broiling any vegetable, remove the pan and preheat the broiler for 15 minutes to ensure a high, even temperature. If vegetables look as if they're browning too quickly, lower the rack or oven shelf; do not lower the broiler temperature.

Sealing vegetables in foil packages is a wonderful way to cook them on the grill. In this way, they partly steam in their own juices and absorb the added flavor of whatever else is tucked within the package—herbs or spices, for example. Use heavy-duty foil, sealed with double folds at the top and ends. Cook the vegetables whole or cut into pieces and try mixing several types in one package.

Vegetables should be grilled 6 inches above coals that have been allowed to burn for 30 to 45 minutes until they are covered with white ash. Cooking times for grilling will vary according to the way you trim the vegetables. Wrapped in foil, fleshy whole or cut-up vegetables such as eggplant, onions, and tomatoes will cook through in 20 to 30 minutes; beets, carrots, and potatoes will take 45 minutes to an hour.

Sliced, unwrapped vegetables such as zucchini and eggplant will take 15 to 20 minutes to cook. Make sure to liberally coat the slices with oil before placing on the grill and to baste frequently in order to prevent from burning. Vegetable slices are done when they can be easily pierced with a fork. Vegetables that have been wrapped in aluminum foil packages are done when they yield easily to gentle pressure.

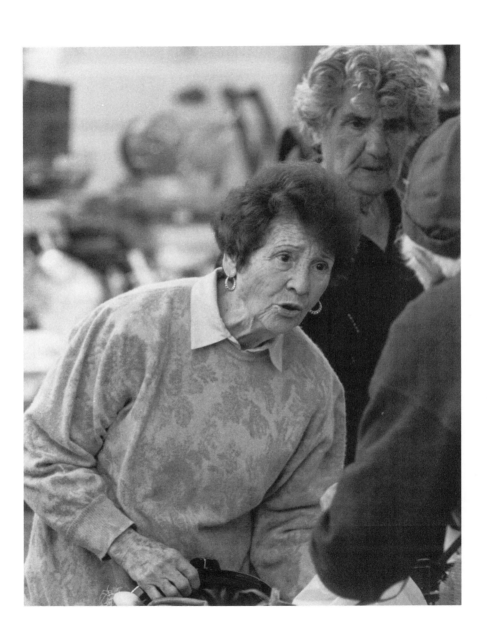

Leaves and Stalks

Some Things Are Better the Old Way

There is a category of older person who, regardless of the Internet and auto-mated checking and wash-and-wear sheets, still prefers to do things the old way. They pay all their bills in person, talk on the telephone only when abso-lutely necessary (and always in a voice loud enough to be heard down the street), dress formally even to empty the mailbox, and never ever eat anything unless they are sitting at a properly set table.

My 83-year-old mother is one of these, and today she wants me to go with her to the cemetery to pay homage to my father who died over fifteen years ago. She wants my opinion of the picture on top of *Babbo*'s tomb. She is not happy with it, she says. "His face is tilted to such an angle that it doesn't look like him."

On the way, we take the long route, walking up the main *viale* to the florist on the corner. It is not her usual flower shop but on Thursdays the proprietor goes to Pisa for a special order of Aurelian lilies and Mother always orders a dozen in a color she refers to as *rosso fegato*, liver red. Today, however, he was unable to ob-tain them, bringing her instead a variety that is paler in color but infinitely more fragrant.

"They simply will not do," she tells him as soon as he removes them from the bucket. From the look on his face, it is clear he had already known this would be the case.

We cross the piazza to another florist, Luca's, and Mother instructs me to buy some purple irises. She cannot buy them herself, she says, because Luca knows she always buys her flowers from Gianfranco, except on Thursdays when she orders lilies from Beppe. "It would not look good," she says. *"Brutta figura."*

I start to protest, to explain that Luca should—and probably would—be happy to sell her his flowers. But then I stop, aware of the fact that she is 83 and has been living this way for a lifetime. *"Quante ne vuoi?"* I ask. How many do you want?

The entrance to the cemetery is lined with acacias overhanging the stone pathway. People arrive and depart constantly, many lingering to chat on one of the numerous stone benches placed at the end of each row of tombs. This is, you see, more than simply a place where the living go to honor the dead. It is a meeting place, a social communion that binds the town's present inhabitants to those who lived as far back as the 1400s. As if to signify this link, bodies here are not in the ground. They're at a halfway point between earth and air, in waist-high marble tombs situated side by side, each with its own flower vase on top, an electrified light, and a framed picture of the person inside.

For years when I was little, I would try walking past the pictures, always pretending a distance made formal by the cold luster of the marble. But my feet would inevitably freeze in the cool, sandy earth, and I would see from the corner of my eye the faces stretching beyond the frames, calling me back. "See me as I was," the cries would meld with the air and seep back through the pores of my skin. "Not as a tablespoon of dust. Spend time with me; include me. Every cell of your body is, after all, one of which I too am part."

"Look at that picture of your father," Mother says now, pulling me away from Paolo Manzini, a good-looking teenager who died in 1963. "Don't you think I should have it redone?"

The curved face of the glass catches the sun's angle. As I lean over *Babbo's* tomb, twisting my face this way and that to get a better look, he appears to me as a giant of a figure, the sun making it seem he might at any moment burst out of his frame and waltz me down the walkway. Looking at it close up, however, I see a man dressed in a fine dark suit and monochromatic tie. His head is tilted to the right and there is a hint of a dimple accompanying his smile. The look on his face says he is happy in the way I always remember him being, without even a minor complexity clouding the horizon.

"The picture is fine," I tell her.

"But it doesn't look like him."

"To me it does."

"Look at it again."

"It looks *exactly* like him," I tell her, knowing that no matter what I say, she will probably dither for another three or four years and then eventually change it.

"Yes, but does it make him look *good*?"

"Wait one second," I say. "Are you talking about whether it looks like him or whether this is the best picture of *Babbo* I've ever seen? If that's what you're asking, I much prefer the small framed photo on your dresser. The one where he is wearing his tux and has that white silk scarf draped around his neck. He is much more handsome there."

"More handsome than *here*?" She points to the photo and turns to face me with a look of abject incredulity. "How can you say that? Look at that gleam in his eyes. Look at his smile, how happy he was that day we went to Cinqueterre. Your father was one of the most handsome men this town has ever seen!"

We begin the daily ritual of shining the marble and arranging the flowers in the granite vase. Excepting rainy days and those when a *tromba d'aria* sweeps down from the Garfagnana, its tight black funnel sometimes raising roofs from houses, she, like the rest of Massarosa's widows, comes to the cemetery to take care of the dead.

She hands me the asters she has just removed from the vase next to the framed photo. "Place these in that pile at the foot of the second row," she directs me.

When I return, she hands me a pot of sandalwood wax and a piece of cotton ragging. She wants me to climb on top of the tomb and put polish on *Babbo's* name. "Make sure you maneuver your finger inside the letters that are closed," she says, making a circular motion with her index finger. "The point at the top of the A, and both loops of the F."

"The letters are like mirrors," I tell her. "They don't need polish."

"They're dirty from yesterday's rain," she insists. "You'll see when you finish, the difference. Do it for your father."

Do it for my father. The words are accompanied by tense movements of her head and especially her eyes. What this means is that people are watching; that I should not let them see me questioning my mother's words; that I should do what my mother tells me like good daughters have done since the time of Lucia de Medici, and if I want the upper hand, I should have daughters of my own.

"Also, check the bulb in the lamp while you're up there. And be careful not to break it!" Her admonition takes me back to last November, when I, in fact, broke the bulb while checking it on the eve of All Soul's Day. Mother was furious—not so much because of the breakage itself (although she does tend towards a certain level of impatience) but because of the All Soul's Day legend which has God gazing with greater favor on those whose tombs are lit, seeing in this display of family caring proof of the soul's inherent worth.

She spent the rest of the day pleading with the local electrician to go to the cemetery and see what he could do. When it turned out he had no replacement for the bulb and neither did any of the local stores—it being the eve of a holiday that, among other things, seriously taxes the reserves of electrical supply stores—she dispatched a friend to Viareggio, the neighboring town, with instructions to keep going up the coast until he found a bulb.

Having finished at the cemetery, we drive to the market. This being Thursday, Viareggio's marketplace is even more hectic than normal. Thursday is known throughout Tuscany as the day reserved for *la piazza*, the day when farmers come from surrounding towns and villages to join with cheese producers, fishermen, and cured meat vendors in creating a colorful festival of sights, smells, and sounds.

Especially sounds.

Whatever else one might say of market day, no one can ignore the accompanying elevation in decibel level—that cacophonous symphony of competing forces, each with its own particular urgency: children crying for yet another *biscottino*; women yelling for service over the heads of those who were there first; men bellowing orders to move this crate over here or back that *camioncino* into there; vendors hawking merchandise ("*Tutto a diecimila lire, diecimila lire, tutto!*" Everything you see, ten thousand lire, ten thousand lire, everything!); and, of course, women haggling.

This last, women haggling, is as much a part of the Tuscan landscape as the aforementioned trip to the cemetery. Without haggling, life in this fair province would be pallid in the extreme, vacuous, mechanical, without tradition. Witness this response from a woman who was scolded by one of Viareggio's fruit vendors for her relentless haggling. *"Oh, ma che ti credi, se non si stiracchia, la democrazia va giú!"* Oh, don't kid yourself, if we ever stop haggling, it will be the end of the Republic!

The haggling itself can take many forms and be motivated by anything from outrage over the stated price to suspicion that the quality is not as good as it once was to quibbling over a statement made by either the vendor or the purchaser (as in: "I picked these artichokes this morning." "Don't tell me you picked them this morning, these artichokes are at least three days old.") or even to arguing over incidents long in the past ("I want the good *baccalà*, not that odious facsimile you pawned off on me last month, calling it San Giovanni. Why, as soon as I put it in my mouth, I knew it was that inferior type imported from Norway.").

As hagglers go, my mother is what I would call quite good. She has, in fact, perfected a technique guaranteed to ward off many of the potential incidents that would warrant a good haggle. She does it, I believe, by inspiring fear in the vendors. *"Non si preoccupi, Signora Valleroni,"* they all say when she complains about the price of polenta. *"Ti faremo un scontino."* Don't worry, Signora Valleroni, we will give you a discount.

The trick lies not so much with appearance, my mother being generally unimposing in both size and shape. Neither does it have much to do with whether or not she is perceived as knowing the difference between superior and inferior quality produce. Like *every* Tuscan of a certain age, Mother is genetically predisposed to, for example, know the difference between full, rounded fennel bulbs and the flatter variety that is infinitely more tender, or between high-starch floury potatoes and the creamier ones used in making perfect *gnocchi*.

No, the secret lies in the eye contact between her and the vendors, a cold, unwavering stare that says, "I am watching every move you make." My mother, you see, trusts nobody. In that, she is quintessentially Tuscan. But whereas others might lean on what they perceive as "good rapport" between themselves and their suppliers, assuming that, since they have dealt with each other for years and will continue to do so for the foreseeable future, they will be taken care of in a somewhat honorable manner, Mother assumes nothing. She approaches the business of shopping for food as though she were descending into a biblical den of thieves.

She arms herself with patience, the patience to survey and observe and note the various vendors' appearances. *"Vedi, quello,"* she'll tell me. *"Quello ha i pantaloni sporchi con la terra fresca."* See that one. That one has fresh dirt on his overalls. The implication, of course, is that he was in the fields this morning and, thus, that his produce is fresher than that of someone who picked it last night.

This is not to say that her criteria always make sense. A notable example of what I consider to be a ridiculous touchstone is when she judges the freshness of bread by whether the vendor lays it round side up or round side down after slicing portions for customers. To my mother, if the bread is returned to the shelf round side down, it flattens and compresses the *midolla*—the pulp—to the point of rendering it overly tough. But ridiculous or not, the fact remains that she always seems to return home with the best of the lot—the sweetest apples, the most succulent asparagus, the freshest *focaccia*, the most savory anchovies.

Another factor in her success lies undoubtedly in the words she chooses to employ when negotiating with the various vendors. Like all Tuscans of her class, she is formal and decorous. On this particular morning, she is surveying the various cheeses on display with an eye to purchasing some *pecorino*. It is fava bean season here, and one of the best ways to enjoy those tiny, early-season delicacies is shelled, peeled, dipped in olive oil, and consumed with a small wedge of one- to two-month-old *pecorino*.

"Mi da un Chilo di pecorino nuovo," she says graciously. I'd like a kilo of very young *pecorino*. Anyone overhearing the exchange would undoubtedly note that she has used the second-person formal rather than second-person familiar in addressing the vendor. Second-person formal is a sign of respect, one used when speaking to elders, professionals, and members of a certain class.

But my mother uses it for more discriminating purposes, namely to seduce vendors into divesting themselves of their very best produce.

The proof of her duplicity lies in the numerous instances when I have witnessed her talking to merchants with whom she has no daily commercial dealings, such as when we attended the village band concert the other night and a candy vendor asked if we wanted to purchase some *croccante*—nut brittle. She, without blinking an eye, said, *"Che tipi n'ai?"*—What kinds do you have?—using second person familiar.

But now she wants something specific, and the tactics have been altered to suit the situation.

"Ho solo questo caciotto e un pó di quello tipo Romano," says the vendor, testing the waters. I only have this *caciotto* and a little of this Roman-style one.

"That's impossible," she says, turning her attention to the two small wooden crates stacked behind the display table. *"E' sicuro?"* Are you sure? (Second person formal.)

His gaze follows hers, and, in the next second, he is bustling to unload a box of *marzolino,* the wonderfully fresh young cheese made only in March and April. *"Caspita, c'e anche quest'altro che me l'ha portato Beppe stamani,"* he stammers. Good gracious, there's also this other one that Beppe brought me just this morning.

Our next stop is Valerio, the cheese vendor known for the excellent quality of his *mascarpone.* In view of the circumstances that have taken place in the last few days, Mother will not, this morning, be purchasing any *mascarpone,* but she is anxious to see the effect of all that publicity.

It was exactly four days ago that the first little boy died from what was ultimately found to be botulism. By yesterday, three more children were dead, and finally, last night, officials from the Interior Ministry confirmed that the deaths had, indeed, been caused by botulism found in a shipment of *mascarpone* cheese produced by Parmalat. Within hours of the report, restaurants throughout Italy had revised their menus to exclude *tiramisú,* the popular dessert made with ground espresso, chocolate, and *mascarpone* cheese.

"E' un disastro," says Valerio when Mother asks how he's doing. It's a disaster. No matter that the botulism was restricted to *mascarpone* made by Parmalat, the giant industrial producer of milk products. No matter also that the outbreak took place in Emilia-Romagna which is over a hundred miles from Tuscany. People are afraid, he says. "And in the name of fear, it becomes very easy to do without a product whose consumption is strictly tied to the concept of *nuova cucina,"* *nouvelle cuisine.*

My mind floats back to two conversations I overheard the day before while waiting on line to buy bread. The first had started with a basic rehash of information regarding the number of people who had died and the efficient manner in which the bacteria had been traced to Parmalat. But it had quickly assumed a more moralistic tone.

"E' la voce di Dio," said one of the two women involved. It is the voice of God.

In her version of events, Parmalat was God's vehicle for delivering the message that Italy has come too far too fast. "Things were better the old way," she declared firmly. "When we all raised our food on our own little plots of dirt and ate only what was natural and in season."

Her companion had unequivocally agreed. "Something is bound to happen when your cheese comes sealed in plastic from a factory," she had added. "Did you see on the news the building where Parmalat makes *mascarpone?* Did you see how big it was?"

The discussion had gone on to include pre-cut vegetables, pre-soaked beans, packaged bread, and the advent of discount stores. "Everybody goes to Sosty," said the first woman, referring to a giant supermarket where fruits and vegetables are sold by the crate for much less than they would cost in traditional village stores. "And they think they have gotten a better deal because they paid less. But once I bought a crate of peaches and, instead of ripening, they rotted! *No no no,* I will continue to buy from Adriana and pay a few thousand lire more, but at least I know where my lettuce is grown."

The second conversation had taken place between two women I know well, one a teacher at the local school and the other an X-ray technician who works in Viareggio's hospital. Both Liliana and Anamaria are married, with children cared for by their mothers to whose houses they were en route for lunch. Like the other two women, Liliana and Anamaria also felt there were larger implications resulting from the Parmalat fiasco.

"*La nuova cucina é un concetto sbagliato dal principio,*" Anamaria said. *Nouvelle cuisine* was a wrong-headed concept from its inception. "What kind of cooking focuses on artistry instead of flavor and on ever-new ingredients at the expense of those we have used for decades to great satisfaction? Its only proponents are people who must always have something new, whose appreciation for food derives from the very fact of its being new rather than an objective evaluation of its merits. No wonder it never really caught on here."

Liliana, a self-described dessert addict, laughingly chided her friend for being overly critical of a type of cooking that "has, after all, created such *meravigli* as *tiramisú* and *panna cotta,*" baked cream tarts. She added, however, that, to a large extent, ingredients such as *mascarpone* were now used "to mask the fact that one either does not know how to cook or does not want to devote the necessary time."

"You see it being thrown into everything," she said. "Penne with shrimp and *mascarpone,* polenta with *mascarpone* and pesto, risotto with squid and *mascarpone.* Things have reached the point that when I see *mascarpone* on a menu, I know the chef is someone who treats cooking like many people treat exercise—the easier the better."

"What do you think will happen?" I ask Valerio, who is making a sign to put in front of his stall that says, "This is not THAT *mascarpone!*" He sighs and says it will probably take a few weeks. "But *mascarpone* is not beef," he says, referring to the "mad cow" scare that took place last year. Then, Italian beef consumption plummeted over fears as to whether the meat had been imported from England. But his reference is equally pointed towards the fact that Tuscans are not known for being big beef (or for that matter, big meat) eaters. "Beef is something Tuscans can do without," he declares. "*Mascarpone* is now in the blood."

Our shopping complete my mother and I return home to the Massorosa and begin making preparations for lunch. Today we're having pasta with artichokes followed by an array of stuffed vegetables (zucchini, zucchini blossoms, potatoes, eggplant, and tomatoes), celeriac salad, and a spectacular puree made from new potatoes and leeks.

As we wait for the pasta water to boil, I plug my laptop's modem into her phone outlet, explaining that I need to check my messages and that it will only take a minute. It is the first time she has ever witnessed the miracle of e-mail, and she hovers over me, pressing for an explanation as to what exactly is going on. "These are letters that have been sent to me," I show her, downloading the day's mail. "And now I am going to write replies and send them."

"Why would you not simply use the telephone?" she asks.

"Because e-mail is cheaper."

"But you cannot hear what the person is saying. How can you know what they really mean?"

"What I lose in inflection, I gain in ease of contact."

"In other words, you can exchange a greater number of words on a greater number of occasions, even though nobody is ever exactly sure what is being said."

"It's like sending a letter," I try. "When you write a letter, there are certain things you give up, one being that your words have to stand on their own, without your voice serving as an amplifier. Right?"

"Yes, but a letter is, by its very nature, a monologue, a format for one to explicate certain thoughts without subjecting them to the back-and-forth dance of conversation. This e-mail, as you explain it, is a substitute for conversation. Did you not just tell me that you use it to *talk* to certain people every day?"

I try another tack. "Well, pretty soon I'll have a little camera on top of the computer and speakers, and then I'll be able to both see and hear who I'm talking to."

I can see she is impressed. But it only lasts for a short time. "However, you will still have to make a sort of appointment to speak, as you do with the telephone. If you call and no one is there, no conversation will take place." She moves back to the stove and begins to throw the pasta into the pot.

"No no no," she says, relinquishing any tiny bit of interest she might have mustered for the subject. "I will stay with talking to people in person. Then I can see them, hear them, smell them, touch them, and when I walk away, know that I have a firm grasp on what transpired."

She lifts out a strand of pasta and tastes to see if it is done. "You can change and refashion and evolve and adapt," she says, taking the colander from the pantry. "But some things are better the old way."

About Leaves and Stalks

Tuscany in springtime is a riot of green. From sugarloaf chicories to bicolor radicchios to curly endives, the unknowing observer could easily be excused for thinking that every leaf in the salad is a one-of-a-kind variety. And in fact, it might just be. There are dozens of Tuscan greens as yet unknown to Americans: *pan di zucchero, dolce bianca, spadona, biondissima, grumolo verde, riccia pancalieri, cartocciate d'ingegnoli, puntarelle, geante maraichere* . . . the list is endless. And while Tuscans have always enjoyed an extravagance of riches where greens are involved, Americans are just catching up.

In this country, in fact, greens (including those grown especially for their leaves, but also the tops of root vegetables) have long been the most underutilized of vegetables. Spinach is tainted with the precocities of childhood. Lettuce, sorrel, and endive are generally reserved for salads. Kale, chard, and mustard greens get boiled to a frazzle. And the more esoteric varieties such as amaranth, chicory, broccoli rabe, and radicchio have yet to gain wide distribution.

The situation is not much better when it comes to stalks. While celery is widely known, it is used mainly as either a flavoring ingredient or as part of a raw vegetable appetizer. Fennel and cardoons are reserved for high-end restaurants. Only artichokes and asparagus have climbed to stardom.

But farmers markets—now part of the urban landscape—are changing all that, and, because of the availability they make possible, restaurants are increasingly prone to experimentation.

The following chapter includes a great variety of greens as well as asparagus, artichokes, celery, and cardoons. In many cases the greens are interchangeable, although they produce uniquely different flavors. Parsley frittata can just as well be made with arugula or chard or watercress; risotto with radicchio also works with amaranth, spinach, and beet greens. But you will never know until you try, and so *avanti!*

Amaranth *Amaranto*

One of the oldest and most common of vegetable greens, amaranth (*Amaranthus gangeticus)* is still quite new to both Tuscans and Americans. Its flavor is very like that of spinach, although it is generally used more for its appearance than its taste; its small, red, lance-shaped leaves are perfect for salads and bedding presentations.

Season: Spring through fall

To Buy: Look for crisp, springy leaves with no hint of wilting or yellowing.

To Prepare: Trim stems and wash well.

Artichokes *Carciofi*

Artichokes (*Cynara scolymus)* are members of the daisy family and a relative of the lowly thistle. Natives of southern Europe and Mediterranean Africa, they are extensively cultivated in this country, mainly in California. Of the budding head, only the bulbous bottoms and fleshy leaf bases are edible. If you try eating any of the spiny leaves, you'll instantly know why the "choke" got its name. Tuscans cultivate a type of artichoke that is, unfortunately, not available in U.S. markets — a thinner, longer, purplish variety called *mazzeferate* that is far more tender and succulent.

Season: Early spring

To Buy: Look for compact, tight leaves, heavy globes for their size, no wrinkling, and few or no brown blemishes. Tuscans judge freshness by rubbing two artichokes together; if they "squeak," they're fresh. Theoretically, the size of an artichoke has nothing to do with its quality, but unless you are going to stuff them (in which case you need larger specimens), stick to the medium-sized or smallish ones. They have little or no chokes (if they are smaller than 2 ounces, you can eat them whole) and need far less peeling and cutting since more of the leaves are edibly tender.

To Prepare: Prepare a bowl filled with 1 quart of water mixed with 1 tablespoon lemon juice. Carefully break off the leaves at the base, discarding them until you come to the pale, tender leaves near the heart. Using a sharp knife, cut 1 inch off the top of the remaining leaves and immediately dip the cut portion in the lemon water. Remove the purple-tipped prickly leaves in the center using your fingers. Then, using a small teaspoon or a melon-ball cutter, scrape out the hairy choke and dip the whole artichoke in the lemon water. Trim the bottom by scraping off the outer skin with a sharp knife. Dip in water and cook according to recipe.

Arugula *Arugula*

Also known as *rocket* or *tiro,* arugula (*Eruca sativa*) is a member of the crucifer family and has a sharp, peppery taste. Tuscans use it in an infinite number of ways — raw in salads, puréed as a pasta sauce, chopped as a pizza topping, shredded into ravioli or calzones, wilted as a bed for mushroom *caciucco* to name a few.

Season: Early spring or fall

To Buy: Arugula has a high water content, so it wilts easily and does not revive. Look for fresh, crisp leaves with no hint of yellow.

To Prepare: Trim off stems and wash in many changes of water, since arugula generally contains a great deal of sand.

Asparagus *Asparago*

Asparagus is a member of the lily family. A native of Europe where it has been in cultivation for over two thousand years, *Asparagus officinalis* was prized by the Greeks and Romans for its slender elegance and vernal taste. There are now three types: green, white, and purple. Appearance notwithstanding, green is still my favorite for its combination of tender texture and woodsy flavor. In Tuscany, asparagus still grows wild and in great profusion, and its emergence from the ground in late winter is cause for great celebration. If you are ever in Tuscany in early spring, make eating wild asparagus one of your highest priorities (preferably in a *frittata*). You will never forget it.

Season: April through June

To Buy: Look for tightly closed, pointed tips and crisp, straight stalks with uniform color. Avoid fat stalks unless purchasing the white variety.

To Prepare: Break off the woody lower stems. Remove the lower scales which may harbor sand, or peel the lower part of the stalk with a vegetable peeler. One way to cook the spears is to tie them into bundles, putting same-sized stalks together. Leave one stalk loose for testing during cooking. Place in fast-boiling salted water and cook over high heat, covered, for 12 to 15 minutes.

Beet Greens *Foglie di Barbabietola*

Although some market vendors sell beets with greens attached, they more often sell the greens as a separate vegetable. Beet greens are similar in taste to chard (alias sea kale beet), which makes sense, since they are in the same family.

Season: May through October

To Buy: Beet greens should be crisp and vividly colored—bright green with red veins. Avoid wilted yellow leaves.

To Prepare: Wash in a few changes of water to remove sand. Drain before using.

Broccoli Rabe *Broccolini di Rapa*

Broccoli rabe is also called turnip broccoli which is a loose translation of its Italian name, *broccolini di rapa*. Not at all part of the broccoli family, broccoli rabe, or simply rabe, is the tender shoot of the wintered-over turnip plant. Like broccoli, it is dark green in color and topped with floret heads, but the heads are tiny, the stalks are much thinner, the leaves are slightly frilled, and, most significantly, the flavor is completely different. Broccoli rabe is a wonderfully bitter, pungently sour vegetable that is at its best when prepared, Tuscan-style, in an exquisitely simple way that allows the full flavor to shine.

Season: Early spring and early fall

To Buy: Look for dark-green leaves and crisp stems that are on the thin side (fat stems tend to be woody and tough). Florets should be closed and green; avoid those with yellow flowers.

To Prepare: Cut off the butt end of any thick stalks. Discard stalks that appear stringy when broken.

Cardoons *Cardoni*

A cardoon (*Cynara cardunculus*) is a tall, thistle-like plant originally from southern Europe. It is a close relative to the artichoke, but, unlike that delicious vegetable, the flower heads are eschewed in favor of the thickened stalk and midrib. Interestingly, cardoons are only referred to as such in Italy, France, and parts of Argentina; elsewhere, they are called noxious weeds. Like some celery and asparagus, the best cardoons are planted deep enough in the ground to maintain the leaves' paleness. In Italy, they are called *gobbi* which means "hunchback." The reference is to the fact that cardoon plants are often bent to the side and covered with dirt until they turn white. The result is a rounded, hunchback-like knob.

Season: October through December

To Buy: Look for long, wide stalks that are a duller green than celery and not quite as stiff but more flexible, like cabbage. Heads should be tightly packed and can range in size from 12 to 18 inches or more in length.

To Prepare: Separate the leaves from the stalk, trim top and bottom, and, with a small paring knife, remove the fibrous string from each stalk. Cut into 2- or 3-inch lengths and immerse in lemon water to prevent darkening until ready to use.

Chard *Bietola*

Also called swiss chard, this subtly tart green is very highly prized by Tuscans, who often use it as two separate vegetables. The leaves are stuffed or steamed or sautéed with garlic and olive oil, while the ribs are fried or gratinated or tossed with spaghetti. It comes in both green and red.

Season: September through November

To Buy: Look for vividly colored, shiny leaves with unblemished ribs.

To Prepare: Remove tough ends of stems and damaged leaves. Wash in several changes of water. If separating leaves from ribs, cut alongside central stem with sharp paring knife.

Chicory *Cicoria*

Chicory (*Cichorium intybus*) is a member of the daisy family and very much confused—both in this country and its native Mediterranean—with endive and escarole which are different members of the same family. Prized for both its bitter, curly, crisp foliage and its elongated taproot (from which the coffee substitute is made), chicory can be white, green, or even rich red. The major cultivated varieties include all red radicchios, Belgian endive (also called *chicon* or Witloof chicory), asparagus chicory, and all chicories grown for their roots.

Season: Spring or fall

To Buy: Choose firm, crisp heads with leaves that are neither too pale nor too dark.

To Prepare: Trim root end and wash leaves in several changes of water.

Dandelions *Dente di Leone*

The dandelion is both the same noxious weed reviled by backyard gardeners and the darling of the culinary world. A member of the huge daisy family, its botanical Tuscan name, *dente di leone,* means lion's tooth, a reference to its jagged leaves. Its vernacular name, *piscialetto* (piss in the bed), takes into account dandelion's well-known use as a diuretic.

Season: April through June

To Buy: The best dandelion heads are small, as they are the least bitter and most tender. Look for crisp, dark-green heads that are not wilted or discolored.

To Prepare: Trim off tough ends of stems. Wash well in several changes of water.

Endive *Indivia*

Endive *(Cichorium endivia)* is an annual or biennial plant that probably originated in India. Before it became an industry of its own and elevated in importance under the Belgian endive moniker, farmers would tie a string around the outside of a mature head of other types of chicory and enclose the heart which then became blanched to a wonderfully pristine white color and developed a notably delicate flavor.

Season: Spring and fall

To Buy: Heads of endive should be crisp and fresh-looking, not limp or wilted. The creamy white spike of an endive should be tightly wrapped, with pale yellow tinting only at the very edges of the leaves. With exposure to light, endive will develop the leaf-green pigment and change color as well as flavor. For this reason, buy only heads that have been wrapped in purple tissue. Avoid green heads.

To Prepare: Remove the damaged outer leaves of endive and wash in many changes of water since this is an excessively sandy vegetable. Endive needs merely to have its bitter, cone-shaped base removed before using.

Escarole *Scarola*

Interestingly enough, escarole and endive are the same plant *(Cichorium endivia),* of the daisy family. Escarole is a broad-leaved variety which, in this country, is sold in somewhat flattened bunches composed of abundant, broad, curly-edged green leaves that shade into a more or less bright yellow center and have a faintly bitter flavor and firm texture.

Season: Spring and fall

To Buy: Choose firm heads with no sign of wilting or discoloration.

To Prepare: Escarole contains more sand and grit than any other vegetable besides spinach. Rinse and drain many times before using, but do not allow to soak for more than 10 minutes: flavor and nutrients leach out quickly.

Kale *Cavolo Riccio*

A member of the widely disparate crucifer family, kale or borecole *(Brassica oleracea acephala)* is actually a sort of nonheading cabbage. The main types available in

Braschette is the Tuscan equivalent of kale.

this country are Scotch (with crumpled, very curly, grayish green leaves), Blue or Siberian (less crumpled and curly than Scotch), and Red Russian (fringe-edged gray-red leaves with red stems). While there is no kale per se in Tuscany, there is a close relative with rounded, wrinkly, very deep-green and purplish leaves called *braschette,* alternately called *cavolo nero* (black cabbage).

Season: Late fall through winter

To Buy: Select only very firm leaves with no sign of yellowing. If possible, use the same day, since, like other greens, kale quickly loses its flavor and nutritional value.

To Prepare: Trim off thick stalks and reserve for soup. Wash leaves in several changes of water.

Lettuce *Lattuga*

There are over 50 different kinds of lettuce (*Lactuca sativa*), but all fall either into the head or loose leaf categories. While mainly salad greens in this country, Tuscans use lettuce in a variety of ways: braised, stuffed, gratinated, grilled, fried, and in soups.

Season: May through November

To Buy: Look for crisp, vividly colored leaves with no hint of wilting or discoloring.

To Prepare: Wash leaves thoroughly just before using. Do not wash to store in refrigerator as this will destroy its nutritional value.

Mustard *Foglie di Senape*

For the purposes of this book, "mustard" applies to the leafy portions of several kinds of cabbage relatives used as greens. Part of the crucifer family, mustard can often be found growing wild, as it does in Tuscany's open fields. Subtly pungent in its youth, this green becomes a real pepper pot when exposed to the summer sun.

Season: April through October

To Buy: Look for crisp, vividly green leaves with no evidence of wilting or yellowing.

To Prepare: Trim off tough stems and wash well in several changes of water.

Nettles *Ortica*

Also known as stinging nettles because of the wickedly stinging hairs that cover the surface of the leaves, nettles *(Urtica)* were brought to this country by European immigrants and immediately became known as a pestiferous weed—an unfortunate situation given its pleasant, spinach-like flavor and wealth of nutrients. Only found in a small number of specialty markets where it is handled with sturdy gloves, nettles' stinging hairs become ineffective after cooking. Used by Tuscans in the same way as other similarly flavored greens.

Season: Nettles are best when young, in early to late spring.

To Buy: Leaves should be crisp and dark green. Avoid any sign of wilting.

To Prepare: Using gloves, trim off any tough stems and wash thoroughly in several changes of water.

Parsley *Prezzemolo*

Though long considered primarily for use as garniture or seasoning, parsley *(Petroselinum hortense,* of the carrot family) has finally become a vegetable in its own right—just as it has always been in Tuscany where you find parsley frittatas, parsley fritters, parsley bread, and parsley ravioli. Two leaf types are generally available as well as parsley root which is similar to celeriac in both flavor and use. Of the leaf types, you should consider only the flat leaf (also called Italian) variety, since curly parsley has virtually no taste.

Season: Fresh parsley is available from June through November; parsley root in late fall and winter.

To Buy: Parsley leaves should be bright green and have no signs of wilt. Parsley roots must be firm and creamy beige with luxuriant tops. Avoid any that feel springy or have excessive mottling.

To Prepare: Wash leaves well and dry before chopping; chopping wet leaves results in mush. For more pungent flavor, use only the leaves (save the stems for soup). Remove the top of the parsley root and only peel the skin if damaged; otherwise grate or dice as per recipe.

Radicchio *Radicchio*

Radicchio *(Cichorium intybus)* is a member of the sunflower family and native to Italy. There are 3 (and counting) types widely available in this country: Verona chicory with short, ruby-red leaves and white ribs and veins; Castelfranco variegated chicory with leaves shaped like the red Verona but white or pale green speckled with deep red spots; and Treviso with slender, dark leaves 3 to 6 inches long attached to a woody root.

Season: May through November

To Buy: Select only firm, brightly colored heads with no drying or browning at leaf's edge.

To Prepare: Separate the leaves (unless grilling) and wash under several changes of water.

Sorrel *Acetosa*

Sorrel *(Rumex scutatus),* or sour grass (their leaves contain oxalic acid), is a decidedly acquired—though delectable—taste. Its puckery, sharp flavor makes it appropriate for use as both a vegetable and an herb. High in vitamin C and impressively packed with minerals, sorrel's uses range from salads to soups to sauces to—sautéed in oil and garlic—side dishes.

Season: Spring and fall

To Buy: Look for lush, full, vividly green leaves with no sign of wilt or yellow. Sorrel wilts immediately upon picking, so this is a somewhat difficult task, but well worth it.

To Prepare: Wash well and spin dry. Trim ends.

Spinach *Spinaci*

There are as many varieties of spinach as techniques for cooking it. A native of southwest Asia, *Spinacea oleracea* was, until recently, a highly unpopular vegetable in this country, both for its acrid taste and for its well-deserved reputation for being notoriously hard to clean. If not for its impressive health benefits (and the public relations effort mounted by Popeye), I doubt it would ever have been redeemed. But redeemed it has been and just in time for our growing love affair with greens of all kinds. The two most widely-available varieties are crinkly leaf or flat leaf. The familiar crinkly leaf, or Savoy, spinach is generally sold in supermarkets in 10-ounce cellophane packages while the slightly more elusive flat leaf comes in bunches and is most easily found in produce markets. Crinkly spinach is drier than flat leaf with thicker, tougher stems; flat leaf is sweeter, less fibrous, and much more tender.

Season: Spring and fall

To Buy: Fresh, crisp, dark-green leaves with short stems. No rot, slime, or badly bruised leaves. Flat leaf spinach is a better buy than the prepackaged crinkly leaf which tends to yield a high proportion of stems.

To Prepare: Remove stems and damaged leaves and wash in several changes of water; spinach is very sandy, so you should use large quantities of water and lift spinach up and down to float off sand and dirt. Lift from water and drain well.

Watercress *Crescione*

"Cress" is a term applied to several different kinds of plants with edible pungent foliage, all members of the same crucifer family and most growing partially submerged in fresh, running streams. In this country, the most common is *Roripa nasturtium* which is sold in tight bunches of crisp, succulent stems set with crunchy little leaves.

Season: Early spring through late fall

To Buy: Leaves should be vivid green—yellowing indicates staleness—and firm to the touch.

To Prepare: Wash in cold water and trim gangly stems.

Quick and Easy

Greens

As any lover of greens will tell you, the best preparation is the simplest: sauté in olive oil and garlic and sprinkle with a little salt. You can apply this treatment to any of the greens in this chapter, although bulkier, more firmly textured varieties such as kale, broccoli rabe, or chard can first be blanched to make them more manageable. In general, use 2–3 cloves of garlic per pound of greens. Sauté in 3–4 tablespoons of extra-virgin oil until soft. Add the greens and toss for 3–5 minutes until just wilted. Season with salt and pepper or drizzle with a little fresh lemon.

Asparagus

One of my earliest food memories is of sitting at the table watching my mother and father divide asparagus stalks between them. One ate only tips; the other preferred the stalks. The asparagus itself would be cooked until tender and brought to the table on a long platter with two small bowls of vinaigrette. If Mother picked up the first piece, she would slice it just under the tip and hand off the stalk to my father; if he was the first to serve himself, the process would be reversed—all of it conducted in concentrated silence. Then, as if on cue, they would each dip their respective pieces like paintbrushes into the vinaigrette bowls, and eat them.

As an adult, I have retained this habit of eating asparagus with vinaigrette; to me, it is the simplest yet most majestic treatment. One difference, however, is that I eat the whole thing.

Cardoons

With such pronounced and distinctive flavor, cardoons can simply be cut into 3–4-inch lengths, boiled in salted water for 30 minutes (or until tender), and cooled to room temperature before eating. If you like, you can also drizzle with a little oil and vinegar or lemon.

Artichokes

Like asparagus and cardoons, artichokes are perfectly wonderful when simply boiled whole for 20–30 minutes and served with vinaigrette.

Clearly, the quality is not as good as it once was.

Frittata di Prezzemolo
Parsley Frittata

Parsley has always been the silent workhorse of the culinary world. Aside from being called upon when a dish requires a little garnishing or a stew a dash of color, its main virtue has been its sub-tlety — the fact that it never overwhelms and so can be paired with a great many things. But parsley is more than just a decorative afterthought. Its surprisingly pungent taste can serve as a recipe's main focus, as the following recipe so aptly demonstrates. Make sure to use flat leaf or Italian parsley; the largely tasteless curled variety should never be used for anything other than garnish.

8 eggs, well beaten	Salt and pepper to taste
1 cup packed chopped parsley*	4 tablespoons extra-virgin olive oil

1. Place the eggs in a large bowl. Add the parsley, season with salt and pepper, and blend thoroughly.

2. Heat the oil in an 8-inch frittata skillet (with rounded sides) over medium heat. Pour the egg and parsley mixture into the skillet and cook until the bottom is slightly browned (use a butter knife to lift the edge when checking).

3. To turn the frittata, slide onto a large plate, cover with another large plate and turn the plates over. Slide the frittata back into the skillet and continue cooking until the bottom is slightly browned (check using the butter knife).**

4. Slice into 4 wedges and serve with salad and hot crusty bread.

SERVES 4   TIME: 30 minutes

LEVEL OF DIFFICULTY: Moderate (because of the turning)

VARIATION: In Tuscany, frittatas are made with everything from *porcini* mushrooms to wild asparagus. Try using any of the greens or stalks included in this chapter.

*When chopping parsley, add a little salt to keep it from sticking to the knife and the cutting board.
**If turning a frittata seems too difficult, cook it in a cast-iron pan and place the pan under the broiler until the top is browned.

Risotto con Radicchio
Risotto with Radicchio

In Tuscany, there are almost as many varieties of radicchio or Italian chicory as there are pecorino cheeses. In this country, where the radicchio craze is just catching on, however, there are three main cultivars: Verona, which comes in tightly packed round heads with rich burgundy leaves, is the best known of the lot, followed by the milder Treviso with elongated leaves that make it look like an overgrown red Belgian endive, and the relative newcomer to the pack, Castelfranco, a spectacular yellow-green variety with red markings and an open flower shape.

The following risotto is both delicious and colorful, its color resulting from the julienned ribbons of radicchio added at the last minute. I would advise using Verona radicchio which is the most pungent of the three varieties, but if Treviso is all you can find, you might want to add a little more salt or grated Parmesan to spice up the flavor. I have also suggested using pale ale as a substitute for white wine. The idea was first suggested to me by Signora Adua Manfredi of Piano di Mommio, and I have used it often as a delicious change of pace.

5–6 cups Basic Vegetable Broth (see page 308)
4 tablespoons extra-virgin olive oil
1 medium onion, finely chopped
1½ cups Arborio rice
½ cup dry white wine or pale ale

1 large head (about 1 pound) Verona radicchio, washed, dried, cored, and julienned
Salt and freshly ground black pepper
½ cup freshly grated Parmigiano-Reggiano

1. Heat the broth in a saucepan and adjust the heat to keep it simmering.

2. Heat the oil in a large, heavy-gauge pot. Add the onion and sauté over low heat until soft and translucent, about 5 minutes. Add the rice and stir until all the kernels are well coated.

3. Add the wine or beer and stir until the rice absorbs all the liquid.

4. Begin adding broth to the rice pot, a few ladles at a time, stirring occasionally and adding additional broth only when the previous liquid has been almost completely absorbed. The heat should be low and the rice gently simmering.

5. Add ¾ of the radicchio at the halfway mark (after the rice has been cooking for about 10 minutes) and stir to blend. Continue adding broth until the rice is

tender and there is still enough broth to produce a slightly runny consistency. You may not need to use all the broth.

6. Season with salt and pepper, add the cheese and remaining radicchio, stir until all ingredients are well blended, and serve immediately in warm bowls.

SERVES 4   TIME: 45–60 minutes   LEVEL OF DIFFICULTY: Moderate

VARIATIONS: In place of radicchio, try using arugula, mustard greens, watercress, dandelions, kale, or chard—or any combination thereof. In the latter two cases, use only the most tender leaves for the julienne.

MAKE AHEAD: Although restaurants generally cook risotto to the halfway point and then finish it to order, I feel that the flavor is definitely affected and would not recommend such a practice unless absolutely necessary. Risotto is quite good when reheated in a double boiler. But the rice continues to absorb liquid even when cold; hence, be sure to add a little hot water or vegetable broth to loosen it up.

Insalata di Lattuga Grigliata
Grilled Hearts of Romaine Salad

I serve this salad towards the end of summer, when the heads of romaine lettuce have reached their explosive peak and I have finally had my fill (well . . . not completely) of baby greens with simple vinaigrette. It makes a lovely and satisfying meal when served after a chilled primo *of soup and accompanied by thick squares of rosemary-scented* focaccia. *While the flavor is best when grilled outdoors over hot coals, an indoor electric grill can also be used.*

2 heads romaine lettuce
1 tablespoon garlic oil*
Salt and freshly ground black
    pepper

4 medium-sized ripe tomatoes,
    quartered
4 tablespoons balsamic
    vinaigrette**

1. Remove the dark outer leaves of the romaine and reserve for another use. The pale green, almost yellow leaves that remain are the heart of the lettuce. Cut the hearts in half, keeping the core intact so the leaves stay attached.

2. Brush the romaine halves with the oil and season with salt and pepper.

3. Grill cut side down over a hot fire for about 5 minutes. Turn and grill other side for another 5 minutes. The leaves should be lightly charred and somewhat tender.

4. Arrange romaine hearts on a platter, garnish with tomato wedges, and drizzle with vinaigrette.

SERVES 4   TIME: 25 minutes   LEVEL OF DIFFICULTY: Easy

VARIATIONS: In place of romaine lettuce, you can also use Treviso radicchio or curly endive, although be prepared for a significantly more pungent flavor if using the endive.

*To make garlic oil, separate and peel the cloves from one medium-sized bulb of garlic. Place them in a clean, empty bottle with a cork (a used wine bottle works well). Fill with olive oil and seal. Refrigerate for 2 weeks before using.
**To make balsamic vinaigrette you will need 1 tablespoon balsamic vinegar, 3 tablespoons extra-virgin olive oil, salt, and freshly-ground black pepper. Slowly whisk the oil into the vinegar to form an emulsion. Season with salt and pepper.

Crostata di Scarola, Cicoria e Acetosa
Bitter Greens Tart

For years, I had always made this as a light, savory, one-crust tart and served it in spring when, by law, every table must have at least two or three dishes incorporating fresh seasonal greens. When I put the first bite in my mouth, it tasted of tender new shoots bursting from the ground and greenish yellow leaves sprouting from branches awakening from winter naps. So imagine my surprise when I was invited to a winter holiday party at the home of my friend, Salvatore Lombardo, who served almost the exact same tart (his mother, Grace's, recipe) but with two crusts (okay, he also added pine nuts). The amazing part was that the same tart now tasted robust and hearty and seemed perfectly at home in a cozy dining room heated by a crackling hearth.

The following recipe makes enough pastry dough for one double-crust, 8-inch tart.

The Crust

2 cups all-purpose flour	¾ cup chilled, unsalted butter
½ teaspoon salt	4–6 tablespoons cold water

1. Mix the flour and salt in a bowl. Cut in the butter until the mixture resembles a coarse meal.

2. Lightly mix in just enough water so that the dough sticks together in a ball. Do not overwork the dough or it will be tough.

3. Divide the dough into 2 balls, one slightly larger than the other. Wrap in plastic and refrigerate until ready to use.

The Tart

3 tablespoons extra-virgin olive oil

2 anchovy fillets (optional)

1 cup thinly sliced onion

2 cloves garlic, minced

3 cups packed escarole, cleaned and roughly chopped

2 cups packed chicory (curly endive), cleaned and roughly chopped

1 cup packed sorrel, cleaned and roughly chopped

Salt and freshly ground black pepper

Optional: ¼ cup packed wild greens (plantains, wild mustard, daisies, lamb's quarters)

½ cup toasted pine nuts

1 egg, lightly beaten

Pastry dough for an 8-inch double crust

Egg wash (1 egg yolk well beaten with 1 tablespoon milk)

1. Pour the oil into a sauté pan large enough to hold the greens. Add the anchovy and cook, mashing it into the oil with the tines of a fork. Add the onion and cook until translucent.

2. Add the garlic, greens, and herbs, season with salt and pepper, and cook until the greens are wilted and tender.

3. Remove from heat. When cool, add the pine nuts and beaten egg.

4. Meanwhile, roll the larger dough ball into at least a 9-inch circle and place in the bottom of an 8-inch tart pan with removable bottom.

5. Roll out the smaller ball of dough for the top crust into a circle slightly larger than 8 inches.

6. Moisten the edges of the bottom crust with water, fill the pastry shell with the bitter greens mixture, and cover the tart with the top crust.

7. Seal the edges by folding and crimping. Trim off any excess.

8. Brush the top of the tart with the egg wash and bake in a 350-degree oven for approximately 1 hour. The crust should be a glossy golden brown.

SERVES 8   TIME: 2½ hours   LEVEL OF DIFFICULTY: Complex

VARIATION: Any combination of greens can be substituted for the escarole and curly endive as long as they are similarly thin-walled (kale would produce a texture that was too heavy). Try using amaranth, arugula, nettles, watercress, or spinach.

MAKE AHEAD: The pastry dough can be made 2 or 3 days in advance, wrapped in plastic, and refrigerated.

Carciofi alla Birra
Beer-Braised Artichokes

People are surprised when a Tuscan recipe contains beer. And yet I can think of 10 beer-infused recipes off the top of my head that I have enjoyed since childhood. The following is one of my favorites, marrying as it does the robust flavor of stout with the equally robust flavor of artichokes and—just like the best of marriages—creating in the end a noticeable third flavor while maintaining the staunch integrity of the original two. In this case, the third flavor is the delicate, almost sweet liquid resulting from the combination of beer, tomato juice, and vegetable broth.

8 medium to small fresh artichokes
1 lemon, cut in half
2 tablespoons extra-virgin olive oil
Salt and freshly ground black
    pepper

4 medium cloves garlic, peeled and
    lightly crushed
¾ cup dark beer, preferably stout
½ cup tomato juice
½–1 cup Basic Vegetable Broth (see
    page 308)

1. Remove the tough outer leaves from the artichokes. Cut in half lengthwise and remove the fuzzy chokes. Rub the cut edges with the lemon to prevent discoloration.

2. Heat the oil in a pan large enough to hold the artichokes in one layer. When the oil is hot, add the artichoke halves, cut side down, season with salt and pepper, and sauté until lightly browned.

3. Turn the halves, add the garlic, and sauté a few more minutes until the garlic is lightly colored.

4. Add the beer, tomato juice, and enough vegetable broth to come halfway up the sides of the artichokes. Bring to a gentle simmer, cover the pan, and cook until tender, about 30–45 minutes depending on the size of the artichokes. The

liquid in the pan should eventually reduce by about ¾, but if it reduces too quickly, add more vegetable broth.

5. Adjust seasoning and serve, spooning the sauce over the artichokes.

SERVES 4   TIME: 1½ hours   LEVEL OF DIFFICULTY: Easy

VARIATIONS: Radicchio or celery may be substituted for the artichokes. For the radicchio, use 4 medium to small heads and halve them, leaving the core intact. Then proceed as for the artichoke hearts. For the celery, separate the ribs from a large stalk of celery and clean. You will need about 12 ribs. Trim the top and bottom from the ribs and cut into approximately 5-inch lengths. Sauté them in the oil lengthwise and proceed as for the artichoke hearts.

Il Fondo Dei di Carciofi Ripiene di Spinaci
Artichoke Bottoms Stuffed with Spinach and Walnut Purée

My favorite part of artichokes has always been the bottoms which contain all the wonderful essence of artichoke flavor with none of the difficulties attending those tough, tongue-discoloring leaves. The following recipe uses a wonderful purée of spinach, walnuts, and cream as a filling for the prepared bottoms and is cooked until the flavors are blended. I have also served artichoke bottoms with cold fillings such as tomato salad, parsley and garlic battuto, or roasted eggplant mash. Do not discard the artichoke tops; use them to make soup or puree the tender parts and use as an alternate to spinach in this recipe.

8 medium-sized artichokes
1 lemon, halved
Juice of one lemon
2 tablespoons extra-virgin olive oil
1 medium-sized onion, minced
1 pound spinach, washed and
    drained

½ cup shelled walnuts, finely
    chopped
¼ cup heavy cream
Salt and freshly ground black
    pepper
4 tablespoons vegetable broth or
    dark beer

1. To peel the artichokes, break off each leaf at the base (bend the leaf back on itself until it snaps, then pull it off towards the base). When most of the outer leaves have been peeled off and the remaining leaves no longer snap, cut off the rest of the cone and rub the cut portions with the lemon to prevent discoloration.*

2. Using a sharp paring knife, trim off all bits of green to expose the more tender, white part of the artichoke bottom. Rub with the lemon.

3. Place the artichoke bottoms in a saucepan with the lemon juice and enough water to cover. Simmer, covered, for 30–45 minutes or until the artichoke bottoms are tender when pierced with a knife. Cool in liquid and reserve.

4. Heat the oil in a skillet over low heat. Sauté the onion until lightly browned. Add the spinach and cook, stirring constantly, until wilted.

5. Place the spinach, walnuts, and cream in a food processor and purée. Season with salt and pepper.

6. Remove the artichoke bottoms from their liquid. Rinse under cold water and remove the choke with a spoon. When finished, you should have 8 perfectly rounded, hollowed-out cups.

7. Preheat the oven to 350 degrees. Fill the artichoke bottoms with spinach cream. Place in a glass baking dish large enough to hold all the bottoms in one layer. Drizzle with the broth or beer, cover with aluminum foil, and bake for 25 minutes, basting occasionally. Just before serving, douse with the remaining liquid from the bottom of the pan.

SERVES 4   TIME: 2 hours   LEVEL OF DIFFICULTY: Moderate

MAKE AHEAD: The artichoke bottoms will keep refrigerated in their cooking liquid for 1 or 2 days.

*Using this method instead of cutting off the leaves with a knife will result in a meatier artichoke bottom because it will leave the tender or edible part of the leaf attached to the bottom of the artichoke.

Insalata Verde S'una Montata di Carote
Wilted Greens Salad on a Bed of Carrot and Rutabaga Spaghetti

The beauty of this dish lies not only in the extraordinary flavor produced by this trio of tangy greens, but also in the visual sensation created by nesting shiny, dark-green leaves on a bed of bright orange carrot and creamy yellow rutabaga strips that have been softened to resemble spaghetti. Served lukewarm, it works equally well as a salad course or, following soup, as a light entrée.

3 medium carrots, peeled
1 large rutabaga, peeled and halved
½ pound mustard greens
½ pound beet greens
½ pound arugula
1 tablespoon balsamic vinegar

1 shallot, peeled and minced
⅛ teaspoon sugar
½ teaspoon stone-ground mustard
Salt and freshly ground black
 pepper
5 tablespoons extra-virgin olive oil

1. Using a mandoline or a cook's knife, cut the carrots into long, very thin strips. Do the same with the rutabaga. Place in a saucepan with enough salted water to cover. Cook, covered, over medium heat until wilted. Drain and set aside in a covered bowl.

2. Meanwhile, remove the stems from the greens and wash them in cold water. Using long metal tongs, lift the greens from the water, and without draining, immediately place in a hot skillet so that they will be cooked in their own water. Cook over medium heat for 3–4 minutes, tossing constantly with tongs until all the greens are wilted. Season with salt and pepper, remove from heat and set aside.

3. To make the vinaigrette, place the vinegar, minced shallot, sugar, mustard, salt and pepper in a small bowl. Slowly whisk in the oil until emulsified.

4. To serve, place ¼ of the carrots and rutabagas on each of 4 salad plates, creating a bedding nest. Make sure that the strands are intertwined so that the colors are blended. Top with a portion of wilted greens, drizzle with vinaigrette, and serve.

SERVES 4   TIME: 30–45 minutes

LEVEL OF DIFFICULTY: Easy

VARIATIONS: Experiment with using sorrel, amaranth, dandelion, chard, or beet greens.

MAKE AHEAD: The carrot and rutabaga spaghetti can be made up to 2 days before and refrigerated. Reheat in a steamer basket. The vinaigrette can also be made 1–2 days in advance.

Valerio Malfi commenting on the Parmalat Scandal: "This is not THAT mascarpone!"

Cardoni con Salsa D'olive e Noci

Cardoon Wedges with
Crushed Olive and Hazelnut Sauce

Adults all have certain memories of foods that were always available in the refrigerator of their childhood, foods geared towards those moments in the late afternoon when you would just have come home from playing and you were suffering from a ravenous appetite but it was not quite yet time for dinner. For many, those foods include fruit or pudding or cheese or even bread slices drizzled with oil. In my house, it was generally little bowls of vegetables marinated in vinaigrette—mushrooms, roasted peppers, eggplant, or (my favorite) boiled cardoons. In the name of progress, I have altered the basic vinaigrette of my reverie and now present one made with olive paste and nuts.

1 medium-sized cardoon
Salt and pepper to taste
1 tablespoon lemon juice
1 tablespoon prepared black olive
 paste

2 ounces shelled hazelnuts, crushed
 with a mortar and pestle to a
 rough paste
1 teaspoon balsamic vinegar
5 tablespoons extra-virgin olive oil
8 leaves chicory, washed and dried

1. Remove the tough outer leaves of the cardoon. Trim the top inch off the head, separate into individual stalks and cut each into lengths 2 or 3 inches long, taking care to remove the fibrous strings. Place in a pot of salted water to which you have added the lemon juice. Cover and cook for 30 minutes or until tender.

2. Place the olive paste, nuts, and vinegar in a mixing bowl and whisk in the oil until blended into a creamy paste.

3. Drain the cardoons and cool to room temperature. Pour the olive sauce over the cardoons and toss until all sections are coated.

4. Arrange the chicory leaves on a platter, top with cardoons, and serve.

SERVES 6 AS A SALAD COURSE   TIME: 1 hour   LEVEL OF DIFFICULTY: Easy

VARIATIONS: If you can find wild yarrow, add 1 tablespoon chopped to the paste in step 2.

MAKE AHEAD: Cardoons can be prepared up to 2 days in advance, refrigerated, and warmed to room temperature before saucing. Sauce can be prepared up to 4 hours in advance.

Pane Ripieno con Broccolini di Rapa
Broccoli Rabe Bread

Tuscan bread bakers are not what I would call culinary innovators. For the most part, they restrict themselves to tried and true—albeit wonderful—recipes. So imagine my surprise when, a few years ago, I came across a shop in Viareggio—Alfio—that, in addition to the traditional recipes, makes a series of breads stuffed with amazing vegetable mixtures. Of the six I have sampled, the following is my favorite.

The Bread

½ teaspoon active dry yeast

½ teaspoon sugar

2 cups bread flour plus additional
    flour for kneading

1 cup whole wheat flour

⅛ teaspoon salt

2 tablespoons extra-virgin olive oil

2 tablespoons coarse-grind polenta
    flour

The Filling

1 pound broccoli rabe

3 tablespoons extra-virgin olive oil

4 cloves garlic, peeled and minced

Salt and pepper to taste

1. Sprinkle the yeast over a half-cup of warm water. Add the sugar and stir until dissolved. Place the cup in a bowl of hot water so that the water reaches up the sides of the cup to the ¾ mark. Let sit until the cup has developed ½ inch of yeasty foam on top.

2. Place both flours in a food processor or a mixer with a dough hook. Add the salt. With the motor running, pour the yeast into the bowl through the feeder tube and immediately pour in another cup of warm water to which you have added 1 tablespoon of the oil. Process until the dough forms a ball.

3. Sprinkle some flour on a table or countertop. Remove the dough from the food processor and, with floured hands, knead for 5 minutes, adding additional flour as necessary. The dough will be ready for rising when it no longer takes up any additional flour.

4. Using the remaining oil, grease the bottom and sides of a large bowl. Place the dough in the bowl, cover, and set in a warm place for 1 hour to rise.

5. Meanwhile, wash the broccoli rabe, spin dry, and chop into small pieces.

6. Heat the oil in a large skillet over medium heat and sauté the garlic for 1 minute. Add the rabe, season with salt and pepper, and sauté for 5–7 minutes until wilted. Transfer from skillet to a bowl and cool to room temperature.

7. When the dough has risen, dust a table or countertop with flour and, using a rolling pin, roll it out to a 16 × 20-inch rectangle.

8. Using a slotted spoon, transfer the broccoli rabe from the bowl and spread it over the surface of the dough. Roll the dough from the short end until you have an evenly shaped cylinder. Fold the ends under to seal.

9. Sprinkle the polenta flour into a baking pan. Place the bread roll on the pan, seam side down. Preheat the oven to 350 degrees and cook the bread for 40 minutes or until the crust is lightly browned. Cool, slice, and serve.

MAKES APPROXIMATELY 14 1-INCH SLICES   TIME: 2½–2⅔ hours

LEVEL OF DIFFICULTY: Difficult

VARIATIONS: Any green can be used to make the filling; try kale, mustard, amaranth, spinach, or watercress. Also try blending greens with other finely chopped vegetables such as onions, peppers, or eggplant. To vary the flavor even further, add some minced parsley or basil.

MAKE AHEAD: The bread dough can be made in advance, wrapped in plastic, and frozen for up to 2 weeks. Thaw to room temperature before using. The rabe can be sautéed up to 2 days in advance and refrigerated until needed. Warm to room temperature before spreading on bread dough.

Carciofi Stufati con Ripieno Croccante
Baked Artichokes with Crispy Stuffing

I have always loved stuffed artichokes but had begun to bore myself with the same old herb and garlic mixtures. One day, my mother made boiled artichokes as an appetizer and, before I was quite finished with mine, brought to the table a platter of fried potatoes she was going to serve with roast chicken. The smell was so good I decided to sneak a potato while my mouth was still filled with artichokes. Lo and behold, I realized how complementary these two flavors could be. Since then, I have rounded out the original idea by adding a wonderful gratinated topping to these potato-stuffed artichokes.

8 medium-sized artichokes
1 lemon, cut in half
6 tablespoons extra-virgin olive oil
1 cup dry white wine
3 sprigs fresh parsley, stems
   removed
2 tablespoons unsalted butter
½ pound Eastern or Yukon Gold
   potatoes, peeled and cut into
   1-inch cubes

1 teaspoon fresh rosemary leaves
1 tablespoon fresh chopped parsley
4 tablespoons freshly grated
   Parmigiano-Reggiano
4 tablespoons unflavored bread
   crumbs
Salt and pepper to taste

1. Remove the tough outer leaves of the artichokes and, using scissors, cut the spines from the remaining leaves. Remove the stems, cutting at such an angle that the artichokes can stand up. Rub cut edges with lemon to prevent discoloration.

2. Place the artichokes in a pot large enough to hold them in one layer. Drizzle 2 tablespoons of the oil over the top and pour in the wine as well as enough water to reach a depth of ½ inch. Add the sprigs of parsley, season with salt and pepper, cover, and cook over medium heat for 30–40 minutes or until the artichokes seem tender when pierced with a fork.

3. Meanwhile, place 2 tablespoons of oil in a skillet along with the butter. When hot, add the potatoes and cook over medium heat, stirring frequently until the potatoes are golden brown on all sides. Sprinkle with the rosemary, season with salt and pepper, and toss to coat.

4. When the artichokes are done, remove them with tongs and discard the cooking liquid. Using a teaspoon or a paring knife, excavate the choke so that the centers are hollow and ready for stuffing.

5. Fill the artichokes with the potatoes and place in a baking pan. Combine the parsley, cheese, and bread crumbs and sprinkle over the potatoes with a generous dusting of black pepper. Drizzle the remaining oil over the top and place in the broiler until the tops are lightly browned.

SERVES 4   TIME: 90 minutes   LEVEL OF DIFFICULTY: Moderate

VARIATIONS: If you can find garlic mustard, add 3 tablespoons, chopped, to the cooked potatoes in Step 3.

MAKE AHEAD: The potatoes can be fried 1 day in advance and refrigerated.

Torta Toscana
Tuscan Spring Tart

When spring arrives, everyone's thoughts turn to Sunday picnics at long wooden tables in open fields. Along with the ubiquitous bread, salads, and sautéed greens, there must always be at least one variation of the following tart which is at its best when consumed with copious quantities of dry white wine. The tart's unique pastry uses no butter, opting instead for a quick, moist dough softened simply with olive oil.

The Dough

4 cups unbleached white flour
½ cup extra-virgin olive oil
Salt and freshly ground black pepper
3 tablespoons cold water

½ pound freshly grated Parmigiano-Reggiano
6 eggs, lightly beaten
1 tablespoon fresh chopped marjoram
Salt and freshly ground black pepper
3 tablespoons extra-virgin olive oil
1 tablespoon unbleached white flour

The Filling

4 pounds chard
½ onion, peeled and finely chopped
3 tablespoons unsalted butter
2 pounds fresh ricotta

1. Place the flour in a large bowl along with the oil, ¼ teaspoon salt, ⅛ teaspoon pepper, and the water. Mix by hand until you have a soft, spongy dough.

2. Divide the dough into 5 equal balls and place the balls on a flat surface. Cover with a wet cloth and, over that, a dry one. Let rest for 30 minutes.

3. In the meantime, clean the chard and remove the central stalks. Blanch in salted water until wilted. Remove with tongs and, when somewhat cool, squeeze "dry." Chop roughly.

4. Sauté the onion in the butter until golden. Add the chard and cook over medium heat, stirring constantly until the chard has assumed the flavor of the sautéed onion. Remove from heat, place in a bowl, and cool to room temperature.

5. Add the ricotta, grated cheese, eggs, and marjoram to the chard. Season with salt and pepper and stir to blend all ingredients.

6. Grease a 9-inch springform pan with oil, dust with flour, and shake to re-

move excess. Roll the first ball of dough into a 9-inch circle to fit the bottom of the pan. Trim off any excess. Place in the tart pan and cover with ¼ of the chard-ricotta mixture, spreading the mixture into an even layer. Drizzle with oil.

7. Preheat the oven to 350 degrees. Roll the remaining balls of dough into 9-inch circles, layering each one in the tart pan and trimming any excess. Cover each with a layer of the chard-ricotta mixture and a drizzle of oil. Make sure the top layer is dough. Drizzle with oil and cook for 1 hour. Serve at room temperature.

SERVES 6   TIME: 2 hours   LEVEL OF DIFFICULTY: Advanced

VARIATIONS: This tart is just as wonderful when made with other greens such as kale, amaranth, mustard, spinach, watercress, or dandelion, although each contributes a different flavor. Also try adding sautéed leeks or asparagus, especially if you can get your hands on some wild specimens.

Fritto Misto
Mixed Fry (Asparagus, Cardoons, Radicchio, Artichokes, and Broccoli Rabe)

My mother has a saying: "Fritto, anche un stivalo." Fried, I would eat even an old shoe. Growing up, I remember huge platters of what is traditionally called a "mixed fry": long, flat pieces of zucchini, small button mushrooms, crunchy wedges of artichokes, thick rectangles of cardoons, all served on a beautiful white platter surrounded by wedges of lemon. The following recipe uses the most simple—and light—of batters for an assemblage of vegetables that vary in both texture and taste.

The Batter

2 cups unbleached white flour
2 tablespoons extra-virgin olive oil
2 tablespoons *grappa* (brandy can be substituted)
2 eggs, separated
½ teaspoon salt
2 cups cold water

The Vegetables

8 very thin asparagus spears
4 medium-sized stalks cardoon
1 head Treviso radicchio
4 medium-sized artichokes
8 stems broccoli rabe (with florets)
Olive oil for frying
Lemon wedges

1. Prepare the batter by placing the flour in a large bowl and adding the oil, grappa, egg yolks (previously lightly beaten), and salt. Mix with a fork, adding water one tablespoon at a time, until you have a thin paste that is neither too pasty nor too watery. Cover and let rest for 1 hour.

2. Meanwhile, prepare the vegetables: Trim the ends from the asparagus and peel the bottom half of the stems. Trim the tops of the cardoon stalks, cut into four equal sections each, and remove the fibrous outer string. Wash the radicchio and cut into eighths. Remove the artichokes' outer leaves, trim the pointy needles, peel the stem, cut into quarters, and remove the choke. Wash the broccoli rabe and cut off the thick stems. Remove any wilted or yellowed leaves.

3. Beat the egg whites until they form stiff peaks and fold into the batter. Heat the oil to a 1-inch depth in a large frying pan.

4. One by one, dip the vegetable pieces into the batter, making sure they are well coated, and fry until golden brown on all sides. Remove to a heated platter lined with paper towels and keep warm. To serve, remove the paper towels and surround with lemon wedges.

SERVES 4

TIME: 1½ hours (not counting the 1 hour during which the batter must rest)

LEVEL OF DIFFICULTY: Moderate

VARIATIONS: Almost any vegetable can be fried, although some, like rutabagas and beets, should be parboiled first.

Crema di Ortiche
Spring Nettles Soup

Nettles are a leafy green whose time has yet to arrive. But I have no doubt that it soon will. Hampered by its design (the leaves sport fiber-thin hairs that deliver a temporary sting when touched), this delicious and nutritious plant is nonetheless a favorite of Tuscans who pluck it from the forest floor (using sturdy gloves) in early spring when the leaves are palm-sized and deliciously subtle. Once picked, the stingers soon lose their potency, and, cooked, no trace remains of the formic acid that created all the fuss in the first place. Rich in vitamin C, betacarotene, and various amino acids, nettles taste somewhat like a sweeter form of spinach and, like spinach, can be eaten raw or cooked. Best when young and tender, they make a delightful springtime soup.

2 medium-sized new red potatoes,
  scrubbed
2 medium onions, peeled but left
  whole
½ pound of nettles, stems removed
  and washed

3 tablespoons unsalted butter
1 quart Basic Vegetable Broth (see
  page 308)
½ teaspoon salt
Fresh ground black pepper
2 one-inch-thick slices day-old
  peasant bread

1. Place the potatoes and onions in a large soup pot and cover with water. Boil until tender. Drain and set aside.

2. Steam the nettles until wilted. Remove with tongs and roughly chop.

3. Heat 1 tablespoon of the butter in a skillet, add the nettles, and sauté for 3 minutes, stirring constantly. Add the salt.

4. Place the potatoes, onions, nettles, and broth in a food processor and puree until smooth. Pour the puree into a soup pot and heat through. Add salt and pepper.

5. Meanwhile, cut each slice of bread into 8 one-inch cubes. Heat the remaining butter in a skillet and pan fry the bread cubes until toasted on all sides.

6. Pour the soup into bowls, top with four croutons each, and serve.

SERVES 4   TIME: 60 minutes   LEVEL OF DIFFICULTY: Easy

VARIATIONS: Any green can be used to make this soup. Try sorrel, arugula, spinach, or amaranth.

MAKE AHEAD: The greens can be sautéed and refrigerated 1 day in advance. The potatoes and onions can be boiled and refrigerated up to 2 days in advance.

Gnocchetti di Erbette
Herb Gnocchi with Tomato Ragu

Gnocchi have long been one of my favorite culinary staples, both because of their wonderful flavor and the relative ease of preparation. But every time I make them, people never fail to respond with visible amazement. "Gnocchi are soooo difficult," they'll say. "You must have worked all day." In fact, I remember preparing the menu for the very first cooking class at our school; when my partner heard me suggest we teach gnocchi-making, she recoiled in horror. "Far too chancy," she warned. "What if they dissolve in the cooking water?" In further discussions, it was revealed that she had never actually made gnocchi, *a fact that surprised me, since I didn't think there was any culinary adventure Sandra had not experienced. When I told her that* gnocchi *were supremely easy, she yielded, but only with a loud harumpfff. "I'll just purchase some pre-made ones from the* alimentari *in case it doesn't work." Needless to say, all went well. But Sandra's sentiment is echoed by even those who make* gnocchi *on a regular basis. I'm not sure why, since I've never found them either difficult or time consuming. You judge, but let me add that, even if the hype were true, these delightful little dumplings would be well worth the effort.*

The Gnocchi

2 pounds fresh mixed herbs
   (arugula, sorrel, lovage, basil,
   mint, yarrow, garlic mustard, or
   watercress), stems removed and
   washed
1 pound fresh sheep's milk ricotta
   (cow's milk ricotta can also be
   used)
1 cup unbleached white flour, plus
   additional flour for kneading
½ cup freshly grated Parmigiano-
   Reggiano
1 egg, lightly beaten
⅛ teaspoon freshly grated nutmeg
Salt and pepper to taste

The Ragu

3 tablespoons extra-virgin olive oil
1 medium onion, minced
1 large can Italian peeled plum
   tomatoes, with liquid
1 dried chili pepper
1 bay leaf
2 cups Basic Vegetable Broth (see
   page 308)
¼ teaspoon salt

To Assemble

6 tablespoons extra-virgin olive oil
4 cloves garlic, minced
Salt and pepper to taste
4 tablespoons freshly chopped
   parsley

1. First make the sauce: sauté the onion in the oil over very low heat until soft. Add the tomatoes, chili pepper, bay leaf, broth, and salt. Cover and cook over low heat for 1 hour.

2. For the *gnocchi*, steam the herbs until wilted. Remove with tongs, wring "dry," and mince finely. Place in a large bowl.

3. Pass the ricotta through a sieve and add to the herbs along with the flour, cheese, egg, nutmeg, and seasoning. Using your hands, blend until you have a thick, homogenous dough. Transfer to a counter dusted with flour.

4. Divide the dough into 6 softball-sized sections. Pinch off walnut-sized pieces

and roll each in the palms of your hands until round. Dust with flour and place on a platter in one layer.

5. Heat to boiling a large pot of salted water. Divide the *gnocchi* into 2 batches; slide the first batch into the water and when they float to the top, remove with a slotted spoon to a platter. Cool to room temperature.

6. When all the *gnocchi* are done, heat 3 tablespoons of the remaining oil in a large skillet. Add half the garlic and sauté for 1 minute. Place half the *gnocchi* (or as many as will fit in one layer) in the skillet and sauté until lightly browned on all sides. Season with salt and pepper and keep warm while sautéeing the remaining batches.

7. To serve, place a bed of tomato *ragu* on a large platter. Arrange the *gnocchi* on top and sprinkle with chopped parsley.

SERVES 6   TIME: 90 minutes   LEVEL OF DIFFICULTY: Advanced

MAKE AHEAD: The *gnocchi* can be made up to 1 day in advance, dusted with flour, covered with plastic, and refrigerated. The tomato *ragu* can be made up to 3 days in advance, refrigerated, and reheated.

Frittata di Asparagi e Spaghetti
Spaghetti and Asparagus Frittata

Spaghetti frittatas have a long-standing tradition in Tuscany, one that originates with mountain peasants who tried to stretch their recipes to feed as many mouths as possible. And what better way to do that than to add a handful of the most quintessential of staples! Now a standard lunchtime item, these crispy frittatas can include anything from mushrooms to wild herbs to whatever vegetable happens to be left over. While most are cooked on top of the stove, the following uses an oven method that makes for easier handling.

9 tablespoons extra-virgin olive oil
2 garlic cloves, minced
¼ cup Gaeta or other black olives, pitted and chopped
1 tablespoon capers, drained and rinsed
1 pound asparagus, thick stems trimmed

6 ounces spaghetti
7 eggs, lightly beaten
3 tablespoons fresh chopped parsley
Salt and freshly ground black pepper

1. Heat 3 tablespoons of oil in a small sauté pan over medium heat. Add the garlic and cook until golden. Add the olives and capers and cook for 3 minutes more, stirring constantly. Transfer to a bowl.

2. Meanwhile, blanch the asparagus in boiling salted water, drain, slice into 1-inch segments, and add to the bowl with the olives and capers.

3. Cook the spaghetti in boiling salted water until tender but firm. Drain, rinse with cold water, and drain again. Add to bowl and stir to blend all ingredients.

4. Preheat broiler. Add eggs and parsley to spaghetti, toss well, and season with salt and pepper. Heat 3 tablespoons of oil in a 12-inch-diameter broilerproof (preferably nonstick) skillet. Add spaghetti mixture and drizzle the remaining oil over the top. Cook over low heat without stirring until almost cooked through, about 8 minutes.

5. Place frittata under broiler and cook until top is golden brown and eggs are set, about 4 minutes. Cool slightly, about 5 minutes. Invert frittata onto platter, cut into wedges, and serve.

SERVES 8   TIME: 60 minutes   LEVEL OF DIFFICULTY: Easy

VARIATIONS: Almost any vegetable can be used in place of the asparagus. Tomatoes, eggplant, mushrooms, arugula, and zucchini would work especially well. If you can find garlic mustard and yarrow, add 1 tablespoon, chopped, of each to the egg and spaghetti mixture in Step 4.

MAKE AHEAD: This frittata is just as good served lukewarm or cold.

Carciofi Chloe Elmo
Artichokes, Chloe Elmo-Style

My dear friend, Doris Woolfe, is not only a great soprano, but a marvelous cook who was much influenced by her time in Italy. When I asked her to contribute a recipe for this book, she sent me the following which is faithfully reproduced in her delightfully chatty style.

"I went to Milan in 1959, after my legato had been ruined by one of the best teachers in New York. The purpose of my journey was to study with one of the great voices of her day, Chloe Elmo, Toscanini's "black alto"—a reference to the color of her voice. She was from Lecce, in the heel of Italy's boot, and a fabulous

My mother begins the daily ritual of shining the marble and arranging the flowers in the vase.

cook. In fact, she was the only person ever allowed by the Taverna della Fenice (across from Venice's former jewel of an opera house) to cook in her rooms for members of her cast. Such is the esteem in which Italy holds her great singers!

"Signora Elmo was not able to solve my problem in the one year I was there; tragically, she had lost her own voice as a result of throat cancer. But we spent one evening together which I will remember for the rest of my days. I had chosen to perform one work in her repertoire, the Verdi *Requiem*, a lovely piece and a new one for me since I am a Mozartian soprano. Cracked as her voice was, the Maestra could not resist joining me, and, while we sang the great "Recordare" duet, I could see the tears coursing down her husband's face as he stood at the door. The music was so beautiful and our hearts so in it, God must have been delighted to welcome her to heaven not long after.

"Anyway, la Maestra taught me how to make these artichokes, and I highly recommend them to you and your readers: Strip 4 artichokes of their outer leaves. Trim off the spiny tops and then cut the bottoms so they will stand in a shallow round casserole or heavy pot. Soak in water and lemon a few minutes. Dry. Whack the artichokes on the bottom to spread the leaves. If they are Italian artichokes, you're ready. If they are the larger American variety, you will have to scoop out the choke with a grapefruit knife or spoon.

"Chop 4–6 cloves of garlic, a hefty bunch of parsley and a few anchovies— chop till you have a smearing-like paste—and then stuff the artichokes. Of course, add a little extra-virgin olive oil. Stand the artichokes close together in the pan, adding a finger of water and a little more oil. Cook 5–10 minutes, covered, over medium flame. If you are using the large artichokes, cook until done, about 20 minutes. Just before serving, choose some beautiful music, pour the wine, cut the bread, and prepare to feast!"

Arancini di Spinachi e Fontina con Salsa Verde

Spinach and Fontina "Oranges" with Parsley and Anchovy Sauce

Named "oranges" because of their round, slightly orange appearance, these croquettes originated in Sicily but have long found a home in Tuscany. Their traditional incarnation included a basic rice and mozzarella filling, but Tuscans chose to color the rice with spinach and use the more flavorful Fontina *for the surprise center. They make a wonderful* antipasto *when served on a bed of greens and accompanied by salsa verde. Note that since Italian oranges are much smaller than ours, the directions call for creating lime-sized balls.*

The "Oranges" (Limes)

1 pound spinach, cleaned and roughly chopped

1 cup Basic Vegetable Broth (see page 308)

2 cups short grain white rice

Salt and freshly ground black pepper to taste

5 eggs

2 ounces freshly grated Parmigiano-Reggiano

¼ pound *Fontina* cheese, cut into 12 cubes

1 cup unflavored bread crumbs

Olive oil for frying

The Dipping Sauce

2 large bunches flat-leaved parsley, cleaned and with stems removed

3 anchovies, drained

5 tablespoons extra-virgin olive oil

1. Purée the spinach in a blender with the vegetable broth.

2. Place the rice in a pot with 2 cups cold water and the spinach purée. Cook over low heat until the rice is tender and has absorbed all the liquid. Stir once during cooking. Remove from heat, transfer to a bowl, season with salt and pepper, and cool to room temperature.

3. Lightly beat 3 of the eggs and add them to the rice along with the grated cheese. Mix well using your hands. Divide the rice mixture into 12 lime-sized balls, press a cube of cheese into the center of each, and roll the balls between the palms of your hands until they are sufficiently round and smooth.

4. Beat the 2 remaining eggs. Dip each ball into the eggs and roll in bread

crumbs to form a thick crust. Fry in ½ inch of oil, turning constantly until all sides are golden brown. Remove with tongs and drain on paper towels.

5. Meanwhile, make the sauce by placing the parsley, anchovies, and oil in a food processor and blend until smooth. Transfer to a decorative bowl.

6. To serve, arrange 10 of the "oranges" in a circle on a bed of greens. Split the remaining two in half and place in the center of the circle in a straight line, overlapping slightly. Accompany with the parsley sauce.

SERVES 6   TIME: 1¼ hours   LEVEL OF DIFFICULTY: Moderate

VARIATIONS: Experiment with other greens in place of spinach. Try watercress, sorrel, or chicory. If you can find garlic mustard and/or plantains, add 1 tablespoon of each, chopped, to the blender in Step 1.

MAKE AHEAD: The rice can be cooked up to 1 day in advance, refrigerated, and returned to room temperature before using.

Sformato di Asparagi con Fonduta di Formaggi
Asparagus Mold with Four-Cheese Sauce

Tuscany's nuova cucina movement has taken traditional foods such as vegetable molds and enhanced their flavor with novel ingredients at the same time as beautifying their presentation by playing shapes against colors. Unlike France's nouvelle cuisine, which suffered from the dual bane of small portions and contrived combinations, nuova cucina appeals to both traditionalists and the culinary avante-garde; both are drawn to the concept of historically prized recipes updated without any loss of flavor or the treasured accessibility that underlies Tuscan cuisine. The following recipe is both delicious and beautiful. And you won't afterwards have to make a bowl of pasta to quell your hunger.

The Asparagus Mold

1 pound asparagus, thick stems removed
3 eggs
½ cup heavy cream
Salt and freshly ground black pepper

The Sauce

2 ounces Gorgonzola
2 ounces Fontina
2 ounces Taleggio
2 ounces Parmigiano-Reggiano
2 egg yolks, well beaten
½ cup milk

Alfio Venturi watches my mother's progress through the market, dreading her arrival at his stand.

1. Parboil the asparagus in salted water. Remove the tips from 6 stalks and set aside. Place the rest in a food processor with the eggs and cream. Blend until smooth. Season with salt and pepper.

2. Preheat the oven to 350 degrees. Grease a 9-inch-diameter mold with butter and fill to the ¾ mark with the asparagus purée. Place the mold in a larger pan filled with water, making sure that the water reaches halfway up the sides of the mold. Bake for 30–40 minutes or until set.

3. To make the sauce, cut all the cheeses into small cubes and place in a double boiler with the eggs and milk. Cook over medium heat for 7 minutes or until the cheeses have melted into a thick consistency.

4. To serve, spread the cheese sauce over the surface of a white, rounded platter. Empty the asparagus mold onto the center of the platter. Decorate the surface of the mold with the reserved asparagus and serve.

SERVES 4   TIME: 1 hour   LEVEL OF DIFFICULTY: Easy

VARIATIONS: Try using artichokes instead of asparagus and various other cheeses for the sauce.

Bietola Ripiena
Stuffed Chard Packets Braised in Red Wine with *Cremini* Mushrooms

Every culture has its tradition of wrapped leaves simmered in a savory sauce. In Tuscany, the leaf of choice is often chard which is large and sturdy enough to contain any combination of stuffing ingredients. The following recipe is a variation on one made for me by a friend in Lucca. In place of Mirella's meat filling, I have substituted saffron and pine nuts which blend beautifully with the wine and mushroom soffrito in which it cooks.

16 large (about 9 inches in diameter) red chard leaves

The Stuffing

3 tablespoons extra-virgin olive oil
1 medium onion, minced
1 small carrot, scraped and minced
1 celery stalk, fibrous string removed and minced
12 strands saffron, soaked in 1 cup hot water for an hour
4 cups cooked short grain rice
½ cup toasted pine nuts, chopped

5 tablespoons fresh chopped parsley
2 eggs, lightly beaten
Salt and freshly ground black pepper

The Mushroom Sauce

2 tablespoons unsalted butter
1½ pounds *cremini* mushrooms, cleaned and minced
1 cup dry red wine
½ cup vegetable stock

1. Parboil the chard leaves until flexible. Refresh in cold water to stop the cooking. Using a sharp paring knife, remove the stems and reserve for another use.

2. For the stuffing: Heat the oil in a skillet. Sauté the onion, carrot, and celery over low heat until the vegetables are soft and the flavors have melded. Transfer to a bowl. Strain the saffron over a glass (reserving the liquid) and add the threads to the bowl along with the rice, pine nuts, parsley, and eggs. Mix well and season with salt and pepper.

3. For the mushroom sauce: Heat the butter in a skillet and, when melted, sauté the mushrooms over low heat until they are soft and paste-like. Add the wine, reserved saffron liquid, and vegetable stock and simmer over medium heat for 10 minutes.

4. Place 4 tablespoons stuffing in the center of each chard leaf. Fold into square packets and place, seam side down, in an ovenproof casserole large enough to hold all of them in one layer. Pack them closely so they cannot unroll. Pour in the mushroom wine sauce un-

The cemetery in Massarosa. My father's final resting place.

til it barely covers the packets. Cover and cook in a preheated 350-degree oven for 1 hour. Serve the packets from the casserole using the braising liquid as a sauce.

SERVES 4   TIME: 2 hours   LEVEL OF DIFFICULTY: Moderate

VARIATIONS: Cabbage leaves can be used in place of chard. Packets can also be cooked over a medium-hot grill or beneath a broiler for 2–3 minutes on each side until browned but not charred.

MAKE AHEAD: The stuffing blend can be prepared up to 4 hours in advance and refrigerated. The chard leaves can be parboiled up to 1 day in advance and refrigerated.

Ragu di Cardone con Sofritto Verde
Ragu of Cardoons with Bitter Green Soffritto

Cardoons are the perfect vegetable for late fall, because of both their flavor—a cross between celery and artichokes—and their marvelous, crunchy texture. The following is a rich, thick stew topped with spicy broccoli rabe. Serve it with hot rustic bread and a bountiful supply of dark red wine.

1 medium cardoon	Salt and pepper to taste
1 tablespoon lemon juice	2 tablespoons extra-virgin olive oil
3 tablespoons unsalted butter	2 cloves garlic, minced
1 pound assorted wild mushrooms, cleaned and thinly sliced	1 fresh chili pepper, seeded, cored, and minced
¼ cup dry white vermouth	½ pound broccoli rabe, washed and with thick stems removed
2 cups Basic Vegetable Broth (see page 308)	

1. Trim the top ½ inch off the cardoon stalks. Separate from the core, cut each stalk into lengths 2 or 3 inches long, remove any fibrous strings, and immediately plunge into boiling salted water to which the lemon juice has been added. Cook for 30 minutes or until tender.

2. Heat 2 tablespoons of the butter in a large skillet. Sauté the mushrooms until soft. Deglaze with vermouth.

3. Drain the cardoons and add to the mushroom skillet along with the vege-table broth and the remaining butter. Bring to a boil and cook, covered, for 30 minutes over medium heat. Season with salt and pepper.

4. Meanwhile, heat the oil in another skillet and sauté the garlic and chili pep-per over low heat for 5 minutes. Add the broccoli rabe and cook for 4 minutes or until wilted. Season with salt and pepper.

5. To serve, divide the cardoon ragu into small casseroles and top with a forkful of sautéed rabe.

SERVES 4   TIME: 1 hour   LEVEL OF DIFFICULTY: Easy

MAKE AHEAD: The cardoon can be blanched 1 day in advance and refrigerated.

CHAPTER FOUR

The Cabbage Family

In the Kitchen at Camporomano

I am generally a very lucky person. Which is why it came as no great surprise, that day in 1994 sitting having tea with Elena Pecchioli, reminiscing about our childhood escapades, when, suddenly, she mentioned how very delightful it would be to have a cooking school on the premises of her 60-acre estate.

Now, Elena and I are good friends, have *always* been good friends. But no matter how much digging into past conversations after that tea I did, I could not recall ever once mentioning my long-held dream to start a cooking school in Tuscany. As Elena later noted, "Good friends inhabit the same thoughts."

And so it came to pass that a cooking school by the name of Toscana Saporita (which means "Delicious Tuscany") took root at Camporomano, a working country estate with thousands of olive trees and more than its share of Old World charm. Of course, it was slightly more difficult than that. For example, our kitchen took slightly longer to construct than we had planned, and so our first classes were held in the main kitchen and dining hall of Elena's private villa—a situation that was, at best, fraught with constant peril.

Elena's mother, you see, was not at all happy having us as co-occupants; at certain moments, in fact, we lived in fear that she might tear down from her palatial apartment on the upper floors and throw us out in the middle of making

97

fresh pasta. It had nothing to do with us invading her private space. She actually *continued* to wish us gone long after we were housed in another of Camporomano's villas and working out of our own kitchen.

To explain the reasons behind the Contessa's antipathy, it would be necessary to review the entire history of Italy's aristocracy, including the expectation on their part that they would never have to think about making money. It has come as a sad blow to people like Elena's mother that her family can no longer live a life of unlimited privilege; that, like it or not, they must adhere to certain financial compromises; that her children have no recourse other than to work for a living.

But while it might have been acceptable for Elena to have sought employment as a diplomat or an art historian, it is—in her mother's mind—beyond imagining that she would take the family's country estate and turn it into a vacation resort catering to foreigners.

"Contessa Pecchioli is absolutely right," my own mother maintains, albeit predictably. "I would feel the same way having strangers traipsing through my rose gardens. What a desecration!"

No matter that it was either that or sell the property to developers. No matter that Elena's actions stem in great part from her sincere love of Camporomano and her desire to keep the estate in the family. No matter that her mother spends three or four months there every year benefiting from the fruits of Elena's shrewd management.

Elena herself is proud of her accomplishments. Truth be told, so are most other members of her family: her brother, Ugo, who handles Camporomano's finances; her father, Gianfranco, who, along with her mother, comes to Camporomano every autumn for the olive and grape harvests; and her 17-year-old son, Niccolo, who shows her off to his friends. "*Solo la mia mamma*," Elena says, shaking her head. Only my mother.

The extent of the Contessa's dissatisfaction with Toscana Saporita was made clear to me during that first-ever cooking school session. She and her husband had only arrived at Camporomano the previous day, having driven over from their residence in Florence with the intent to stay for two or three weeks. Walking back from the vegetable garden, I saw her headed towards the pool.

"*Buon giorno, Contessa*," I said, my arms filled with ripe red tomatoes and snippets of basil. "Our class is just about ready to prepare lunch. Won't you join us?"

She halted abruptly, her body tensing visibly. "*Lo so quelche stai facendo. E no, non credo che potro' venire."* I *know* what you are doing here. And no, I do not think I will be joining you.

But more important than her disdainful expression was the fact that she addressed me using the informal "you"—a conversational turn of phrase that is abjectly inappropriate outside one's family, except when speaking to children or hired help. "Maybe she just slipped," said my friend Janet. "Or maybe that's just the way she talks to everybody."

It is a hard thing to explain to a non-Tuscan, but neither of those options are the least bit plausible. Tuscan adults of a certain class never use the informal "you" even when chatting with life-long friends. "No," I told Janet. "Much as I would like to think otherwise, she used *tu* in order to make a point."

I did not tell my mother who would either have been furious at Elena's mother or, more likely, furious at me for having provoked such a display of bad manners.

It was the Contessa who first reacted to the idea of a cooking school with the disbelieving attitude I would have expected of Tuscans in general. "Adult men and women are coming to Camporomano to learn how to cook?" she said with as much incredulity as could be squeezed into that brief query. "Who has been preparing their food until now?"

I did not interpret her question as a slight to our students, but rather as evidence of one of the great many differences between Tuscans and Americans. The fact is that, despite a lifestyle largely precluding daily meal preparation, the Contessa is a marvelous cook. As is Elena, her brother Ugo, and her father Gianfranco. "*Siamo nati cuochi*," brags Gianfranco. Tuscans are born knowing how to cook. His declaration crosses gender, class, and age lines and applies even to those who, for all intents and purposes, have never cooked a single meal in their lives.

The awareness of food—how it is grown, selected, and prepared—truly permeates every Tuscan soul to the point where I once heard my uncle Dante (a non-cook) orating with great certainty about the thickness of the skin walls of two different types of red peppers and how that determined their suitability for roasting. The amazing part of the story is not only that he was right, but that his knowledge about those peppers transcended a good many thoroughbred cooks'.

Since the Contessa's question, I have often run up against a similar look of amazement when people find out I have a cooking school catering to adults. Even my partner, Sandra, whose mentality is as American as the proverbial apple pie in spite of having spent all of her 31 years living about 2 miles away from the school, even Sandra professes surprise at the stream of Americans interested in learning to cook, Tuscan-style.

On the one hand, everyone is always thrilled to see Americans sincerely interested in food preparation (Tuscans still believe Americans eat nothing but hot dogs and hamburgers). But there is also a hint of condescension layered into the praise. *"Che ne s'hanno l'Americani,"* sneered a local vegetable vendor upon my grilling him as to whether or not he had used chemicals to grow his leeks. What would Americans know? Of course, being Tuscan, he probably would have said that about anybody, including Umbrians, who live just next door.

People here are also amazed that Americans would travel over 4,000 miles simply to learn to cook. "Why wouldn't they simply take lessons in their *own* country?" asked Sandra's mother when we first told her we were starting a school. "There are a great many Tuscans residing in the United States. Why not study with them and save their vacations for rest and relaxation?"

I have repeatedly tried to explain that Americans like to combine their education and travel experiences—learning Portuguese while housed in a villa on the Algarve, for example, or studying piano in a Viennese conservatory, or even exploring the decline of the Central American rainforest while trekking through Costa Rica. It is a very hard concept to convey, especially because Tuscans view holidays as holidays and education as work. They cannot understand why anyone would prefer staying in a working agricultural estate instead of a fine hotel. That some people might also like to help out with such things as harvesting olives or making wine—and often pay to do so—is beyond comprehension.

Once I suggested to a Tuscan strawberry farmer that he advertise for people to help pick his crops. "It would certainly be nice," he said, "but how could I afford to pay them?"

"Where I come from, they often pay you, just for the experience," I told him. He didn't believe me.

Guests at Camporomano can view people picking olives and grapes (students in our Harvest Festival cooking classes even pick their own). They can also watch as the olives are turned into oil in the estate's 300-year-old press and the grapes crushed for what will eventually become a light, fruity red wine. Because the farm actually produces oil and wine, it qualifies under Italy's recently enacted *Agriturismo* laws which have enabled dozens of estates throughout Tuscany to transform themselves into resorts.

Agriturismo, or agricultural tourism, began officially in 1985 with the passing of regional and national laws to preserve Italy's historic rural environments, depopulated in the postwar move to industrial cities. Tax breaks and other incentives have since been provided to those who restore old farm buildings for the purpose of housing visitors.

The Italian government is promoting *Agriturismo* in hopes that it will stimulate ailing rural communities and provide additional income for struggling farmers. Not out of a spirit of altruism, however. If successful, *Agriturismo* would allow the government to reduce farm subsidies and hence their bloated level of debt. Under the new laws, working estates are not allowed to build any new structures but must restore existing ones.

At Camporomano, seven old stone houses, ranging in size from one to four bedrooms, have been transformed into charmingly decorated, cozy guesthouses. In addition, Elena has completely refurbished the large villa opposite her own to house our cooking school, and painted it in the maroon and almond stripe motif that dates back over 300 years.

Elena's family has owned Camporomano since the 18th century when one of her ancestors, the Marchese Ludovico Garzoni, purchased it as an autumnal vacation spot. "Garzoni was the Italian ambassador to Paris and the governor of Livorno," Elena says proudly. "He loved to come for the *vendemmia* (grape harvest) and usually stayed for a month or two afterwards."

Garzoni's picture is part of a genealogical portrait hanging over the 16th-century writing desk in Elena's reception hall. The canvas is dark with centuries' worth of grit, but you can still pick out the women with their jeweled tiaras and the men with their fur robes and gold crowns. Elena points out her favorites: the Duke of Lucca, a 12th century iconoclast responsible for many of that walled city's architectural splendors, Count Gustavo Parravacini, her great uncle who married Emilia Garzoni and came to live at Camporomano, and Giuseppe Garzoni, a member of the Senate during the wars between the Guelphs and the Ghibellines.

"Sometimes I wonder if Americans aren't better off simply having a mere 200 years of history," she says, laughing.

This week, Toscana Saporita's guests include Tom Milson, a 51-year-old pathologist from Kenosha, Wisconsin; Tom's mother, Mary, who lives just outside

Philadelphia; Vivian Kremer, a San Francisco stock broker; Vivian's architect boy-friend Robert, who has just spent the last six months travelling through Europe; Micki Benowitz from New York's Upper West Side; Lucy Stamb from Douglas Manor, Queens; Doris Woolfe, a New York City social worker; Doris' boss, and Diane Vevurkis.

We spent the first morning strolling among the olive trees, searching for ramps (wild native leeks), and the first sprigs of wild asparagus. The sun was high, and, by 10:00 A.M., everyone had stripped down to bare arms. At one point, we spotted Mariano—Camporomano's caretaker—in the distance leading a contin-gent of about 35 light-gray cows. *"Ciao, Americani,"* he yelled, and we all waved back. The cows, Sandra explained, serve as organic lawn mowers: Mariano lets them clean up the grass and weeds beneath certain sections of olive trees, and then he rotates them to the next area, and so on. "Free fertilizer," he always jokes. "That's why Camporomano's olive oil has such a distinct earthy flavor."

Lucy was the first to spot a cluster of ramps, whose leaves resemble lily of the valley while the bulb is similar to that of a scallion. "They taste like an earthy mix of garlic, leek, and dandelion," Sandra explained over breakfast, "and they're only in season from the middle of March to late May, after which they grow too strong in flavor." Our plan was to turn them into a wonderful lunch, drizzled with oil and grilled over olive wood along with new spring onions, the wild asparagus, artichokes, and radicchio. "I get more because I found them," teased Lucy.

At the end of an hour, everybody's basket was filled to overflowing with ramps, dandelions, sorrel, garlic mustard, plantains, sweet cicely, and an abun-dance of long thin wild asparagus. We took them back to the kitchen and began our lesson about spring vegetables. "Tuscans go a little mad in springtime," San-dra explained. "In part it is the weather, but it is also knowing that, for the next seven months, everything they eat will be fresh, young, and prepared in the sim-ple way that defines Tuscan cooking."

Two hours later, we were sitting out on Camporomano's main lawn feasting on homemade (or, in this case, student-made) green *taglierini* with parsley, spin-ach and wild herb pesto. This was followed by a mountain of grilled spring veg-etables, served with rosemary rolls, bitter greens salad, and—of course—an abundance of excellent local wines. To complete the picture, we made ourselves a fragrant compote of fresh fruits poached in red wine and served it with iced goblets of *grappa* made by Sandra's uncle, Duilio.

"And now you expect us to climb into a van and tour Lucca?" said Doris as she folded her apron and looked lovingly at the chaises lining the pool.

Today's class is on making fresh tortellini, and we have invited a friend of Sandra's mother to help with the teaching, a woman named Amelia who is noted throughout the Lucchesia for her perfectly shaped tortellini rosettes. Amelia arrived two hours before classtime to make absolutely certain we had what we needed in terms of both kitchen accoutrements and ingredients. It didn't matter that we had called her just yesterday to assure her we lacked for nothing.

At one point during the conversation, I heard Sandra talking in a measured monotone I knew all too well: "Yes, Amelia, we have rolling pins; yes, Amelia, we have pasta machines; yes, we have enough flour." Eventually, though, she lost it. "We're a cooking school!" Sandra pointed out in a thoroughly exasperated voice. "We have *everything* you could possibly need!" There was a pause, and then I saw her body tense and heard what I think were her teeth grinding against each other. "Yes, Amelia, we have olive oil."

Amelia does not speak English, and so our job—Sandra's and mine—is to translate her directions, which are as vivid as they are plentiful. In short order and to everyone's delight, Amelia quickly establishes herself as the Lucrezia Borgia of the kitchen: her control is absolute. *Di a quello li che le deve prima piegare e poi girare. Perché non ha ancora capito?* Tell that one that he has to first fold the tortellini before turning them around his finger. What will it take to make him understand? Diplomatic she is not.

We work for five hours on those tortellini, and Amelia eventually enraptures the class both with her mastery and her hilarious stories. Once, when Lucy points out that while the tortellini are works of art, they are also very time-consuming for the everyday cook, Amelia remarks that it was nothing unusual for "women of her time" to spend an entire day making "one or two thousand rosettes." And frequently it got to be too much for them to handle. As usual, she illustrates her point with a story, this time, the tale of Beppina Mafaldi, an old woman in her village:

"Beppina's husband Pietro would always come home for lunch and expect his meal to be sitting on the table. One day, Beppina was working at the stove, stirring the polenta. Her three small children were all sick, and she was holding one in her arms while the other stood at her side, crying and pulling on her skirts for attention.

"Pietro entered the house and went straight to the table. 'Why isn't the polenta yet ready,' he demanded in a loud, impatient voice as he turned to his newspaper. Beppina cracked. She put down her baby, picked up the *mestola* (a long wooden spoon used for stirring polenta), ran out to the dining room, and began beating Pietro over the head. 'Why isn't it ready?' she screamed. 'Why isn't it ready? Why do you *think* it isn't ready?'

"Pietro ran out of the house and into the courtyard. But Beppina ran right after him and continued hitting him with the hot spoon as all the neighbors watched in amazement.

"*Beh*, the poor man sustained painful burns all over his face and neck and was the laughingstock of the neighborhood for quite some time. But when anyone subsequently asked Beppina if she was sorry for what she had done, she always answered, '*O figlia mia* (oh daughter of mine), if I had only known then what I know now, I would have done it much sooner. Now when Pietro comes home and his dinner is not yet ready, he sits meekly at the table and patiently reads his paper. 'No need to rush,' he says and sometimes even offers to help!"

We *do* encounter one small problem with making the tortellini, and that is the clash between Amelia's desire to teach the students to make perfectly identical rosettes and the tendency on their part to experiment with more creative shapes. We have run into this situation before—specifically when another local woman came to the school to teach *gnocchi*-making—and we always just chalk it up to a clash between cultural values.

Simply put, Tuscans feel there is one right way to do things and all other ways are wrong. Hence, tortellini rosettes are made like this and not like that. Feeling comfortable enough with their knowledge of the basic technique, however, Doris soon begins experimenting with double rosettes, and, following Doris' lead, Diane commences crimping the edges of the pasta to give the rosettes a somewhat frilly look.

"They are not doing it right," Amelia complains when she realizes she is losing control of the situation. The problem, of course, is that she needs a translator to convey the full force of her message. "You *have* to tell them," she pleads with Sandra who after a few whispered asides simply declares that the students have already demonstrated their mastery of the "right" way and that it is fine for them to engage in a little experimentation—experimentation founded on a thorough understanding of the basics is what makes good cooks.

Amelia eventually cedes, and with a degree of graciousness I had not expected ("*Si chiameranno tortellini Americani,*" she says, celebrating the students' creations. We'll call them Tortellini, American-style). I can already predict, however, that the next time she comes to do a lesson, she will stress even more insistently that *this* is the way we do it.

Later that afternoon, I am in the herb garden with a few of the students explaining the use of *nepitella*, a mint-like herb used by Tuscans whenever mushrooms are included as part of a recipe. "Its flavor contains overtones of marjoram, oregano, and a hint of fresh sage," I tell them. "But it is very hard to find *nepitella* back home, so your best bet is to try experimenting with various types of mint."

Just at that moment, I turn and see Elena's mother standing approximately two feet away. "If they cannot find *nepitella* where herbs are sold," she says in a quiet, authoritative voice, "they can try talking to flower growers. I know from when I was last in America that *nepitella* is commonly used as what they call 'a ground-covering plant.'"

To say I am startled would be a gross understatement. Not only was I unaware that Elena's mother understood English, but I truly had no idea she had ever visited America. "I will tell them that, Contessa," I say cautiously.

But she has already turned and walked off after motioning for the students to follow. "I show you nepeta," she is saying in very good English and pointing to the flower garden alongside her villa.

When I have regained my composure and caught up with them, she is giving the students a horticultural primer. "Nepeta is member of the catnip family," she says, smiling. "You call nepeta; we call *nepitella,* but all the same. My husband use for tea—very good." She passes a sprig under each person's nose. "Like strong mint, no?"

That evening, we serve *tortellini in brodo* (Tortellini in Broth) as a first course and everyone, naturally, asks for seconds. By popular demand, Amelia stays to dine with us, and she is joined by her husband, Armando, and his friend, Santi. Also at the table are Elena, her brother, Ugo, her father, Gianfranco, and—in a turn of events that Elena has deemed "*miracoloso*"—her mother, dressed in a long, flowing silk skirt and looking every inch the Contessa.

At one point, when we have finished the main course and are setting up for dessert and coffee, I see Gianfranco and Ugo standing in the corner, kissing Lucy and Diane's hands. "Our own versions of Mastroianni," Sandra explains to Tom. "Oozing patrician charm from every pore."

Later, Gianfranco, with his wife's blessing, will take the class on a tour of his palatial apartments—a tour that will leave them breathless with wonder at being in what Micki will refer to as "a living museum." After that, the students, Sandra, and I will climb into the van and head for the *Sagra delle Castagne*—the Chestnut Country Fair held in nearby Barghecchia—where we will eat roasted chestnuts, sip *vin santo,* and dance in a 13th century piazza to a local orchestra playing waltzes and tangos.

But, for now, the moon is visible through the glass doors and Ugo is pouring brandy to accompany the *dolce di ciliegie* (cherry tart) we made for dessert.

"What happened?" Elena whispers when she accompanies me to get the canister of tea. "I have never seen my mother like this."

"No idea," I tell her, reaching for the sugar. "But let's not anger the gods with our need for too many answers."

She rolls her eyes. "No," she says. "Let's just go back to the table and watch her charm the students as if it were an everyday occurrence." She throws back her head and breaks into a wide grin. "Even the gods would not have an answer for this!"

About the Cabbage Family

Cabbage plants are much beloved by Tuscans, especially when the leaves have fallen from the trees and children begin appearing in their cold weather woolens. Crispness is the watchword for this pungent family whose vegetables come from different parts of the plant. Head cabbages—red, green, and Savoy varieties as well as their miniature version, brussels sprouts—are the tightly rolled leaves of the plant, while with kohlrabi (the German name for "cabbage-turnip") the bulbous plant stem is the favored part. Broccoli consists of green buds on a fleshy stalk, and cauliflowers are actually compressed flowers.

Broccoli Broccoli

Broccoli (*Brassica oleracea*) is technically a long-season cauliflower; the English, in fact, often refer to it as winter cauliflower. Although the Romans have prized a different variety of broccoli for over 2,000 years, the broccoli that we know today, with its large heads, only became popular in this country when California's

Italians began planting it in large quantities in the 1930s. While the new purple broccoli makes a colorful addition to any garden, I generally restrict my purchases to the green variety which produces larger, more mature heads; purple broccoli tends to flower immediately upon reaching maturity, which means it either needs to be picked at the very moment of maturation or, more likely, in an unripe state.

Season: June through July and September through November

To Buy: Broccoli heads should be dark-green (or purple) with firm stalks and tightly closed buds. Avoid any with woody stems, yellow or open-cored branches, or strong smells.

To Prepare: Wash well and soak in salted water for 30 minutes if necessary to remove insects (as in organic heads). Cut off the tough butt end of the central stalk. Break the head into florets and peel the floret stalks; peel the main stem as well. The trick is to cook broccoli as quickly as possible to maintain its color and crispness.

Brussels Sprouts *Cavoletti di Bruxelles*

Part of the cabbage, kale, and cauliflower family, brussels sprouts have been around since the 13th century and are prized for their miniature cabbage-like heads which cook quickly and taste like a milder, sweeter version of their cousin, green cabbage.

Season: September through November

To Buy: Brussels sprouts should be vivid green in color, firm to the touch, and unwrinkled. Best if still on the stem since they lose their unique flavor almost immediately upon being picked.

To Prepare: Pick off the stem, trim bottom ends, and remove any yellowed outer leaves (but don't cut off too much of the bottom or you will lose too many leaves). For more even cooking, pierce the base with a sharp knife point. Rinse well.

Cabbage, Green, Red, or Savoy *Cavolo*

Cabbages are exceedingly adaptable plants that grow under even the most adverse conditions and, hence, are one of the few vegetables cultivated in almost all parts of the globe. The first cabbages grew straight up rather than as heads. Known as *caulia* to the Latins, they had very thick stalks and tall, oblong heads much like Chinese bok choy.

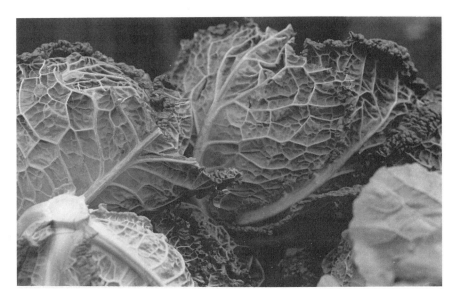

Savoy cabbage.

Season: September through November

To Buy: Choose only firm heads that seem heavy for their size. Heads should have good color (not too light which signifies overmaturation and not too dark which means it has yet to mature) and crisp, finely ribbed leaves.

To Prepare: Remove coarse or discolored outer leaves. Remove core and rinse whole, or cut into quarters and remove core before rinsing. For wedges, core is left in but with bottom trimmed, to hold sections together. To reduce gastric irritation, add an onion when blanching or boiling cabbage.

Cauliflower *Cavolfiore*

Mark Twain once said, "Cauliflower is simply a cabbage with a college education," and, indeed, cauliflower takes its name from the Latin *cavoli a fiore*—cabbage that blooms like a flower. While in this country we tend to prize only large, pure-white heads, Tuscans (who cultivate cauliflower to a tremendous extent) favor small heads that are light green or purple. Romanesco cauliflower varieties, which are now widely available in this country, are lime green and have smaller heads.

Season: September through November

To Buy: Choose only heads that are pure white (or lime green) in color, not yellow or brownish. The buds should be fine-grained, crisp, and tightly closed; the leaves, fresh green and well-trimmed. Avoid any that have a strong smell and those whose clusters have begun to separate from each other.

To Prepare: Remove leaves and trim tough part of stalk. Cut away discolored parts. Wash and separate into florets, leaving a portion of the center stalk attached to each one. Peel the attached stems, making a 1-inch slit through the stems of any fat pieces to facilitate cooking. If cooking whole, cut out center of stalk for more even cooking.

Kohlrabi *Cavolrape*

A close relative of the common cabbage, kohlrabi (*Brassica oleracea caulo-rapa*) has such a strange spaceship-like appearance that it is often described as a turnip growing on a cabbage root, although its flavor is more delicate and subtle than either of those vegetables. Both stem and leaf can be used; the former, usually white and beautifully flushed with purple, adapts to a variety of uses, from mashed to steamed to raw to sautéed to stuffed.

Season: Late summer through fall

To Buy: Look for crisp firm specimens that are 2 to 3 inches in diameter and have a uniform light-green color. Larger ones are often woody.

To Prepare: Peel like a turnip, being sure to remove the full thickness of skin.

Quick and Easy

Broccoli

Broccoli is one of the most versatile of vegetables. Raw florets are a wonderful addition to a fresh salad, as are parboiled, julienned stems. Sautéed in garlic and olive oil and tossed with pasta and fresh grated Parmigiano-Reggiano, broccoli assumes the mantle of a classic. Boiled (or steamed) and drizzled with olive oil and lemon, broccoli florets make the perfect cold-season side dish. And who could live without broccoli as an addition to a platter of crudités?

Brussels Sprouts and Cabbage (Red, Green, and Savoy Varieties)

Like greens, brussels sprouts and cabbage are most often eaten sautéed in garlic and oil and seasoned with a little salt. Prepared this way, they make excellent toppings for pasta, especially when dusted with grated *pecorino* cheese. Boiled (or steamed) until wilted, brussels sprouts and cabbages also form an essential part of boiled vegetable salads which generally include potatoes, onions, carrots, cabbage, and, often, broccoli rabe. Place all the vegetables (except for broccoli rabe) in a large pot and boil (or steam) until all are tender. Add the broccoli rabe 4 or 5 minutes before completion. Cut into bite-sized pieces and toss with olive oil, salt, pepper, and—if desired—a squeeze of fresh lemon. Like their American counterparts, Tuscans also use shredded cabbage to make coleslaw, although Tuscans substitute oil and vinegar for mayonnaise.

Cauliflower

There are few vegetables as attractive or flavorful as a whole head of cauliflower, boiled until just tender (or if cooked as florets, reassembled with toothpicks) and served simply with a drizzle of oil, salt, and freshly ground white pepper. If desired, add a pinch of freshly ground nutmeg. Raw (or blanched) florets also form a welcome addition to salads or platters of crudités.

Kohlrabi

Boiled in salted water until tender, kohlrabi can be mashed or riced with a modicum of butter and seasoning. It can be thinly sliced and sautéed in garlic and oil, or cut into wedges and served as a raw appetizer with parsley or garlic sauce (see chapter on Basic Sauces).

"How much olive oil?" Sandra and students at Toscana Saporita.

Cavolfiore in Padella
con Erbe Selvatiche e Acciughe
Pan-Fried Romanesco Cauliflower
with Wild Herbs and Anchovies

Cauliflower is a vegetable for those who love beauty as well as flavor. Whether the pure white version or the lime green Romanesco variety used in this recipe, cauliflower never fails to make a distinct fashion statement. Legend, in fact, has it that maidens in ancient Rome pressed small, perfectly shaped heads into their decolletage to call attention to their precious gifts. Beauty aside, the "cabbage that blooms like a flower" is one of nature's foremost culinary delights and never more delicious than in this simple recipe where it is sautéed with a number of wild herbs and seasoned to perfection with anchovies.

2 small heads Romanesco cauliflower	¼ teaspoon fresh chopped purslane
3 tablespoons extra-virgin olive oil	¼ teaspoon fresh chopped borage
1 clove garlic, mashed	3 anchovy fillets, drained and chopped
½ cup dry white wine	
¼ teaspoon fresh chopped lovage	

1. Using a small knife, separate the cauliflower into small florets. Place in a steamer basket and cook over boiling water for 5 minutes or until tender. Remove from heat and dice the florets.

2. Heat the oil in a skillet. Sauté the garlic for 1 minute over medium flame. Add the cauliflower and continue to sauté, stirring, for 5 minutes.

3. Add the wine, herbs, and anchovies and sauté until the wine has evaporated, about 2 minutes. The cauliflower should be crisp but tender. Transfer to a warm serving dish and serve hot.

SERVES 4   TIME: 35–45 minutes   LEVEL OF DIFFICULTY: Easy

VARIATIONS: Try using other herb combinations such as marjoram/basil, sage/thyme, or parsley/mint.

MAKE AHEAD: The cauliflower can be steamed 1 day in advance and refrigerated.

Cavolo in Umido con Vino Rosso e Castagne
Braised Red Cabbage with Chestnuts and Red Wine

Cabbage only comes into its true flavor after the heads have shivered through a few light frosts. True Tuscan connoisseurs always wait until school children begin wearing their wool uniforms — the navy blue jumpers and cardigan sweaters that presage the arrival of winter. Small wonder, then, that the following recipe so successfully pairs this most colorful of cabbages with that other seasonal harbinger, chestnuts. To best capture the mood, serve it in a decorative earthenware casserole with plenty of sturdy bread to soak up the sauce and a carafe or two of full-bodied red wine.

2 ounces dried *porcini* mushrooms

3 tablespoons extra-virgin olive oil

1 medium onion, minced

1 medium-sized red cabbage (about 2½ pounds), core removed and shredded

1½ cups dry red wine

1½ cups Basic Vegetable Broth (see page 308)

2 tablespoons red wine vinegar

¼ teaspoon freshly grated nutmeg

½ teaspoon salt

Freshly ground black pepper

2 pounds chestnuts, parboiled for 10 minutes, outer and inner skins removed

1. Preheat oven to 350 degrees.

2. Soak the mushrooms in warm water for 1 hour. Drain, rinse, squeeze "dry," and mince. Filter the liquid and reserve.

3. In a heavy 3-quart ovenproof casserole that has a tightly fitting cover, heat the oil and sauté the mushrooms and onion for 5 minutes over low heat, stirring frequently until the onions are soft and buttery. Stir in the cabbage and cook for 10 minutes.

3. Add the wine, broth, vinegar, nutmeg, salt, and a generous grinding of pepper. Cover and place in the oven for 2 hours. Make sure that the liquids are not cooking away too fast; if so, add more broth.

4. Gently stir in the chestnuts and cook, covered, for another hour or until the cabbage is tender and most of the liquid absorbed. Adjust seasoning and serve.

SERVES 6   TIME: 4¼ hours   LEVEL OF DIFFICULTY: Easy

MAKE AHEAD: Chestnuts can be skinned 1 day in advance.

Ravioli di Broccoli Profumati con Limoncino e Scalogne

Broccoli Ravioli Perfumed with Shallots and Lemon Balm

As basil is to a platter of fresh tomatoes and bufala mozzarella, so, too, is lemon balm to this wonderful dish of delicate ravioli filled with broccoli and bedded on polenta soffrito. Like basil, lemon balm exudes an unmistakable fragrance that perfumes anything with which it comes into contact. Also like basil, lemon balm shines whether cooked or raw. In this dish, it is used both as part of the filling and as a delicate cushion underlying the ravioli. Lemon balm should be available at your local farmer's market, but if you have trouble getting some you can substitute it with 8 fresh mint leaves and a teaspoon of lemon zest.

The Dough

1 cup unbleached white flour
4 tablespoons extra-virgin olive oil
½ cup semolina
¼ teaspoon salt
Cold water

The Filling

1 pound broccoli, stems removed
    and reserved for another use
¼ teaspoon fresh grated nutmeg
1 tablespoon minced shallot
2 tablespoons extra-virgin olive oil
8 leaves lemon balm, minced
Salt to taste

The Sauce

2 tablespoons extra-virgin olive oil
2 large shallots, peeled and minced
1 medium carrot, scraped and
    minced
1 small celery stalk, fibrous string
    removed and minced
1 cup Basic Vegetable Broth (see
    page 308)
2 tablespoons fine-ground
    polenta
Salt and freshly ground black
    pepper
16 leaves lemon balm

1. Place all the ingredients for the dough in a large bowl. Using your hands, mix until well blended, adding water as necessary to create a soft, springy dough. Rub some olive oil on the dough and in an oiled bowl covered with a dish towel, let the dough rest for 30 minutes.

2. Meanwhile, cook the broccoli florets in boiling salted water until tender. Drain and chop finely. Add the remaining filling ingredients and blend well.

3. Roll the dough into a 12-inch square approximately ⅛ inch thick. Using a juice

glass or ravioli cutter, cut 12 3-inch-diameter (approximately) circles. Fill each circle with 1 teaspoon broccoli filling, making sure to place the filling only on one half of the circle. Using your finger or a small pastry brush, moisten the outside rim of the circle with water. Fold the ravioli in half and press shut.

4. To make the sauce, heat the oil in a skillet and sauté the shallots, carrot, and celery over low heat for 7 minutes or until soft. Add the broth and whisk in the polenta, stirring to create a soupy paste. Season with salt and pepper. Chiffonade the lemon balm leaves by shredding finely with a sharp knife.

5. Cook the ravioli for 6–8 minutes in a large pot of boiling salted water. Remove carefully with a slotted spoon to a heated platter.

6. To serve, spoon 2 tablespoons sauce onto each of 4 plates, top with a few slivers of lemon balm chiffonade, and arrange three ravioli in a triangular pattern.

SERVES 4   TIME: 1¼ hour   LEVEL OF DIFFICULTY: Moderate

MAKE AHEAD: Both the filling and the sauce can be made 6 hours in advance and refrigerated.

Verza Ripiena
Whole Savoy Cabbage Stuffed with Sorrel, Rice, and Wild Mushrooms

Cabbage, that staple of peasant cooking, comes to center stage in this extravagant and delicious one-dish meal. Large heads of curly Savoy are stuffed, wrapped in cheesecloth, poached in a tasty broth, brought to the table whole, and then sliced into wedges for serving. Leftovers are equally good—some say better—the next day.

1 cup long grain white rice
2 quarts plus 2½ cups Basic Vegetable Broth (see page 308)
1 large head Savoy cabbage (5–6 pounds)
3 tablespoons extra-virgin olive oil
1 medium onion, minced
Salt and freshly ground black pepper

1 pound mixed wild mushrooms, cleaned and chopped
½ pound sorrel, cleaned and roughly chopped
¼ pound walnuts, chopped
3 tablespoons fresh chopped parsley
¼ cup heavy cream
1 cup dry white wine

1. Cook the rice until tender in 2½ cups of the broth. Remove from heat and cool.

2. Trim the stem of the cabbage and remove any damaged leaves. Simmer the cabbage in salted water for 10–15 minutes until the outer leaves are supple. Take the cabbage out of the pot and drain it. Set aside any leaves that have detached. When the cabbage is cool enough to handle, place it on a large piece of cheesecloth.

3. Gently pull back the outer leaves of the cabbage, one by one, until you reach the firm heart of inner leaves which will be slightly larger than a fist. With a sharp knife, cut the heart from the stem, leaving the outer leaves attached. Chop the heart finely, squeeze to remove any excess water, and set aside.

4. Heat the oil in a skillet. Sauté the onions for 5 minutes over a low flame. Add the chopped cabbage heart, cover, and cook for 8–10 minutes until the cabbage is wilted. Season with salt and pepper.

5. Uncover and add the mushrooms. Increase the heat to medium and sauté, stirring frequently, for 5–6 minutes. The mushrooms should be soft but not mushy. Add the sorrel, walnuts, and parsley and sauté for another minute, stirring constantly, until the sorrel has wilted.

6. Transfer the mushroom cabbage mixture to a large bowl. Add the cooked rice, cream, and wine and stir until all ingredients are well blended.

7. Pack all but 5 tablespoons of the stuffing into the hollow center of the cabbage, molding it into a ball about the same size and shape as the excavated heart. To help keep the stuffing intact, press one or two large leaves over it, using leaves that broke off during the preliminary simmering (or detach a few outer leaves). Secure them by pressing the remaining stuffing around their edges and folding a few outer leaves over it.

8. Gently fold all the outer leaves back into place. Overlap them to enclose the stuffing completely and to give the cabbage its original rounded shape. Pull the four edges of the cheesecloth together at the top and tie them.

9. Heat the remaining broth to boiling in a pot large enough to hold the cabbage. Gently lower the cabbage into the broth, reduce the heat to simmer, and cook the cabbage, uncovered, for 2 hours.

10. To remove the cabbage, push the prongs of a large fork through the top of the cheesecloth. Use a bowl to catch the drippings and transfer the cabbage to a colander. Drain for 5–10 minutes. Reserve the broth.

11. To unwrap the cabbage, place it in a bowl, untie the cheesecloth, and lay a plate over the top. Turn over plate and bowl together. Lift away the bowl and remove the cheesecloth. Finally, replace the bowl and invert plate and bowl once more so that the cabbage is stem side down.

12. Slice into wedges and pour a little of the cooking liquid over each wedge before serving.

SERVES 8   TIME: 4 hours

LEVEL OF DIFFICULTY: Advanced

VARIATIONS: Green cabbage can be used in place of Savoy, and you can include almost any vegetable in the stuffing. Try chard with tomatoes and olive paste, or lettuce with peas and spinach. Also try adding dried fruit (raisins, prunes), various types of cheeses, and other kinds of nuts. Bread crumbs can be used in place of rice.

MAKE AHEAD: The cabbage can be stuffed and tied with cheesecloth 1 day in advance and refrigerated.

Amelia Baltieri instructing the students: "Tortellini rosettes are not made like that."

Calzonetti con Cavolo Rosso e Caprese
Calzonetti (bite-sized calzones) Stuffed with Red Cabbage and Chevre

Calzones are half-moon-shaped stuffed pizzas native to southern Italy. Their size varies from 6 to 8 inches in length and fillings include anything from four cheeses to the standard tomatoes and mozzarella. A few years ago, I began to notice that Tuscans had appropriated the idea of calzone and pressed them into use as a cocktail party appetizer. The Tuscan version, however, is much smaller in size and wrapped around largely vegetable fillings. The result is a marvelous slightly-larger-than bite-sized nibble.

The Dough

1 tablespoon yeast

1½ cups warm water

4 cups unbleached all-purpose flour, plus flour for kneading

2 tablespoons extra-virgin olive oil, plus additional oil to grease the bowl

1 teaspoon salt

The Stuffing

3 tablespoons extra-virgin olive oil

1 medium onion, minced

1 small head red cabbage (approximately 2 pounds), cored and finely chopped

½ tablespoon lemon juice

2 tablespoons balsamic vinegar

Salt and freshly ground black pepper

1 pound chevre

2 tablespoons fresh chopped parsley

Extra-virgin olive oil

Coarse-grind polenta for sprinkling

1. To make the dough, sprinkle the yeast over ½ cup of warm water in a 4-ounce glass. Place the glass in a larger bowl containing enough hot water to come up to the halfway mark on the glass. Set aside for 15 minutes.

2. Place the flour in a large bowl (or in a food processor). Add the yeast, 1 cup warm water, oil, and salt. Mix (or process) until you have a soft dough. Add additional warm water as necessary. Turn the dough out onto a floured surface and knead until smooth, taking in as much of the remaining flour as the dough will absorb, about 7 minutes. Place the dough in a clean bowl that has been well coated with olive oil. Cover with a damp towel and place in a warm spot to rise for 2 hours.

3. Meanwhile, make the filling. Heat the oil in a skillet and sauté the onion over low heat for 7 minutes or until soft. Add the cabbage and lemon juice, cover and sauté for 10 minutes until the cabbage is wilted. Stir in the vinegar, season with salt and pepper, transfer to a bowl, and bring to room temperature.

4. Crumble the chevre into the cooled cabbage and toss with the parsley.

5. Roll the dough into sixteen 4-inch rounds. Brush each with a little oil.

6. Preheat the oven to 500 degrees. Divide the cabbage and chevre among the 16 rounds, placing it on half the dough and leaving about a ½-inch margin. Fold the dough over and press with your fingers to seal the edges tightly. Brush each calzonetti with a little oil and set them on a baking sheet (or pizza stone) that has been sprinkled with coarse-grind polenta. Bake for 15 minutes or until the crust turns golden. Serve immediately.

SERVES 4   TIME: 3¼ hours   LEVEL OF DIFFICULTY: Moderate

VARIATIONS: The possibilities are infinite when it comes to stuffing mixtures. Try red onions, mushrooms, black olives, and fresh mozzarella. Or lemon zest, olive oil, sesame seeds, chopped greens, and thyme. Also try serving with a dipping sauce.

MAKE AHEAD: Pizza dough can be made 1 day in advance and refrigerated in a plastic bag sealed tightly to prevent the dough from expanding further. It can also be frozen and thawed when needed. The cabbage filling can be prepared up to 3 days in advance and refrigerated.

Cavolrape Ripiene
Stuffed Kohlrabi

Kohlrabi has aptly been described as a turnip growing on a cabbage root, although its flavor is more delicate and more subtle than either of those vegetables. It is a handsome vegetable and one that can be used in a myriad of ways, including mashed or riced like potatoes, sliced and sautéed in butter, battered and fried as part of a fritto misto, or grated raw over a bed of salad greens. The following recipe can be served as an appetizer or as a main dish, accompanied by a cold, fresh string bean salad.

4 medium-sized kohlrabi (3-inch diameter)
½ loaf long Italian bread, coarsely broken
1 pint heavy cream
¼ cup plus 2 tablespoons extra-virgin olive oil
1 pound *cremini* mushrooms, minced

Freshly ground black pepper
1 egg yolk
1 cup freshly grated Parmigiano-Reggiano
1 tablespoon chopped parsley
½ cup unflavored bread crumbs
¼ cup Basic Vegetable Broth (see page 308)

1. Cut a thin slice off the bottom of each kohlrabi so that they stand flat and upright. Put them in lightly salted boiling water. Cook, uncovered, over medium heat for 30 minutes or until tender.

2. Meanwhile, soak the bread in the cream for ½ hour. Shred the softened bread until it is almost a paste and set aside.

3. Hollow out each kohlrabi from the stem end, leaving the shell about ½ inch thick. Chop the scooped-out flesh and set aside.

4. Place 2 tablespoons oil in a skillet and sauté the mushrooms over low heat for 5 minutes or until soft and paste-like. Season with pepper and bring to room temperature.

5. Add the mushrooms to the bread along with the egg yolk, cheese, parsley, and chopped kohlrabi. Mix well.

6. Fill the kohlrabi with the bread and mushroom mixture. Place in a well-greased baking dish and sprinkle with bread crumbs. Pour the oil and broth into the dish and bake in a 425-degree oven for 15 minutes, basting occasionally. Spoon sauce over the kohlrabi and serve.

SERVES 4   TIME: 90 minutes   LEVEL OF DIFFICULTY: Moderate

MAKE AHEAD: The kohlrabi can be boiled and hollowed out 1 day in advance.

Nidi D'uccello
Pasta Nests with Creamy Cauliflower and Bechamel

When my friend, Sheila, saw me making these pasta nests, she asked whether the flavor was any different than it would be if the pasta was simply tossed and baked without taking the time to twirl it into nests. "Well, no," I had to reply. "Probably not." But then I thought about it again: Does presentation affect flavor? And having restructured the question into this saner, more creative framework, I retracted my previous answer. "Actually," I told her, "it does. After all, don't you usually have a better day when you're looking your best?"

1 head white cauliflower
1 tablespoon white vinegar
4 tablespoons extra-virgin olive oil
3 cloves garlic, minced
¼ teaspoon fresh chopped oregano
Salt and freshly ground black pepper

2 tablespoons butter, plus 2 ounces butter cut into 8 thin pats
3 tablespoons unbleached flour
2 cups milk
1 pound vermicelli
½ cup freshly grated Parmigiano-Reggiano

1. Break the cauliflower into florets, slashing any thick stalks lengthwise so all parts cook evenly. Boil until just tender in salted water with vinegar added (to keep the cauliflower white). Drain and chop finely.

2. Heat the oil in a large skillet. Sauté the garlic over low heat until soft. Add the cauliflower and sauté for 5 minutes, stirring frequently. Add the oregano, season with salt and pepper, and set aside.

3. Make the bechamel by melting 2 tablespoons butter in another skillet. Add the flour and stir with a fork to paste-like consistency. Whisk in the milk, pouring in a steady stream until the sauce has thickened. Keep warm.

4. Meanwhile cook the pasta until very *al dente*. Drain.

5. Preheat the oven to 350 degrees. Grease an 8 × 16-inch baking pan and spread 2 tablespoons of the bechamel sauce over the surface.

6. To assemble the pasta nests, twirl 10 strands into a nest with an open center. Place the nest in the baking dish and fill with cauliflower. Repeat until you have 16 nests. Pour the remainder of the bechamel over the nests, sprinkle with cheese, dust with pepper, and bake for 20 minutes. Serve immediately.

SERVES 4   TIME: 75–90 minutes   LEVEL OF DIFFICULTY: Easy

MAKE AHEAD: The cauliflower can be cooked up to 4 hours in advance and refrigerated.

The "organic lawnmowers" of Camporomano.

Cavoletti di Bruxelles alla Toscana
Brussels Sprouts with Caramelized Red Onions, Apples, and Red Wine

When I was a child, I always thought Brussels sprouts were baby cabbages, so tiny, well formed, and manageable were they on my plate. Now, of course, I know that I was right, although they're the kind of babies whose adolescence endures into perpetuity (very much like some humans'). The following recipe pairs their sweet, mild, autumnal flavor with those other late season favorites, apples, and red wine.

3 tablespoons unsalted butter
1 medium red onion, diced
1 teaspoon sugar
2 greening or other tart apples, diced

1 pound Brussels sprouts, stems trimmed and cut in half
2 cups dry red wine
½ teaspoon salt
½ teaspoon freshly ground black pepper

1. Melt the butter in a large, nonaluminum skillet over medium heat. Add the onion, increase the heat and sauté, stirring constantly for 3 minutes or until the onion begins to brown. Add the sugar and increase the heat to high. Sauté, stirring constantly, until the onion caramelizes, about 2 minutes.

2. Add the apples and sauté for 3 minutes, until softened.

3. Add the Brussels sprouts, stirring gently to blend, and sauté for 3 or 4 minutes.

4. Pour the wine over the sprouts and add the salt and pepper. Reduce the heat to low, cover, and simmer for 10–15 minutes or until the sprouts can easily be pierced with a fork.

5. Using a slotted spoon, transfer the contents of the pan to a heated platter. Increase the heat to medium and cook until the pan juices are reduced by half. Make sure to scrape up any bits of food. Pour the reduced juices over the sprouts and serve.

SERVES 4   TIME: 45–60 minutes   LEVEL OF DIFFICULTY: Easy

VARIATION: Greens such as beet leaves can also be added with the wine in Step 4.

Zuppa di Versa e Porri Selvaggi
Savoy Cabbage and Wild Leek Soup

In addition to sheltering chestnuts, wild asparagus, and porcini *mushrooms, Tuscany's forests also produce copious quantities of ramps or wild leeks. During their very brief season (mid-March to the end of May), ramps can be found on almost every menu, often in conjunction with cabbage in a hearty soup that can serve as a one-dish meal.*

6 tablespoons extra-virgin olive oil	1 quart Basic Vegetable Broth (see
1 large onion, minced	page 308)
1 medium head Savoy cabbage,	1 tablespoon fresh chopped parsley
cored and coarsely chopped	8 ¾-inch-thick slices day-old
½ teaspoon salt	peasant bread
1 cup finely chopped, cleaned	4 garlic cloves, halved
ramps (wild leeks), including	
green parts	

1. Heat 3 tablespoons of the oil in a large skillet. Add the onion and sauté over low heat for 5 minutes, stirring frequently until soft and creamy.

2. Add the cabbage and sprinkle with salt. Increase the heat to medium, cover, and cook until the cabbage has wilted, 6 or 7 minutes.

3. Meanwhile, heat the remaining oil in a small nonstick skillet. Add the ramps, cover with a tight-fitting lid, and sweat over low heat for 5 minutes or until translucent.

4. In a large soup pot, bring the broth to boiling. Transfer the cabbage and its cooking liquid to the boiling broth. Reduce the heat to low and simmer, uncovered, for 20 minutes.

5. Transfer the sweated ramps and their juices to the soup pot. Stir to blend. Remove from heat and stir in the parsley. Set aside.

6. Toast the bread on both sides and immediately rub with garlic. Place 2 slices in each of 4 soup bowls. Pour the soup over the bread and serve immediately.

SERVES 4   TIME: 1 hour   LEVEL OF DIFFICULTY: Easy

VARIATIONS: If you can't find ramps, you can use a combination of scallions and shallots.

Broccoli al'Olive
Broccoli Florets Roasted with Black Olive Sauce

My love affair with broccoli dates back to my youth, when I would hold the stalk in my hand and nibble at the florets as if I were eating an ice cream cone. The variety of the vegetable that we enjoy today, with its large florets, is a fairly new phenomenon that comes to us courtesy of producer Albert Broccoli's (of James Bond fame) Calabrian grandfather, who first crossed cauliflower and rabe and named the new vegetable after himself. All I can say is, thank you, Signore Broccoli.

The following recipe is one of my favorites, both for its simplicity and intensely concentrated flavor. The broccoli is slowly pan fried in a slightly thinned black olive paste until it takes on an almost crispy texture.

2 medium-sized heads broccoli, trimmed and cut into florets
3 tablespoons extra-virgin olive oil
2 cloves garlic, minced

3 ounces black olive paste
2–4 tablespoons Basic Vegetable Broth (see page 308)

1. Parboil the broccoli in a large quantity of salted water. Drain thoroughly.

2. Heat the oil in a large skillet. Sauté the garlic over low heat for 5 minutes or until soft. Add the olive paste and whisk in 1 tablespoon of the broth.

3. Increase the heat to medium. Add the broccoli and sauté for 15 minutes, turning frequently until the florets are coated with the olive sauce and lightly browned. The sauce should be fairly dry at all times; add more broth if necessary to keep from sticking.

SERVES 4   TIME: 25 minutes   LEVEL OF DIFFICULTY: Easy

VARIATIONS: Other vegetables can also benefit from this technique. Try asparagus, string beans, or celery.

MAKE AHEAD: The broccoli can be parboiled earlier in the day. Refresh in ice water and drain before storing.

CHAPTER FIVE

Roots, Tubers, and Bulbs

Full Stomachs, Warm Feet, Cold Judgment

"Ethics takes precedence over the rising of the sun," said Petrarch, giving voice to a sentiment with which I have always agreed. Until now, that is. Now I am standing alongside my cousin, Loredana, in the middle of a bucolic fruit orchard which is itself surrounded by an endless circumference of greenery. Accompanying us on this April morning filled with the fragrance of ripening apricots is a boorish, fifty-something real estate broker—Ugolino by name—who has finally, with this piece of property, stumbled onto something that might conceivably be of interest to us.

The orchard is located in what is called the *bonifica*, a vast tract of former swampland transformed by Mussolini over 60 years ago into prime agricultural terrain. Actually, swamplands once covered much of Tuscany; in the Lucchesia, they sprawled over much of the land between the Apuan foothills and the Tyrhennian Coast around Lake Massaciuccoli. In some cases, where the land was less swampy than elsewhere, workers had previously grown rice, benefiting from the mild climate and the protection offered by the high peaks of the Apuan chain. But rice never compensated for the fact that little else could be grown there.

Until Mussolini. Il Duce undertook a complex and far-reaching project involving the installation of thousands of pumps designed to suck water from the swampy plains into specially constructed canals (most of the pumps are today still in operation). Once the land had been drained, it was tilled and readied for planting, and, as a result, land that was historically unusable was soon blanketed with hectares of corn and lettuce and zucchini and fruit trees. *"Chi si marita sta contento un giorno, ma chi puo piantare un orto sta contento per tutta la vita,"* Mussolini is reputed to have said in announcing his plan to provide Tuscans with plantable land. He who marries is happy for one day, but he who can plant food is content for the rest of his life.

This particular orchard is located just a few miles from our family's ancestral home in Massarosa. Loredana's intent is to build a small *rustico* to which she can flee when life in Milan becomes unbearable. *"Vivere in un frutteto e sempre stato un sogno,"* she whispered into my hair when we were sitting in Ugolino's office. Living in an orchard has always been my dream. The problem lies with the zoning, which—at least for now—prohibits the construction of permanent housing in agricultural areas. Trailers are fine, as are *prefabbricate*, pre-constructed wooden houses.

The center of the orchard sports an *annesso agricolo,* a shack built of corrugated metal in which tools are stored. Ugolino is pushing hard to convince Loredana that she could take the first step towards an eventual house by immediately wiring the shack with electricity and arranging for the installation of indoor plumbing. Both these things, he claims, would be permitted without question, since even bureaucrats understand that working an orchard often means being there past dark and afterwards needing to wash up. *"Puoi, fai un altro passo,"* he says with a disingenuous wink. Then you take another step. By which he means committing herself to building the house in stages, each stage initially against the law but transformed into legality after the payment of certain fines.

Neither of us appreciates his furtive suggestions. I, particularly, would like nothing better than to pooh-pooh his proposed course of action from a position rooted in moral rectitude. Two factors stand in the way, however. One concerns the fact that the strategy he espouses is as much an accepted part of everyday Tuscan existence as is haggling with the market vendor over the price of artichokes.

No matter the circumstances, legal building permits are virtually nonexistent in this part of Tuscany, local governments having shrewdly decided they had more to gain by forcing people to build illegally and then collecting the resultant fines. In this way, they benefit not only from a certain short-term cash flow, but lock in place a perpetual source of revenue. As the system now exists, people can make only one small alteration at any given time (enclosing an outdoor sink for example, or tiling a roof that was previously corrugated metal); if they take too large a step, they risk having their cheekiness reduced to rubble by ever-vigilant building inspectors. But small steps merely draw fines whose eventual payments culminate not only in the stamp of legitimacy but the license to proceed to Phase Two, which eventually draws more fines, and so on.

But there is a more important factor at play, one that Loredana and I have spent much time discussing before even contacting Ugolino. The fact is, Loredana would like nothing better than to build in an area whose primary attraction lies in there being no other houses nearby. Viewed through this window, one can even say that the provincial government has acted very shrewdly in its tight-fisted approach to building permits. And yet here she is, plotting to subvert the process because, as she puts it, "I would only be removing two or three trees and bringing in a small, pre-built wooden cottage." In her mind—and in mine—the ecological impact would be minimal. But it is still a rationalization no matter how you arrange the arguments.

We are about to leave, but just as Ugolino starts the car and asks, again, if we mind his smoking (we have already said yes three previous times), a large grizzled man comes trudging through the trees, waving his arms and positioning himself directly in our path. He is, Ugolino explains through clenched teeth, the orchard's caretaker, Ennio, and it is clear from the nature of the conversation between the two that we are the first potential buyers to have visited the property in quite some time.

Ennio is nonetheless worried; in the space of three minutes, he has already asked three times if we have come to a decision. As we eventually learn, he is not actually employed as a caretaker in the strict sense of the word. The owner apparently wants nothing to do with either the orchard or the fruit it produces. So, under a legal system known as *mezzadria*, Ennio—a marble cutter by day—rents the land from him and, along with his family and in his spare time, does what is necessary to ensure the highest level of production.

Under the terms of a typical *mezzadria* agreement, Ennio's responsibilities would include pruning the trees, cutting the weeds, buying and applying fertilizer, picking the produce, trucking it to market, and negotiating for the best price. The resultant profits would then be divided into three parts, one reverting to the owner. In many cases, such as when the orchard in question contains olive trees or grape vines, owners may choose to take their share in merchandise instead of money: in liters of oil or casks of wine. As Ugolino later tells us, however, the owner of *this* particular orchard takes nothing, neither fruit nor money. Ennio apparently does such a good job caring for the trees that the owner is more than content just knowing his investment is safe.

"*Allora*," says Ennio, resting his massive arms on the car roof above Loredana's head. "*Se vi posso aiutare in qualsiasi modo . . .*" If there is anything I can do to help. He strains for a certain lightness of tone, but the concern for his future is obvious in the way his eyes follow our every movement.

Ugolino is just about to, once again, start the motor when Loredana decides to ask Ennio about water and electricity—about whether their installation would be as easy to arrange as Ugolino maintains. "*E non si sa*," Ennio shrugs, showing the natural discomfort experienced by men unaccustomed to discussing technical details with women. It is hard to say.

"*Vieni*," he says, "*vi spiego come sono le cose*" (Follow me, I'll explain to you how things are), and, much to Ugolino's chagrin, she gets out of the car and hurries away. Really, I would like to follow, but I decided instead to stay behind and calm Ugolino's fears.

As he and I position ourselves at the edge of the orchard (Ugolino lighting up yet another cigarette), we are treated to the lyrical sight of a hardworking field-worker—a member of Ennio's family, I presume—wielding her sickle, cutting away shrubby undergrowth, cleaning the land with, no doubt, the same thoroughness as she cleans her home. There is a beauty to her movements and a grace not unlike that of a dancer. I am, however, reminded of a conversation with my friend, Carlo, wherein he castigated my romantic notions regarding the lives of peasants. "Do you think they'd agree their lives are worthy of painted landscapes?" he asked. "How would you feel hearing someone like you wax poetic about the 'honesty' of their work, listening to a woman dressed in an Armani blazer describe their movements as 'lyrical?'"

When Loredana and Ennio are finished, and she returns to the car, it is with a far different version of the possibilities than that conveyed by Ugolino who, nonetheless, continues to adhere to his stated position. "*Cosa v'aspettate*," he says, flashing a sardonic grin. "What were you expecting—that Ennio, whose interests lie, naturally, in his wallet, would tell you anything other than there will be insurmountable problems if you buy this land?"

His point is well taken.

"Go to the *comune*," he says. The City Hall. "There you will find the answers to all your questions."

We already know—and so does he—that City Hall has no answers to anything, least of all the viability of placing a house in an orchard with rural zoning. But there is clearly no point in discussing it further.

The next afternoon, we are seated around the big wooden table in Loredana's parents' dining room, eleven of us celebrating the 100th anniversary of L'Alpini—the mountaineer army regiments most noted for their heroic efforts during the World War II resistance movement. My uncle, Roberto, Loredana's father, served as a captain in the 23rd Division, which, after a brutal 2-month siege, finally succeeded in routing the Germans from the hills around Stazzema. Earlier this morning, our family joined hundreds of people who had turned out to see L'Alpini marching down Massarosa's main street. *Zio* Roberto marched in front of the eight remaining members of his Division, each of them dressed in their black felt helmets outfitted with a tassel of luminescent pheasant plumes. There were bands and speeches and people leaning out of windows decorated with chains of red, white, and green flags. Sixteen other regiments had come from various parts of northern Tuscany to join in the festivities.

An excellent musician, *Zio* Roberto has been entertaining us with his accordion playing in the break between courses. We are about to move to dessert—*latte alla portoghese (crème caramel)* and a spectacular *torta della nonna* (chocolate cake layered with rum cream and toasted pine nuts)—when we hear a voice at the door. "*Permesso!*"

It is Ennio bearing a crate of exquisitely fragrant apricots. "I just picked them this morning," he explains, his eyes fixed on Loredana, "and called Ugolino to find out where you lived."

Loredana is speechless, she who can rattle on about anything at the drop of a hat.

"*Non dovevi aver disturbato,*" she finally manages to blurt out. You really shouldn't have troubled yourself.

She introduces him to everyone at the table, showering him with praise for taking such splendid care of the orchard. "*Volete un po di dolce?*" she concludes, pointing to the table laden with desserts. But he is embarrassed and declines to join us, saying he will otherwise be late for his midday game of cards. "*Ciao,*" he says, hurrying out the door.

By this time, Loredana's brother, Luca, has filled a bowl with apricots and set them in the center of the table. As the rest of our family oohs and aahs over their pale pink perfection, Loredana and I stare at each other in a confusing mixture of guilt and helplessness.

"He obviously thinks he would lose the orchard if I bought it," she says, moving to sit next to me at the head of the table. "Should I have said something?"

Her question implies a certain degree of indecisiveness, but we both know that the answer is fixed and determined. In theory, yes, she should have said something. "I am a single working woman who lives in Milan," she should have said. "I have neither time nor interest in working the orchard and would be ecstatic if you would assent to continuing with the same agreement you had with the previous owner."

I myself might have added a clause guaranteeing that a crate or two of apricots be left aside for me during the height of the season—apricots, in my eyes, being surpassed only by the David in terms of sensual perfection.

But it would all have come to naught because this is, after all, Tuscany, a land where words are as plentiful as the grains of sand on the Versilian Coast—and equally as substantial! Ennio would have shaken her hand and declared with a great display of seriousness his absolute faith in her assurances. And in the very next moment, he would have begun scheming to undermine any possibility of an actual property sale, believing with an incontrovertible fervor that as soon as she took control, she would oust him from his position. Furthermore, the very fact of her having tried to reassure him in the first place would serve as proof that she intended the exact opposite.

And if the sale ever *did* go through and she began taking the necessary steps, as per Ugolino's advice, to eventually situate a house there, you could be sure that Ennio would alert the authorities the instant she skirted the law.

There is an old Tuscan proverb that says: "*Fidarsi e un gallant uomo, ma non fidarsi e un gallant uomo e mezzo.*" Trusting is a gallant man, but not trusting is a gallant man and a half. Even more telling is a description of the existential state considered by Tuscans to be perfection personified: *pancia piena, pieni caldi, e testa fredda.* Full stomach, warm feet, and cold judgment.

"Nobody here trusts anybody," says Loredana as we move to clear away the dessert dishes. "I'm not talking about a situation where you buy a skirt in a small village, and you're short 10,000 lire, and the clerk says, 'Take the skirt and pay me tomorrow.' What I'm referring to is more fundamental.

"Our entire bureaucratic system is based on cynicism and a lack of trust," she says, shaking her head in exasperation. "Whatever needs doing ultimately requires endless reams of official paper assurances that what anyone has said is so, from paying one's taxes to selling a car." By way of example, she tells me the story of her friend Cinzia who recently decided to buy a *cinquecento* from a woman whose husband had just died. "The first obstacle lay in the widow, who was the sole owner of the car, having to go to City Hall for a certificate certifying her widowhood, for which she had to stand in line 90 minutes and pay $15.

"Then it was Cinzia's turn to stand in line, this time for two certificates of residency, each of which needed $18 in *bolle* [stamps affixed to a document asserting that you are who you say you are and live where you say you live]. Unfortunately for Cinzia, the certificates were issued in the wrong name, a fact she discovered only when she returned to the ACI [Automobile Club] office and the clerk realized that the spelling of her name did not correspond to that on her *codice fiscale* [a kind of Social Security card]. So she had to go back to City Hall and wait as the clerk steamed the six stamps from the certificates, dried them, and then pasted them onto the new pages.

"Back in the ACI office, she and the widow handed the clerk the accumulated documents [nine in all] and Cinzia paid the normal $400 fee for transferring the car's ownership. Then, of course, she had to deal with registering the car and securing insurance."

Loredana's story held no surprises. I myself have had more than a few experiences with Italian bureaucracy, most recently when I tried to take books out of the library in Lucca. I, too, had to go to my local City Hall for the ubiquitous residency certificate affixed with 20,000 lira's worth of *bolle*. Then, because my house is in Massarosa, I also had to go to City Hall in Lucca for a *tesserino,* a sort of library card which required another 30,000 lire in *bolle.* By the time I actually arrived at the library, it was, of course, time for lunch, and I had to wait until 3:30 for it to reopen.

"People live in New York their entire lives and *never* see the inside of City Hall!" I say, adding that the problem lies not only in the theoretical implications underlying a lack of trust—the disturbing need people feel to have government guarantees backing up any official transaction—but in the financial windfall reaped by a government whose economic stability has come to depend on a continuing climate of distrust.

Loredana shakes her head as if she cannot even bear to discuss the subject further. *"No no no,"* she says with great finality. *"Non si po piu andare avanti cosi."* We can no longer go on this way.

Not wanting to enter into yet another discussion about how things will have to change—an assertion I've been hearing since I was a child with virtually no significant results—I shift the topic back to the problem at hand. "Why don't you try driving back up to the orchard tomorrow and talking to Ennio," I suggest. "If you really make it clear to him that, apart from words, there is no logical reason to fear your taking possession of the land, maybe the two of you could come to some kind of accommodation."

"Ehi," she says, stretching it out to four syllables.

A bristling sensation overtakes my spine. I *hate* that term, *ehi*, especially as spoken with the ubiquitous rolling of the eyes! In Tuscany, you hear it wherever you go, whenever anyone says something like, "The electrician said he would come tomorrow," or "I think I really have a chance at getting this job." Its intent lies somewhere between "what, are you crazy?" and "how naive can you get?" No matter that the doubt expressed often turns out to have been well-founded. It is not the doubting itself that irks me, but the surrounding air of skepticism, the suggestion that you are somewhat slow of mind for not having realized the fu-tility of thinking positively.

"You know," I say with controlled fury, "you were complaining before about cynicism and the lack of trust. Yet every time anyone makes a suggestion de-signed to improve the situation, you respond with *ehi*. You don't really want to solve the problem; all you want to do is complain."

"You are *sooo* American," she says, laughing. "Only Americans dare to assume that every problem has a solution. Wait until your country has a few hundred more years to its credit. Then you will understand."

"So, in your mind, there's nothing to be done about Italy's economic prob-lems or, for that matter, your problems with Ennio?"

"I never said the situation was without hope. Only that the solutions are not as simplistic as you make them out to be. When you have a history as long and as complicated as ours, more factors come into play, and there is more to gain by taking your time with the considerations. We have already tried many of the things you try in your country and know from experience they will not work."

She notes my grimacing but presses on nonetheless.

"The best comparison I can give you is that of a parent and a child. The child is optimistic because it has not yet experienced a great number of outcomes, positive or negative. That is not to say that the child's optimism won't sometimes make the situation a success, but the odds against it, as perceived by the parent, are great enough to negate choosing that particular course of action."

This is not a new discussion for us. As a matter of fact, Loredana and I travel over this same terrain at least once whenever we spend extended time together. The last time I visited her in Milan, the discussion centered on the differences between Americans and Italians when it comes to conjuring up new ideas. "I abhor the fact that everything is immediately deemed impossible here," I said after an evening spent with friends of hers from work. "In New York, when someone suggests an idea for a new business or a new approach to doing something, everyone always says, 'Great! Do it!' Here, the discussion immediately centers on the impossibility of overcoming the obstacles."

"Things *are* more impossible here than they are in New York."

"*Nothing* is impossible if you truly want to do it."

"But that's what I mean when I say you are so American. Being American means having a mindset made up of 40 percent optimism, 40 percent naiveté and 20 percent luck."

We talked long into the night that visit, but as the sun came up over the Duomo down the street from her condominium, we remained rooted in the same judgments: she is pessimistic, and I am naive.

We have just finished setting the dessert plates in the dishwasher when Loredana's brother comes bounding into the kitchen. "You *have* to taste this chamomile *grappa* that Giovanni brought," he says, brandishing the bottle. "Incredible!"

Neither of us responds. He walks further into the room, looking from me to her, from her to me. He steps into the chasm between us and stands there, completely silent, observing. Suddenly he scrunches up his shoulders and pretends to shiver. "Brrrr," he says, laughing. "Is it me or is it extremely chilly in here?" He looks at both of us, standing on opposite sides of the room. "Are you two fighting again?"

"Let me guess," he says, resting the *grappa* on the counter. "She," he points to Loredana, "is rooted in an irrelevant history. And you," he nods his head in my direction, "are like a jackrabbit, always leaping forward without concern for where you're going." He throws up his hands, palms upturned. "Am I right?"

I try not to laugh, and I can sense Loredana is trying too, but we are helpless before Luca's charms.

"You know," he says, sensing victory. "Other people's earliest memories are of trips to the country or of being given a warm velvet blanket. Mine are of you two fighting. The Americans versus the Italians; all your fights were always about the same thing." He purses his lips and affects a high, squeaky voice. "*We* do things better. No, *we* do them better. The thing that makes me laugh the most is that you are so much alike."

He pours the *grappa* into two small glasses. "Here, taste this and then come back inside. We're about to launch into a discussion of the Maastrict Treaty. I'm *sure* you two will have a lot to contribute."

We spend the rest of the afternoon sitting around a table filled with highly opinionated people arguing about the pros and cons of Italy joining the European Economic Community. When the guests have gone and Loredana and I are alone (except for Luca and her parents who are watching the Italian soccer team trounce the Brazilians on TV) I ask about her plans for the following day. "I thought we might take a drive up to the orchard to talk with Ennio," she says. "I was thinking that if you give him your honesty speech, and I provide the cynicism, maybe we'll succeed in shaking his equilibrium to the point where he might actually listen. What do you think?"

About Roots, Tubers, and Bulbs

Like their American counterparts, Tuscan restaurants are only now beginning to come to terms with the culinary possibilities inherent in root vegetables. One of the main problems, at least with Tuscans, has been their great love of the greens sprouting from the tops of these vegetables. But you can't have your cake and eat it too; if you keep cutting the greens, the root has to work twice as hard to make new greens and never quite matures.

Impatience aside, root vegetables are now all the rage in Tuscany. Whether because of the area's *nuova cucina* movement and its proponents' desire for constant experimentation or because root crops are so healthy or simply because they're so incredibly delicious, it's hard to find a restaurant anywhere in Tuscany without at least a root vegetable stew on the menu, especially in fall and winter.

I am tempted to say that root vegetables are my favorites—crunchy carrots, creamy rutabagas, tangy beets, delicate salsify—but as I think it through, I realize I could probably say that about every vegetable in this book. Suffice to say, they're *among* my favorites.

Beets Barbe Rosse

In earlier times, beets were prized only for their red-veined outer leaves; the roots—referred to in 58 A.D. by Pliny the Elder as "the crimson nether parts"—were relegated to medicinal use. Today, beets *(Beta vulgaris)* are divided into three categories: those grown for the high sugar content of their tuberous roots, those prized for their large, delicious leaves, and those reserved strictly for the spectacular ornamental value provided by their red, green, and yellow iridescent leaves. In addition to the standard red beets, golden carrot-colored ones are now available as well as striped red ones.

Season: July through October

To Buy: Look for smooth, firm roots and crisp green or reddish green tops. Avoid roots whose flesh has been cut or nicked in any way or large, rough roots which often tend to be woody.

To Prepare: Cut off the tops, leaving 1 inch of stem attached to the beets. Leave roots on and take care not to break the skin or the beet will bleed into the cooking liquid. Do not peel. Scrub well and cook before peeling. Remove beet stains on your hands by rubbing with salt and washing in soap and water. A little bleach will immediately remove stains from utensils.

Carrots Carote

Daucus carota is part of the umbellifrous family which also includes caraway, celery, chervil, fennel, parsley, parsnips, and the delicate Queen Anne's lace as well as the deadly hemlock. Long considered a "bad weed," carrots have also gone through periods, notably in the Middle Ages, when they were thought to have aphrodisiacal powers, probably because of their obviously erotic design. Unlike some other root vegetables, carrots lose flavor very soon after being pulled from the earth. Use as soon as possible. Also, remove carrot tops immediately as leaving them on turns the carrots limp and lifeless. Do not discard, however. Chop into salads or use for the carrot-top soup on the following pages.

Season: July through November

To Buy: Carrots should be bright orange in color, crisp, straight and well-shaped with a smooth surface. Best is to buy with tops intact and let the health of the greens serve as an indicator of the carrots' freshness. Old carrots are usually cracked and covered with tiny white roots. Avoid very large carrots which are often woody.

To Prepare: Trim top and bottom ends. Pare with a hand peeler or, if serving steamed, peel after cooking by rubbing off the skins under running water.

ROOTS, TUBERS & BULBS

135

Celeriac *Cedano Rapa*

Also known as celery root or turnip-rooted celery, celeriac (*Apium graveolens*) is a type of celery cultivated for the enlarged root rather than for the stalks and foliage. Used by the ancient Greeks, Romans, and Egyptians, this strange, bulbous vegetable has a pronounced celery taste with a fuller, creamier texture that has long been prized by Europeans and, now, also appreciated by us.

Season: September through April, but best in the fall

To Buy: Bulbs should be firm and heavy and on the smallish side; large ones are often soft and spongy in the center

To Prepare: Trim top and bottom ends. Remove the skin with a sharp paring knife. If not using immediately, place the celery roots in lemon water to avoid discoloration.

Fennel *Finocchio*

The name fennel covers both the herb and the vegetable. The former is a common or wild strain grown for its seeds and leaves. Florence or sweet fennel resembles a squat version of celery and, itself, comes in two types: a flat, long variety that is somewhat tough and stringy, and a squat, bulbous version that is crisper, sweeter, and the only one considered by Tuscans to be worthy of most fennel dishes (the other is reserved for soups or stews). The Tuscan name for fennel, *finocchio,* means "fine eye," a reference to the belief that eating fennel improves the eyesight.

Season: September through November

To Buy: Only buy if the stalks are intact because the fennel will have more flavor that way. Also, bulbs tend to lose moisture faster after the stalks are removed. Look for firm bulbs and avoid any that have mottling or evidence that the outer leaves were removed (done with old fennels to give the appearance of youth). A fennel bulb should feel heavy with moisture, which indicates that it was recently picked.

To Prepare: Trim the stalks, leaving the bulbs intact. Remove any dry, discolored, or pulpy outer leaves and pare the root ends to remove tough, fibrous portions. Core and slice in half or quarters as per recipe. Save the feathery fronds for other uses.

Garlic *Aglio*

Garlic (*Allium sativum*) is a member of the lily family and a close relative of the onion. Its curative properties are legendary and involve thwarting blood pressure, asthma, and the common cold. There are over 250 different strains, each requiring a cold, dormant period in order to perform. Garlic cloves can be used whole, sliced, slivered, chopped, minced, pressed, or pounded, and each technique results in a different taste. Garlic's heat comes from sulfur compounds in the cell walls. When the walls are broken and come into contact with air, the flavor intensifies. The more cells broken and the more violent the break, the hotter the taste. Conversely, if cells are broken cleanly and gently, the taste is milder. Elephant garlic is exactly what its name implies, garlic that is about 8 times bigger than regular. But bigger doesn't mean more powerful. Closely related to leeks, elephant garlic has a sweeter, milder taste that, in combination with its size, makes it perfect for stuffing.

Season: July through September

To Buy: Skins should be white or pink with no brown spots, soft areas, or spoilage. Avoid any that have extremely dry skin or sprouts.

To Prepare: Separate cloves one by one as needed. To peel cloves, crush ever so slightly with palm of hand or side of heavy knife. Peel and trim root ends.

NOTE: The USDA has warned that minced garlic in oil—without some kind of acid, like vinegar or lemon juice to inhibit bacterial growth—can cause botulism. Avoid garlic products that don't contain citric or phosphoric acids and discard any garlic oil prepared without added acids.

Horseradish *Rapano*

A weedy plant with a knobby, elongated root, horseradish (*Armoracia rusticana* of the cabbage family) is known for the pungent "heat" it imparts to food. Long used as an appetite stimulant, a sinus clearer, and a digestive, it generally comes in fresh, grated, and powdered forms. Home growers keep the roots in sand buckets in the cellar where they last as long as a year.

Season: Late summer

To Buy: Select roots that are creamy pale, exceptionally firm, and free of spongy or soft spots. Avoid sprouting, greenish-tinged horseradish which may be bitter and requires deep peeling.

To Prepare: Trim off ends and, using a very sharp knife, pare off the knobby outer skin. Be prepared for significant eye-watering and sinus-clearing.

Leeks *Porri*

Members of the lily family, leeks (*Allium porrum*) have been cultivated in Mediterranean and North African regions since prehistoric times. These overgrown scallions are an indispensable part of the Tuscan kitchen where they are both used on their own (gratinated, sautéed, or simply steamed) and as flavoring agents in soups and stews.

Season: April through June and September through November

To Buy: Select only those with fresh green leaves and 2 to 3 inches of white. The white part should be crisp and tender, not fibrous.

To Prepare: Cut off roots and green tops (reserve the green for soup). Cut them in half, lengthwise, to within 2 inches of the base, separate the layers slightly, and rinse under running water to remove all embedded soil.

Onions *Cipolla*

Until recently, onions *(Allium cepa)* have played strictly a background role in culinary circles, serving more as a flavoring agent than as a vegetable in its own right. No longer. As new varieties continue to be introduced, this valuable member of the lily family has finally fulfilled the destiny to which its name aspired: onion stems from the Latin *unus* which means "one." Used as babies, new spring onions are cause for celebration. Pulled from the ground as substantial bulbs, they inspire tears of joy (to go with the tears shed during preparation). My favorites are the sweet, red Italian variety which are milder than any of their compatriots.

Season: Spring through summer

To Buy: Avoid onions that are sprouting or have soft spots. Spring onions should have fresh-looking greens and firm, clean bulbs.

To Prepare: For dry onions, cut off root and stem ends. Peel, wash, and cut or slice as needed. For spring onions, cut off roots and wilted end of green tops.

Parsley Root *Radice di Prezzemolo*

Above ground it looks like flat-leaf parsley, but below you'll find a slender cylindrical root similar to a parsnip with white skin and flesh and a musky sweet aroma. Widely used in European kitchens, parsley root *(Petroselinum hortense)* can be eaten raw, steamed, or cooked in hearty soups, stews, or fanciful soufflés. Also known as Hamburg parsley.

Season: Fall

To Buy: Look for firm, creamy beige roots with luxuriant tops. Avoid any that are forked or have black, fungus-like spots.

To Prepare: Do not trim tops until ready to prepare the roots. Does not need peeling unless the skin is in especially bad shape. Place cut roots in lemon water to prevent discoloration.

Parsnips *Pastinaca*

Parsnips (*Pastinaca sativa*) originated in Europe where they were prized long before the advent of Christianity. Romans were fond of them, and, in fact, the Emperor Tiberius had the roots specially imported from France and Germany to his clifftop eyrie on the Isle of Capri. Roots are often left in the ground over the winter before being dug in springtime. Their texture, raw, is like that of a spongy carrot, but their flavor can only be described as uniquely parsnip.

Season: Spring

To Buy: Look for firm, smooth, well-shaped roots of equal size and with light, uniform color. Large ones are often woody.

To Prepare: Trim tops and peel.

Potatoes *Patate*

Although many people believe the potato originated in Ireland, it is, in fact, a native of the high valleys of Peru, Bolivia, and Chile. A member of the nightshade family, potatoes (*Solanum tuberosum*) have a colorful history. The Spaniards, who found it in Peru, introduced the plant to Europe in the 16th century where it was cultivated largely as a curiosity and reported to be deadly poisonous. It was introduced into Ireland by the Royal Society of London to avoid the famines that periodically swept the island and became such an instant success that the potato blight of 1846 caused the starvation deaths of 600,000 people. Reintroduced to the Americas in 1719, potatoes are now available in more than 28 varieties.

Season: New potatoes are harvested in late summer.

To Buy: Potatoes are classified according to starch content. The amount of starch determines their use. High-starch-content types such as Russet or Burbank are long, regularly shaped with slightly rough skin, and light, dry, and mealy when cooked. They are ideal for baking and the best potatoes for french fries since the high starch content produces an even golden color and good texture. Medium-starch potatoes such as Eastern, Yukon Gold, Yellow Finnish, or Peruvian Blue are irregularly shaped and good for pureeing or mashing. Low-starch varieties such as La Rouge, Ruby Crescent, New Reds, and Fingerlings are small, round in shape, and with thin smooth skins. They hold their shape well when cooked and have firm, moist textures. Low-starch potatoes are good for salads and any preparation where the potato must hold its shape. Do not use for deep frying, since the high sugar content and absence of starch will cause dark streaks and poor texture.

Regardless of which potato you choose, select only those that are firm and smooth, not soft or shrivelled. They should have dry skins, shallow eyes, no sprouts (sprouting potatoes are high in sugar), no green color (green areas contain solanine which has a bitter taste and is poisonous in large quantities; all green parts should be cut off before using), and an absence of cracks, blemishes, and rotten spots.

Also, be careful when buying potatoes labeled "new." The only truly "new" potatoes are those that were picked when the vine was still green and the sugar had not yet turned to starch. Many potatoes sold as "new" are merely small, mature potatoes, usually red.

Loredana Francesconi: "Things are more impossible here than they are in New York."

To Prepare: Wash thoroughly with a brush to remove any traces of dirt.

Radishes *Ravanelli*

Radishes (*Raphanus sativus*) are part of the crucifer family and popular in virtually all parts of the globe. Red-skinned varieties are the most common in American markets, although it is also possible to buy long-rooted white-skinned, elongated red-and-white-striped, softball-sized black-skinned, and carrot-shaped purple-skinned radishes.

Season: Spring or fall

To Buy: Look for radishes that are firm, tender, and crisp with good shape and color.

To Prepare: Cut off root and stem ends and wash.

Rutabaga *Rapa Gialla*

Though most people think of rutabagas and turnips as one and the same vegetable, they are in fact, completely different species. Rutabagas (*Brassica campestris*), or yellow turnip (although there are also white-fleshed varieties), are recently developed vegetables originating in Scandinavia or Russia. Abundantly and distinctly flavored, they usually arrive in our markets from Canada and are waxed to retard spoilage.

Season: July through October is when they're at their best.

To Buy: Fresh rutabagas (almost impossible to get) should be uniformly round, crisp, and firm.

To Prepare: Trim roots and ends. Peel with a sharp knife. If buying waxed, make sure to cut off enough skin to remove all traces.

Salsify *Sassefrica*

Also known as oyster plant and vegetable oyster, salsify (*Tragopogon porrifolius*) has recently come into great popularity for the delicate (some say oyster-like) flavor of its fleshy taproots, up to 10 inches in length and 2 inches in diameter on top. The skin is grayish white or grayish yellow and the flesh is white with a milky white juice.

Scorzonera or black salsify (*Scorzonera hispanica*) is a black-skinned related plant favored by Tuscans for its sultry sweet and buttery texture. Both types can be enjoyed raw, but it is more common to boil or steam them.

Season: Autumn to early spring

To Buy: Choose firm, smooth roots that suggest a crisp, juicy interior. Avoid wrinkled, limp, or flabby ones.

To Prepare: Trim the ends, then scrub and scrape the roots before cooking or after blanching. Since it oxidizes rapidly, slice the vegetable into lemon water.

Shallots *Scalogni*

Shallots (*Allium ascalonicum*) are close relatives of onions and garlic. Small, pointed, and borne in tight little clumps, they are cultivated for the grayish or brownish bulbs (cloves) utilized for flavoring sautés, braises, sauces, and stews. Their flavor is reminiscent of a mild onion with a touch of garlic added for good measure.

Season: July through November

To Buy: Choose only firm bulbs with no soft spots, bruising, discoloration, or sprouting.

To Prepare: Cut off the tops and tails. Peel with fingernails, pulling away the first layer of flesh with the skin that is usually firmly attached to it. Or blanch in boiling water for 30 seconds and pull off peel.

Turnips *Rapi*

Turnips (*Brassica rapa*) are one of the oldest known vegetables, having been cultivated for more than 4,000 years. Popular for both their bulb and their refreshing greens, turnips have white or purple-white roots and are best when only about 2 inches in diameter.

Season: Spring or fall

To Buy: Look for firm, unblemished skin and uniformly shaped, smallish roots. Wrinkled skin is a sign that the turnips have lost their moisture and that the texture will be spongy. If possible, choose those with leaves attached. Roots should feel weighty.

To Prepare: Trim tops and root ends. Peel before using unless you're using baby specimens.

Quick and Easy

Beets

Baby beets with their young leaves still attached can be steamed quickly and eaten drizzled with butter. Medium-sized and large, mature beets can be boiled whole for 35–50 minutes then peeled, sliced, and eaten with a drizzle of olive oil and a dusting of chopped parsley. They can also be oven roasted wrapped in foil, peeled, sliced, and eaten drizzled with garlic oil. Foil-wrapped whole beets (baby or mature) can also be grilled. Grated beets make wonderful cold salads; they can also be cooked like spaghetti and topped with sauce.

Carrots

Carrots are wonderful sliced, diced, julienned, shredded, or whole. And any of those options have two further options: cook or eat raw. Steamed sliced carrots need nothing more than a drizzle of oil, salt, and pepper. Cook 1 pound shredded carrots in 1 quart boiling salted water for 10 minutes, add 3 tablespoons butter, 2 tablespoons minced parsley, and serve. Baby carrots can be parboiled for 5 minutes, dipped in egg and milk, rolled in bread crumbs, and fried until tender.

Living in a fruit orchard has always been Loredana's dream.

Miniature roots can also be parboiled, sautéed in butter for 5 minutes, and simmered in port.

Celeriac

Most often used shredded, in salads, celeriac is also wonderful cut into cubes and eaten raw, with salt. Crisp fritters can be made from the pureed vegetable, or the puree can be added to mashed potatoes with or without roasted garlic. Diced celeriac can be braised in chicken stock and served with chopped parsley.

Fennel

Parboiled fennel can be mixed with chopped fronds, diced tomatoes, and other greens for a wonderful salad. It can also be simply drizzled with olive oil and sprinkled with grated parmesan. Braised fennel (in broth or beer) makes a wonderful accompaniment to risotto. If you like, add a little cream just before serving. Sliced thinly and basted with oil, fennel is particularly good grilled, as it is roasted alone or with other vegetables. Sauté it with onions and garlic and serve it on pasta, or use it to accompany a dish of plain white beans drizzled with oil. Pureed fennel makes a perfect soup or sauce base, and raw fennel is a work of art when paired with Gorgonzola.

Garlic

Roast a few bulbs in the oven and eat the sweet, soft flesh with cheese and bread. Hollow out particularly large bulbs, stuff with seasoned ricotta, and bake for 20 minutes. Make easy garlic soup by sautéeing thinly sliced cloves in oil, adding broth, and sprinkling the finished product with chopped parsley. Mash garlic cloves with walnuts, salt, and a little cream and stir into lentil soup. For effortless garlic bread, place a few sliced cloves in a paper bag with hot bread for 10 minutes. The bread will be magically flavored with the scent of garlic. Individual cloves can be braised in butter over low heat for 10–15 minutes until very tender.

Horseradish

Shred into mashed potatoes, add to beans and lentils while cooking, stir into vinaigrettes, and use to spice up vegetable purees. Puree with sugar, vinegar, lemon juice, salt, and pepper and spread on hot crusty bread. For a pleasurably different taste, try stirring the grated root into cooked apples. A particularly inventive use for the grated root is to press it onto vegetables about to be fried before dipping in batter.

Leeks

The classic Tuscan preparation for leeks is to parboil and drizzle with a simple vinaigrette. Sautéed leeks can be used as a sauce for pasta or combined with vegetable broth, sprinkled with parmesan, and served over bread as a soup. Braise leeks in vegetable broth and olive oil for 15–20 minutes over low heat. Grilled leeks are one of the wonders of the world.

Onions

Mix sautéed onions with ricotta and use as a filling for calzone or a topping for pizza. Cut large onions into thick slices, baste with olive oil, and grill. Make sweet and sour pickles from peeled small white onions by boiling for 2 hours with 2 tablespoons vinegar, 2 teaspoons sugar, salt, and pepper and adding water as necessary. The pickles are done when brown and tender. Braise onions in a mix of vegetable broth and beer until soft. Stir raw minced onions into cooked onion soup for a little extra zest.

Parsley Root

Blanch parsley root cubes and puree with butter and cream. Cut into slices and add to slowly sweated shallots sprinkled with fresh thyme. Sauté cubes over very low heat until caramelized and serve over croutons sprinkled with chopped nuts.

Parsnips

Parboil slices and sauté in butter, or puree and combine with chopped parsley, minced nuts, and lemon zest. Make parsnip chips by frying very thin slices (soak in ice water for an hour first) in hot oil. Shred, parboil, and use in salads. Thread slices onto skewers, alternating with cherry tomatoes, and grill.

Potatoes

Mix mashed potatoes with roasted garlic or give them a ribbon of color by quickly stirring them through with red pepper puree. Pan fry until almost done and complete the cooking by braising in a cup of dry white wine. Parboil whole potatoes, cut into chunks, and roast in the oven with olive oil, minced garlic, and dried sage. Boil new red potatoes until tender, slice, and combine with pitted black olives, chopped parsley, and vinaigrette. Make a fresh herb puree, rub onto oiled potato cubes, and roast for 45 minutes, turning occasionally.

Radishes

Core and stuff with parsley butter. Cut into thin slices and fry in very hot oil. Shred into salads or soups. Make radish pancakes by combining shredded radishes with minced onions, flour, and egg and frying on a hot griddle. Marinate in olive oil, wine vinegar, and brown sugar.

Rutabagas/Turnips

Make into chips by slicing into thin strips and frying in hot olive oil. Shred into salads or boil until tender and mash with roasted garlic, potatoes, and diced horseradish. Baby turnips can be eaten raw, like radishes or carrots. Oven roast larger plants with herbs or cut into cubes and gratinate with bechamel topping. Add chunks to barley or onion soup, or toss into long-simmering stews.

Salsify

Grate into salads or mix with flour and egg and make salsify fritters. Sauté thin slices in olive oil and finish with a dash of truffle oil. Simmer diced salsify in cream until tender and spoon over pasta or polenta.

Shallots

Cut into thin slices and fry. Mince finely and mix with vinaigrette. Roast whole by itself or with other root vegetables. Wrap in foil with lemon thyme and grill. Sauté shallot halves with mushrooms and use as a topping for pizza.

Where we found Doris every day after lunch.

Insalata di Barbe Grattate con Gremolata
Grated Beet Salad with Pears, Chives, and Hazelnuts

Oven-roasted beets take more than 2 hours to cook; boiled or steamed, almost an hour. But grated beets are ready in less than 15 minutes and, when paired with warm pears and a gremolata of chopped chives and crushed hazelnuts, make a wonderfully refreshing dinner salad.

S
O
L
O

V
E
R
D
U
R
A

1½ pounds fresh beets, tops
   removed
6 tablespoons extra-virgin olive
   oil
Salt and freshly ground black
   pepper
1 teaspoon red wine vinegar

1 tablespoon unsalted butter
2 Comice pears, stemmed, cored,
   and halved lengthwise
4 tablespoons finely minced chives
½ cup crushed hazelnuts
2 teaspoons balsamic or raspberry
   vinegar

1. Peel and grate the beets using a food processor or a mandoline. Heat 2 table-spoons of the oil in a large skillet, add the beets, and toss to coat with oil. Season with salt, pepper, and the red wine vinegar and mix well. Add ¼ cup water, cover, and cook over medium heat for 10 minutes or until tender. Toss occasionally, being careful not to mash the beets.

2. Meanwhile heat the butter in another skillet and add the pears, cut side down, in a single layer. Cook over medium heat for 2 or 3 minutes, shaking the pan every now and then to prevent sticking. Turn and cook for an additional minute. Remove from heat and cut each pear lengthwise into thin slices. Set aside.

3. Place the chives in a small bowl. Add the hazelnuts, the remaining oil, and the vinegar. Beat with a fork until smooth.

4. Divide the beets into 4 portions and place each on the center of a plate. Arrange a few pear slices alongside, drizzle with the vinaigrette, and serve.

SERVES 4   TIME: 25 minutes   LEVEL OF DIFFICULTY: Easy

VARIATIONS: The beets can also be laid on a bed of greens; try sorrel, beet greens, and chicory.

MAKE AHEAD: The beets can be cooked up to 6 hours in advance, refrigerated, and warmed before serving.

Briosce di Patate
Potato Brioches

Tuscan breakfasts can consist of just about anything from tomato focaccia to tiny rice custards to apple pastries to the following brioche, which works equally well as an appetizer served with cheese and pickled vegetables. I always make many more than I need and freeze the rest for unexpected brunch guests.

2 pounds Eastern or other all-purpose potato, peeled and quartered

¼ cup unsalted butter, softened, plus butter for greasing muffin tin

Salt and freshly ground black pepper

⅛ teaspoon fresh ground nutmeg

1 teaspoon baking powder

1 egg yolk, lightly beaten

¼ pound fresh *bufala* mozzarella, cut into 1-inch cubes

2 tablespoons unflavored bread crumbs

Assorted cheese wedges for garnish (Taleggio or Gouda or Emmethal)

Edible daisies for garnish

1. Boil the potatoes in a large quantity of water for 15 minutes or until tender. Drain and return to the pot in one layer. Place the pot over a very low flame for 2–3 minutes to dry the potatoes.

2. Force the potatoes through a ricer and place the mash in a saucepan with the butter, salt, pepper, nutmeg, baking powder, and egg yolk. Mix well.

3. Preheat the oven to 400 degrees. Grease an 8-muffin tin and fill each cup to the ¾ mark with potato batter. Press one mozzarella cube in the center of each and sprinkle the bread crumbs over the top. Bake for 8–10 minutes or until golden brown. Immediately remove from the tin and place on a rack to cool. Serve with wedges of cheese and place a few daisies on each plate.

MAKES 8 BRIOCHES   TIME: 60 minutes   LEVEL OF DIFFICULTY: Moderate

VARIATIONS: Slice the cap off the brioche and fill with anything from tuna fish salad to mushroom bechamel. Serve as an appetizer.

MAKE AHEAD: The potatoes can be boiled 1 day in advance, refrigerated, and returned to room temperature before Step 2.

Minestra di Foglie di Carote
Carrot-Top and Rice Soup

There is a Tuscan saying: Non si tira via niente—*nothing gets thrown away—that is particularly appropriate vis-à-vis this soup. Carrot tops are almost always discarded. But why? They have the same sweet-earthy taste but with a hint of green that makes them perfect for soups or vegetable sautés. Try the following recipe and let it spur your creativity as to how else to use these delicate frilly leaves.*

3 tablespoons extra-virgin olive oil
1 medium onion, minced
2 small carrots, diced
1 stalk celery, diced
3 cloves garlic, minced
½ teaspoon salt
½ teaspoon freshly ground black
   pepper

6 cups Basic Vegetable Broth (see
   page 308)
½ cup short grain rice
1½ cups chopped carrot tops
4 tablespoons fresh grated
   Parmigiano-Reggiano

1. Heat the oil in a large, heavy-gauge soup pot. Sauté the onion, carrots, celery, and garlic for 5 minutes over low heat until translucent. Add the salt and pepper, pour in the broth, and bring to a boil.

2. Add the rice to the broth and cook for 15 minutes or until the rice is almost tender. Add the carrot tops and cook for 5 more minutes, mixing well.

3. When the rice is done, pour the soup into four bowls, sprinkle with cheese, and serve.

SERVES 4   TIME: 45–60 minutes

LEVEL OF DIFFICULTY: Easy

VARIATIONS: Instead of rice, add 2 pounds cubed potatoes at the same time as the broth. Or serve the soup over garlic-rubbed bread.

Count Gianfranco Pecchioli and his daughter, Elena, at their estate in Camporomano.

Scorzonera Salsa Vellutata
Scorzonera Veloute

Two years ago, when I first tried to grow scorzonera, *or black salsify, from seeds brought back from Tuscany, nothing came up. I later realized that when the plants first sprouted, the leaves looked a lot like thin blades of grass and I pulled them, thinking they were weeds. This past year was better, and I harvested a healthy crop of 8-inch-long roots. For the next few days, we had salsify at almost every meal, but the following dish—salsify rounds in a rich creamy sauce—was one of my very favorites.*

1½ pounds *scorzonera* or black salsify, peeled and cut into 3 chunks each

2 tablespoons fresh lemon juice

3 tablespoons unsalted butter

2 tablespoons unbleached flour

4 tablespoons heavy cream

½ cup Basic Vegetable Broth (see page 308)

Salt and freshly ground black pepper

⅛ teaspoon fresh grated nutmeg

4 tablespoons fresh chopped parsley

1. Place the salsify in a large amount of water to which the lemon juice has been added. Bring to a boil and cook over medium heat for 30 minutes. Drain, cool to room temperature, cut into thin rounds, and set aside.

2. Melt the butter in a large skillet. Whisk in the flour and then the cream until a thick paste has been created. Add the broth, bring to a boil, and cook for 3 minutes, whisking constantly. Season with salt, pepper, and the nutmeg.

3. Reduce the heat to low. Add the salsify rounds to the skillet and cook for 10 minutes, stirring frequently. Transfer to a serving platter, sprinkle with parsley, and serve.

SERVES 4   TIME: 90 minutes   LEVEL OF DIFFICULTY: Moderate

VARIATIONS: Use as a topping for spinach pasta.

Gnocchetti di Rafano in Brodo
Horseradish Gnocchetti in Broth

Horseradish is not used a great deal in Tuscany, but every now and then you come across a chef in love with its particular pungency. Such was the case the night I went to Trattoria Giovanni in Gualdo, a small hilltop village above Viareggio. A longtime personal friend, Giovanni uses horseradish in making everything from crusts for his vegetable tarts to cream sauces for crostini *appetizers to the following dish of tiny, spicy* gnocchetti *oven-baked in vegetable broth.*

2 Eastern or other all-purpose
   potatoes
2 eggs, lightly beaten
2 tablespoons grated horseradish

Salt and freshly ground black
   pepper
4 cups Basic Vegetable Broth (see
   page 308)
½ cup unbleached flour

1. Boil the potatoes in salted water for 40 minutes or until tender. Drain, peel, and cool to room temperature.

2. Force the potatoes through a food mill and place the puree in a bowl along with the eggs, horseradish, salt, and pepper.

3. Heat the broth in a saucepan. Lower the heat and maintain at a simmer.

4. Place the flour in a heap on a pastry board and add the potato mash. Knead thoroughly until the mixture is well blended, smooth, soft, and elastic. Roll into strips about ½ inch in diameter. Cut into pieces ½ inch wide.

5. Drop the *gnocchetti* into a generous amount of boiling salted water and stir gently with a wooden spoon. Let cook for about 3 minutes during which time they will rise to the surface. Remove with a slotted spoon and place in an oven-proof baking dish.

6. Preheat the oven to 350 degrees. Pour the broth over the *gnocchetti*, bake for 30 minutes, and serve.

SERVES 4   TIME: 1½ hours   LEVEL OF DIFFICULTY: Advanced

VARIATIONS: The cooked *gnocchetti* can also be served with melted butter and grated Parmesan instead of being baked in broth.

MAKE AHEAD: The uncooked *gnocchetti* can be made through Step 4 up to 1 day in advance and refrigerated, covered with plastic wrap.

Napoleani di Barbe Gialle
Golden Beet Napoleons with Root Vegetable Sauce

This elegant dish is made from the humblest of ingredients, beets (albeit that beautiful golden variety), and takes surprisingly little time. And yet its presentation—creamy beet purée sandwiched between crisp layers of fried beet chips—suggests you worked for hours. The idea comes from those wonderful desserts made from cream and rum and powdered sugar and layered between paper-thin sheets of pastry and is the outgrowth of having harvested too many beets last summer.

The Sauce

1 parsley root, diced
1 celery root, peeled and chopped
2 parsnips, peeled and chopped
2 carrots, scraped and chopped
2 medium onions, peeled and diced
2 tablespoons unsalted butter
1 tablespoon flour
2 tablespoons heavy cream
Salt and freshly ground black
    pepper

The Napoleons

2 pounds golden beets
1 tablespoon extra-virgin olive oil,
    plus olive oil for frying
2 tablespoons unsalted butter
Salt and freshly ground black
    pepper
16 chives for garnish

1. To make the sauce, preheat the oven to 350 degrees. Brush (or spray) the bottom of an ovenproof baking pan with extra-virgin olive oil, add the vegetables, and bake for 45–60 minutes or until browned, stirring occasionally. Add water to cover and simmer for 3 hours. Strain and reduce by half.

2. Meanwhile, place all but one of the beets in a saucepan with enough water to cover. Boil for 45 minutes or until tender. Remove with tongs, cool, and peel. Puree until smooth in a food processor, adding oil through the feeding tube. Stir in the butter, season with salt and pepper, and set aside.

3. Peel the remaining beet and cut into ⅛-inch-thick slices. Place ½ inch oil in a frying pan and heat to 325 degrees. Deep fry the beet slices until crisp, pressing them with a spatula to keep from curling up. Drain on paper towels, cover with a weight, and keep warm.

4. Melt the 2 tablespoons butter in a skillet over medium heat. Whisk the flour and add ½ cup of the root vegetable broth, stirring constantly until thick. Add the cream, season with salt and pepper, and heat through.

4. To assemble, place a beet chip on each plate, top with a dollop of beet puree, and lay another beet chip on top. Drizzle a tablespoon of sauce over the beet chip and serve garnished with the chives.

SERVES 4   TIME: 3½ hours

LEVEL OF DIFFICULTY: Advanced

VARIATIONS: Use reduced Basic Vegetable Broth (see page 308) or any other good-quality canned broth, reduced, in place of root stock.

MAKE AHEAD: The stock can be made ahead of time and frozen until use.

Patate Nuove con Peperoncino
New Red Potatoes with Chili Peppers

This is a classic potato dish throughout Tuscany, although the use and amount of chili may vary depending on one's feeling for heat. Served in summer when the first potatoes are deemed ready ("Only when the earth has been 55 degrees or more for at least one month's time"), the sweetness of the potatoes makes a fine companion for the spiciness of the chili.

4 tablespoons extra-virgin olive oil	½ teaspoon freshly chopped red
2 pounds small, new red potatoes,	chili pepper
quartered	Salt and freshly ground black
	pepper

1. Heat the oil in a nonstick skillet until hot enough to sizzle a piece of potato. Add the potatoes, turn the heat to medium, and sauté the potatoes, turning often, until evening browned, about 10 minutes.

2. Sprinkle with the red pepper, cover, and cook until the potatoes are tender, about 15–20 minutes. Sprinkle with salt and pepper.

SERVES 4   TIME: 30–35 minutes depending on the size of the potatoes

LEVEL OF DIFFICULTY: Easy

VARIATIONS: Use ½ teaspoon dried crushed sage in place of chili.

Carote Arrostite con Limoni e Olive
Roasted Carrots with Lemon and Olives

While root vegetables are generally thought of as long-growing, fall-maturing crops, there is a refreshing tendency nowadays to pull the roots while still babies and feast on summer sweetness. For those of us who are gardeners, eating baby vegetables not only satisfies our impatience with waiting through two entire seasons, but also our gluttony since there are two crops to harvest instead of one. I simply plant the seeds in April, eat the first carrots or beets or turnips in June, plant again, and harvest in September.

The following is a wonderful recipe for those first baby carrots (if you can stop yourself from eating the entire harvest raw). Roasted with garlic, olive oil, and lemon, the carrots are given a final burst of flavor with the addition of tangy Gaeta olives.

1 pound baby carrots, tops removed
10 garlic cloves, bruised with the
    side of a knife
3 tablespoons extra-virgin olive oil
4 paper-thin slices lemon, halved

Salt and freshly ground black
    pepper
3 ounces Gaeta or other small black
    olive, pitted and minced

A breather before the Torta della Nonna: Uncle Roberto plays "Malaguena."

1. Preheat oven to 350 degrees. Combine carrots, garlic, oil, and lemon in a shallow ovenproof baking dish. Season with salt and pepper and stir to blend. Bake, stirring occasionally, until carrots are tender and lightly browned, about 45 minutes.

2. Add the olives and bake 10 minutes longer. Serve immediately.

SERVES 4   TIME: 60 minutes

LEVEL OF DIFFICULTY: Easy

MAKE AHEAD: Carrots can be made 2–3 hours in advance and served at room temperature. If refrigerated, they can be reheated in the oven or in a skillet brushed with 1 tablespoon oil.

153

Frittelle di Rapa Bianca
Turnip Fritters with Tomato Lemon Sauce

Fritters are a Tuscan mainstay, whether made from chestnuts, baccalà (codfish), or, as suggested here, turnips. I can remember many a winter afternoon sneaking into the kitchen when these fritters were being made and sliding one off the platter when the cook's back was turned. There were never any left over at my house, no matter how many were made, so I have absolutely no advice as to what to do should you make too many. Which is impossible, of course.

The Sauce

8 canned Italian plum tomatoes,
    squeezed and with liquid
½ cup Basic Vegetable Broth (see
    page 308)
Juice of 1 lemon
1 teaspoon fresh chopped oregano
Salt and freshly ground black
    pepper

The Fritters

1½ pounds turnips, peeled and
    shredded in a food processor
1 medium onion, minced
½ cup finely chopped scallion tops
    (use the white part elsewhere)
3 eggs, lightly beaten
¼ cup unbleached flour
1 small, fresh red chili, minced
½ teaspoon salt
Vegetable oil for frying

1. To make the sauce, combine all ingredients in a saucepan and simmer over low heat for 15 minutes, stirring occasionally.

2. For the fritters, place all ingredients save the oil in a large bowl and mix well. The batter will be somewhat loose.

3. Heat ¼ cup oil over high heat. Spoon ¼ cup of the batter into the skillet at a time, putting as many fritters in the pan as can fit without crowding. Cook until lightly browned on one side (3–5 minutes), turn with a spatula and brown the other side. Drain the fritters on paper towels. Repeat with remaining batter until all the fritters are cooked. Top with tomato-lemon sauce and serve.

MAKES ABOUT 12 FRITTERS   TIME: 60 minutes   LEVEL OF DIFFICULTY: Moderate

VARIATIONS: Turnip fritters make a wonderful accompaniment to soup when placed on the side of the bowl in place of bread.

MAKE AHEAD: The sauce can be made up to 1 day in advance, refrigerated, and reheated.

Puré di Pastinaca con Salvia Fritta
Parsnip Purée with Fried Sage

For years, I thought parsnips had to be frozen in the ground in order to be good. So at the end of every summer, when the parsnips in my garden were big enough to seem ready for harvest, I would dutifully leave them until spring. Ultimately, I learned that it doesn't make any difference, and so, last year, I ate them all in October. Which was very good. But then came spring, and there was nothing to dig up, and I had to console myself with all those wonderful memories, of which the following was definitely one: smooth, creamy parsnip purée accompanied by crisp leaves of fried sage.

2 pounds parsnips, peeled and cut into thirds
1 cup tightly packed fresh parsley leaves

Salt and freshly ground black pepper
4 tablespoons unsalted butter
Olive oil for frying
24 large fresh sage leaves

1. Place the parsnips in a large saucepan, cover with water, add salt, and bring to a boil. Lower the heat to medium and cook for 10–15 minutes or until tender. Drain.

2. Place the parsnips and parsley in a food processor and purée. Season with salt and pepper and whip in the butter. Keep warm.

3. Pour ½ inch olive oil into a skillet and place over medium heat. When the oil is hot enough, add as many sage leaves as will comfortably fit and fry for 10–15 seconds or until just crisp. Remove with tongs and drain on paper towels.

SERVES 4   TIME: 45 minutes

LEVEL OF DIFFICULTY: Moderate

VARIATIONS: For a spicier flavor, purée the parsnips with 2 cloves garlic and ½ of a red chili pepper.

Luca, the family peacemaker: "Have some of this grappa, you two, and stop fighting."

Pizza con Cipolline Primaverile
Pizza with Spring Onions

I grow a prodigious number of onions of all varieties, and it takes all the discipline I can muster to leave them in the ground beyond the stage when the tops are flush with the vivid green of youth. My tendency is always to wander down to that particular plot and just pull out dozens at a time. Why? The reasons are endless, ranging from simply basting with olive oil and cooking on the grill (possibly my favorite use) to braising in beer and serving with pecorino cheese. The following is a Tuscan classic; once you try it, it will become a repertoire regular. I guarantee it.

2 dozen young spring onions
6 tablespoons extra-virgin olive oil
1 recipe Basic Pizza Dough (see page 314)

¼ pound Gaeta or other black olive, pitted and minced
3 ounces goat cheese, crumbled
Salt and freshly ground black pepper

1. Preheat the oven to 500 degrees. If using a pizza stone or pizza tiles, place these in the oven.

2. Baste the onions with 2 tablespoons of the oil and grill on an outdoor barbecue or indoor electric model.

3. Meanwhile, spread the dough into a circle ⅛ inch thick and 16 inches in diameter. Place on a pizza peel and brush the surface with 2 tablespoons of the oil.

4. Arrange the onions on the pizza and dot with olives and cheese. Drizzle the remaining oil over the surface and season with salt and pepper.

5. Slide the pizza onto the stone and bake for 10–15 minutes or until crust is bubbly and cooked. Slice and serve immediately.

SERVES 4   TIME: 30–40 minutes   LEVEL OF DIFFICULTY: Moderate

VARIATIONS: In lieu of grilling, the onions can also be sautéed in a skillet until tender. If you don't have a pizza peel, stone, or tiles, place the pizza in a baking pan in Step 3. There is, however, no comparison between cooking pizza on a stone which creates both bottom heat and a porous, humidifying surface that prevents the pizza from drying out.

Finocchio Grattugiato
Fennel Gratin

Tuscans love fennel and eat it as an appetizer, a between-course palate freshener, and a digestive. No part of the vegetable goes unheralded: in addition to myriad uses for the bulb, the seeds are added to sausage and the fronds chopped into soups, sauces, and stews. But it is the bulb that sees the most use, and the following recipe is one of the most frequent and beloved preparations.

2 bulbs fennel, tough outer layer removed and quartered
3 tablespoons extra-virgin olive oil

Salt and freshly ground black pepper
¼ cup freshly grated Parmigiano-Reggiano

1. Preheat the oven to 350 degrees. Boil the fennel in salted water until tender, about 10 minutes. Drain and place in greased, ovenproof baking pan in one layer.

2. Drizzle the oil over the top, season with salt and pepper, sprinkle with cheese, and bake for 15–20 minutes or until the cheese is melted and bubbly. Serve immediately.

SERVES 4   TIME: 30 minutes   LEVEL OF DIFFICULTY: Easy

VARIATIONS: For a richer, creamier taste, dot with 2 tablespoons butter in addition to the oil before baking.

Scalogne Ripiene
Baked Stuffed Shallots

The weather last summer was absolutely perfect for growing shallots. There was plenty of sun, and it rained just enough for the sandy soil to dry out between waterings. By late July, I had an amazing crop of bulbs whose cloves were all at least 2 inches in diameter. (I grow two types: the long, frog's leg gray shallots and the oval type with pinkish skin sometimes known as "multiplier onions.") Anyway, this cornucopia of riches caused me to wonder why their use was always restricted to that of behind-the-scenes flavoring agent. Why not center stage? And so it came to me: I'll stuff them with some kind of creamy mixture and bake. Everyone at the table that night was very pleased.

16 shallot cloves, at least 2 inches in diameter, tops and roots removed and peeled
¼ pound fresh ricotta
2 ounces freshly grated Parmigiano-Reggiano
3 tablespoons fresh chopped parsley
Salt and freshly ground black pepper
3 tablespoons extra-virgin olive oil
Parsley sprigs for garnish

1. Cut a very thin slice from the surface of each shallot clove so they can stand up in the baking pan. Using a melon baller, hollow out the inside of each clove, leaving at least 2 layers of shell intact.

2. Preheat the oven to 350 degrees. Place the ricotta, grated cheese, parsley, salt, and pepper in a bowl and mix well. Stuff the shallots with the cheese mixture. Place in an ovenproof baking pan in one layer, drizzle with oil, and cover with foil. Bake for 15 minutes, remove the foil and bake for another 10–15 minutes, until golden brown.

3. Place 4 shallots on each plate, garnish with parsley, and serve.

SERVES 4   TIME: 60 minutes

LEVEL OF DIFFICULTY:
Moderate

VARIATIONS: The shallots can also be oven braised in a ¼-cup mixture of white wine and Basic Vegetable Broth. As with the above recipe, cover the pan for 15 minutes, remove the foil and continue to bake until golden.

MAKE AHEAD: Shallots can be stuffed 6 hours in advance and refrigerated.

"Now that's a good form of exercise," says Adriana as we pass bicyclists on the steep, winding road to Colognora.

Ravanelli in Umido
Radishes Braised in Root Vegetable Broth

All radishes can be cooked, and to wonderful effect. A favorite version is this simple braising in root vegetable broth (if you made the recipe on page 308 you should have a few cups left over) thickened with a little heavy cream.

4 tablespoons unsalted butter
¾ cup finely minced shallots
24 red or pink radishes at least
  1½ inches in diameter, tops
  removed and scrubbed
½ cup Basic Root Vegetable Broth
  (see page 308)

2 tablespoons heavy cream
Salt and freshly ground black
  pepper
12 very thin asparagus, cooked until
  tender and bound with a chive
  blade into bundles of 3, for
  garnish

1. Heat the butter in a large skillet. Sauté the shallots over low heat for 5 minutes or until translucent. Add the radishes in one layer and the broth, increase the heat to medium, cover, and cook for 2 minutes. Lower the heat and braise until tender, about 5 minutes. Using a slotted spoon, transfer the radishes to a heated platter.

2. Simmer the broth until it is reduced by half. Stir in the cream, season with salt and pepper, and simmer for one minute longer. Pour over the radishes and serve, garnished with asparagus bundles.

SERVES 4   TIME: 40–45 minutes   LEVEL OF DIFFICULTY: Easy

VARIATIONS: The radishes can also be served in a simple root broth reduction thickened with a tablespoon or two of pureed parsnip or turnip.

Sformato di Rape Bianche e Cipolle Rosse
Turnip and Red Onion Terrine

Layered vegetable terrines are limited only by the imagination in terms of color, texture, appearance, and taste. All that's necessary is to have one ingredient acting as a binding agent between the layers. The following is a colorful and delicious terrine that alternates layers of turnips with cara-

melized red onions, spinach, roasted garlic, and carrots. Served on a bed of beet purée, it makes a perfectly elegant appetizer.

1 turnip (about 1 pound), peeled and cubed
2 eggs, lightly beaten
¼ cup heavy cream
1 tablespoon fresh chopped thyme
Salt and freshly ground black pepper
3 tablespoons unsalted butter
1 medium red onion, diced
1 teaspoon sugar

3 medium carrots, scraped and roughly chopped
8 ounces spinach, washed and roughly chopped
¼ cup unflavored fresh bread crumbs
3 medium-sized beets, tops trimmed
8 leaves fresh sage

1. Boil the turnip in salted water until tender, about 20 minutes. Drain and purée in a food processor. Cool to room temperature. Beat the eggs with the cream and add to the food processor with the thyme, salt, and pepper. Mix well and set aside.

2. In a nonaluminum skillet, melt butter over medium heat. Add onion, increase heat, and sauté, stirring frequently, until it begins to brown, about 4 minutes. Add sugar and increase heat and sauté until onions begin to caramelize, about 2 minutes. Cool to room temperature and set aside.

3. Cook and purée the carrots in the same way as the turnip. Season with salt and pepper and set aside.

4. Blanch the spinach, squeeze out excess liquid, and purée. Season with salt and pepper and set aside.

5. Preheat the oven to 350 degrees. To assemble the terrine, butter a 9 × 5-inch loaf pan and spread the bread crumbs over the bottom. Spread half the carrots over the bread crumbs and cover with a fourth of the turnip puree. Add half the spinach, another fourth of the turnip puree, and top with all the onions. Continue the layers: turnips, spinach, turnips, and finally carrots until all ingredients are used up.

6. Cover the pan tightly with foil and cut a small slit on top for steam to escape. Place the terrine in a larger pan and add enough boiling water to reach the 2-inch mark on the loaf pan. Bake for 40 minutes.

7. Remove the terrine from the oven and press down the contents with a flat weight.* Cool for 2 hours and then refrigerate overnight. Unmold the terrine onto a platter and slice. Serve on a bed of beet purée and garnish with the fresh sage.

SERVES 4   TIME: 2 hours (exclusive of overnight refrigeration)

LEVEL OF DIFFICULTY: Advanced

VARIATIONS: The terrine can also be used as a party spread served with crackers or wedges of *pecorino* cheese.

MAKE AHEAD: The turnips, spinach, carrots, onions, and beets can all be prepared 1 day in advance and refrigerated. Return to room temperature before assembling.

*In lieu of a flat weight used strictly for culinary purposes, you can use a thin piece of wood or cardboard weighted down with a large can of tomatoes.

Carote al Parmigiano
Braised Carrots with Parmesan Cheese

Are raw carrots sweeter than cooked? I can never decide the answer. Biting into a raw carrot—especially when newly pulled from the earth—creates a sensation at once so sweet and crispy as to leave me almost breathless. On the other hand, what better way to bring out sweetness than to cook briefly and in a flavored broth? Ah life! So full of unresolvable conflicts.

8 medium-sized carrots, scraped
   and cut on the diagonal into
   ¼-inch slices
2 cups Basic Vegetable Broth (see
   page 308)
1 tablespoon unsalted butter

Salt and freshly ground black
   pepper
¼ cup freshly grated Parmigiano-
   Reggiano
8 3-inch sprigs fresh rosemary

1. Place the carrots in a saucepan with the broth and butter. Season with salt and pepper, cover, and cook for 15 minutes over medium-low heat.

2. Stir in the cheese and cook for 5 minutes longer or until all the liquid is gone.

When done, the carrots will be dry and somewhat wrinkly. Serve immediately, garnished with sprigs of rosemary.

SERVES 4   TIME: 30 minutes   LEVEL OF DIFFICULTY: Easy

VARIATIONS: Prepare without the cheese but add 1 tablespoon fresh chopped parsley leaves instead. Can also be puréed and served as is, or as a stuffing for zucchini.

Sassefrica Saltata con Porri e Erbe
Salsify Sautéed with Leeks and Herbs

There is a general consensus that salsify tastes very much like oysters, which is why it is alter-nately referred to as the oyster plant. I disagree. To me, the flavor is more akin to that of scallops or even tender white asparagus. Be that as it may, Americans are very lucky that it is finally available in local markets, although, generally, it still comes from abroad, from Belgium or Holland. The following recipe is a wonderful combination of salsify, leeks, and fresh herbs that is very easy and delightfully delicious. It works just as well whether you use white salsify or the more slender, less hairy black version.

1 pound salsify, scraped or peeled
4 tablespoons lemon juice
2 tablespoons extra-virgin olive oil
2 cloves garlic, sliced in half length-wise
2 medium-sized leeks, cleaned and thinly sliced (white parts only)

1 tablespoon chopped fresh sage
1 tablespoon chopped fresh parsley
1 tablespoon chopped fresh dill
Salt and freshly ground black pepper
Edible daisies for garnish

1. Cut the salsify into 1-inch cubes and immediately dip in water acidified with half the lemon juice. Drain and cook in boiling salted water for 15 minutes or un-til tender.

2. Meanwhile, heat the oil in a heavy skillet. Sauté the garlic for 3 minutes over low heat. Remove the garlic with a slotted spoon and discard. Add the leeks and cook for 10 minutes, stirring frequently until soft.

3. Drain the cooked salsify and add to the skillet with the sage, parsley, and dill.

Sauté for 5 minutes, stirring constantly until the salsify is lightly browned. Season with salt and pepper, transfer to a warm serving platter, and drizzle with the remaining lemon juice. Garnish with daisies and serve immediately.

SERVES 4   TIME: 40 minutes   LEVEL OF DIFFICULTY: Easy

VARIATIONS: Salsify prepared this way can also be used as a topping for pasta. If you can find wild herbs such as yarrow or garlic mustard, use them in place of, or in addition to, the sage and parsley.

Cipolle con Ripieno di Capellini d'Angelo
Onion Bowls Stuffed with Spinach Angel Hair Pasta and Fennel Fronds

This recipe comes courtesy of my friend Adriana del Prato who is a stalwart proponent of traditionalism in every area of her life except for food. Dinners at her house are always an exercise in pushing the envelope of the possible. Witness the following onion "bowls" overflowing with creamy angel hair pasta and served with lids askew.

4 large onions
½ teaspoon fresh chopped lemon
    thyme (or ¼ teaspoon regular
    thyme and ¼ teaspoon lemon
    zest)
2 tablespoons unsalted butter
Salt and freshly ground black
    pepper
3 tablespoons extra-virgin olive oil

2 cloves garlic, minced
4 tablespoons chopped fennel
    fronds
¼ cup Basic Vegetable Broth (see
    page 308)
¼ cup heavy cream
¼ pound spinach angel hair pasta
4 tablespoons fresh grated
    Parmigiano-Reggiano

1. Preheat the oven to 350 degrees. Carefully cut a 1-inch slice off the stem end of each onion. Slice enough of the root off the bottom so they will stand up on their own. Remove the dry outer skin but leave the inner skin on both the bottoms and lids.

2. Using a sharp knife and/or a tablespoon, carve out the insides of each onion, leaving about 2 outside layers all around. Reserve the insides of the onion. Make

sure to not cut all the way to the bottom. Sprinkle some lemon thyme in the openings and place a piece of butter in each cavity. Arrange the onions in a small, ovenproof baking dish, sprinkle generously with salt and pepper, and replace the onion lids. Cover tightly with foil and bake until onions are tender, about 40 minutes.

3. Meanwhile, mince the onion insides. Heat the oil in a skillet and sauté the onion and garlic for 5 minutes over low heat. Add the fennel fronds and cook for 1 minute more, stirring constantly. Pour in the broth and heat through. Add the cream and simmer until thickened. Remove from heat and set aside.

4. Cook the pasta in salted water for 7 minutes or until *al dente*. Drain and add to the fennel cream. Toss with the cheese.

5. When the onions are done, place one on each plate. Remove the lids and fill each cavity with pasta, letting some of the pasta hang over the side. Replace the lid so that it sits a little askew. Serve immediately.

SERVES 4   TIME: 60 minutes   LEVEL OF DIFFICULTY: Moderate

VARIATIONS: Onions and pasta are each complete dishes on their own and can individually be served independent of each other. If serving the onions as a side dish, cut into quarters and arrange in an overlapping pattern.

Cipolle al Forno con Salsa Balsamica
Roasted Red Onions with Balsamic Vinegar

When onions are roasted, they lose much of their strong taste and become deliciously sweet and caramelized. In the following recipe, their natural sweetness is enhanced even further by the addition of a balsamic-based vinaigrette which gives it a slightly tart glaze. This is a perfect dish to serve with simple pastas sauced with parsley and garlic or a light cheese sauce.

2 large Vidalia or other sweet onions
3 tablespoons balsamic vinegar
2 tablespoons extra-virgin olive oil
1 teaspoon coarse salt

1 teaspoon freshly ground black pepper
4 sprigs fresh thyme
1 tablespoon capers, drained and minced

1. Preheat oven to 450 degrees. Cut off tops of onions, keeping roots intact. Peel and cut in half, slicing directly through the root. Slice each half in 6 wedges, keeping some of the root so that the wedges remain intact. Arrange the wedges in a single layer in a large, shallow, ovenproof pan, overlapping the edges.

2. In a small bowl, whisk the oil into the vinegar. Season with salt and pepper and drizzle over the onions. Tuck the thyme sprigs in among the wedges. Cover tightly with foil and roast for 40 minutes, basting once or twice during that period.

3. Uncover the onions, baste with pan juices, and roast for 10 minutes longer.

4. When the onions are tender, remove from oven and cool for 10 minutes. Sprinkle with capers and a few more grindings of pepper and serve.

SERVES 4   TIME: 1 hour   LEVEL OF DIFFICULTY: Easy

VARIATIONS: Roasted onions make a wonderful topping for pizza or pasta, sprinkled with some grated cheese.

MAKE AHEAD: The onions can be made up to 2 days in advance and served cold or reheated in the oven.

Pods and Seeds

An Inch Towards Modernity?

"Canyon Ranch is a concept that has yet to find its expression in Tuscany," says my friend, Adriana, a few days after returning from a stay in one of America's most popular health resorts. "For sure, we have expensive health spas, but none where a week's stay is priced in direct opposition to the amount of food consumed."

I have heard her tell the story of Canyon Ranch three times already, and, each time, the part that causes the greatest snickering is that she paid more than $4,000 for a week, during which she ate almost nothing. Not voluntarily, mind you. On the contrary. Like most Tuscans, Adriana loves eating, although you would never know it looking at her slim, fit figure.

No, the problem lay instead in the American connotation of "health spa" as a place where people go to lose weight. "There were twice daily weigh-ins," she said. "And at mealtimes we were fed mainly small bowls of soup and salad with oil-free lemon dressing. The daily schedule was exhausting: early morning yoga, mid-morning water aerobics, afternoon hikes, tennis at dusk. By dinnertime, I needed a big bowl of pasta followed by a thick slice of veal roast, not a dry piece of grilled chicken with a few wisps of arugula drizzled once again with lemon."

Adriana is in the process of constructing a health spa on a mountaintop overlooking the 15th-century village of Pietrasanta. She bought the land in 1995 and labored for over two years to get the necessary permits to reconstruct the 400-year-old farmhouse whose interior walls had crumbled to the ground.

Work began in earnest in October of 1996, and, as of now, the projected date of opening is sometime in autumn of 1999.

In the meantime, she has traveled to many countries comparing various types of health spas. "Except for those in the United States, most of the ones I visited were structured approximately along the lines of what I have in mind—mineral baths, sun rooms, massages, mud treatments, good food, and rest. To my way of thinking, one goes to a health spa to be treated luxuriously, not to undergo the kind of training regimen favored by the military."

Adriana has spent a great deal of time in America; before deciding to open her own spa, she worked for a number of years as an overseas representative for Olivetti, the Italian electronics firm. At one point, she was in New York for almost three consecutive months and the two of us spent numerous evenings hunched over the tables of local restaurants. Her observations on American life have always seemed to me to be overly harsh: we work too hard, play too little, eat poorly, take things too seriously, live too far away from our families, and have absolutely no sense of tradition.

I am not saying she's wrong. In fact, I think her analysis is in keeping with why so many Americans have fallen uncontrollably in love with Tuscany—whether or not they have ever been here. They believe the Tuscan lifestyle to be a loosely constructed pastiche of laughing people sitting at long tables with friends and family, eating good, plentiful food of the type that must obviously not be very fattening, given the negligible numbers of truly overweight people in any given village. Of course, there is an abundance of wine, unlimited sun, and, maybe, in the distance, even a few happy farmers carting olives off to the press.

Her point is well taken, however. To a large extent, Americans have become the kind of people who do not walk in the park unless it is part of an exercise routine. Every minute has a purpose, and the purpose is never simple enjoyment. Our lives revolve around set goals—extravagant dreams in whose name we are willing to sacrifice away both the present and any form of tradition that does not accommodate our direction. Our health spas perfectly reflect this mentality. Instead of offering us simple pleasures, time to daydream, and a healthy dollop of pampering, we gravitate towards either gluttonous excess or spartan regimentation. As Adriana so aptly puts it, "Americans pay for discipline. Why not discipline *yourself* and spend your money on luxury?"

European health spas apparently agree, none more so than Montecatini Terme, an elegant, international spa resort that was—and still is—a legend.

Montecatini is Tuscany's most glamorous thermal spa, host to kings and maharajas, musicians and writers, divas and the divine. Its fame dates back to the 1300s when the properties of its healing waters were popularized by an astute doctor named Ugolino Simoni. "Curative for anyone suffering from ailments of the liver, intestines, and stomach," he postured. His advice lives on in the hearts of the rich and glamorous, who can generally be seen strolling the resort's manicured pathways, glass in hand.

Just outside the resort, on Viale A. Diaz, you can take a funicular railway up to Montecatini Alto (also called Valdinievole, "Valley of the Mists"). This sister village was the setting for one of the major battles between the Guelphs and the Ghibellines: the Pisan Ghibellines defeated the Guelphs of Lucca here in 1316. It also served as the subject for Leonardo da Vinci's very first drawing. In fact, it is believed that da Vinci's lifelong fascination with canals, locks, currents, dams, and the misty watery backgrounds of his most famous paintings originate in a childhood spent contemplating precisely this view from his nearby hometown of Vinci. One of his notebooks even contains a design sketch for a fountain to be placed in the rotunda adjoining Montecatini's baths; 380 years later, the fountain is currently being built of Carrara marble and will serve as a monument to da Vinci's genius.

Montecatini's greatest strength lies in the fact that its prescription for health is the same as it has been for centuries: relaxing, strolling through the gardens, listening to a little music, lingering in a cafe, enjoying the magnificent panoramas of the surrounding countryside, and indulging in a bit of the old *dolce far niente* (the sweetness of doing nothing). Its ambience draws heavily on a Belle Epoque nostalgia for days when the spa literally seethed with dukes, politicians, literati, and actresses. Afternoons and evenings are highlighted by pop and classical music concerts, fashion shows, and art exhibits, all held in a spectacular outdoor rotunda. Famous authors frequently present their latest books here. For those who want something a little more active, there is a golf course, numerous swimming pools, a squash court, mud baths, and even a small race course (for trotters).

Whenever I come here, I am reminded of that wonderful movie with Marcello Mastroianni and Sophia Loren, *A Special Day*. Loren plays a poor southern Italian woman married to a lower-class boor and living in a four-room hovel with her in-laws and dozens of screaming children. This grim existence—made to look even more so by the film's black-and-white photography—comes to a temporary halt when Loren develops tuberculosis and is sent north to a beauti- fully quiet health spa. There she meets Mastroianni (also recovering from some sort of illness), and the two spend their afternoons strolling in perfectly main- tained gardens, sitting in softly lit rooms with beautiful floor-to-ceiling windows, and, of course, falling in love. Eventually, however, Loren gets better and—in a tearjerker ending without rival—has to leave the spa to return to her old life.

When I first saw the movie, I was appropriately heartbroken, especially dur- ing the final scene when Mastroianni sees her off to the train. But I was also struck by the concept of a health-care system which, even in these days of fiscal retrenchment, continues to prescribe and pay for spa holidays when rest and relaxation are deemed to be the most efficacious cure. How brilliant, I thought then! Twenty years later, I still feel the same way, maybe even more so.

In addition to its general air of peace and tranquility, Montecatini's prescrip- tion for health includes a regimen favored by the ancient Romans but pooh- poohed by the majority of Americans: "taking the waters," by which is meant drinking or soaking in waters rich in minerals and trace elements. The Romans so believed in the waters' curative properties that much of the plunder accumu- lated from conquering the world was spent on building ever more beautiful fountains. As if to prove their importance, Montecatini's water dispensers are lined up like so many grande dames next to each other and adjoining the main rotunda.

Grouped according to water properties—*Stabilimento Torretta, Stabilimento Tamerici,* etcetera—the dispensers are built in spectacularly classical style and set among gardens and parks with the gorgeous Tuscan countryside rising behind. Each individual dispenser has two gold spigots set beneath huge mosaics trum- peting the salubrious effect of that particular water. There is "Wisdom," "Long Life," "Agility," and, of course, "Beauty"—*La Bellezza.*

"Americans think it is a joke," Adriana tells me on the first day of the three we spent in Montecatini. "They refuse to acknowledge that mere water can do as much for them as imbibing a pitcher of Brunello." She shakes her head in disbe- lief. "When people have been doing something for 3,000 years, how can anyone just dismiss it out of hand?"

I ask about the waters, and she tells me they either come from deep calcare- ous strata or spring from the sandstone through alluvial sand and gravel. "They reach the surface purified by the subsoil," she says. "They're free of bacterial im- purities and enriched with minerals like sodium, chlorine, iodine, lithium, and phosphates. Generally, they are said to most benefit those with diseases of the joints and limbs, but they have also been known to help those with metabolic disturbances and problems related to the stomach and intestines."

"It sounds far too easy," I tell her. "Americans have a saying, 'No pain, no gain.'"

"I know," she says. "When I was in New York for that one long stretch, I took out a 3-month subscription at one of your gyms, remember? I even had a personal trainer who, I believe to this day, descended from the Fascists. 'Do a few more,' he would always say, regardless of what the exercise was or how many I'd done." She shakes her head and breaks into a hearty laugh. "Once, I stopped in the middle of sit-ups and asked why he was pushing me to do more than my body felt it could handle. 'Easy,' he said with such precise certainty, 'because that's how you raise your threshold level.' 'And do I keep raising to infinity?' I asked. He took a while, but then he said, 'No, at some point you plateau out.' So I asked him what the difference was between plateauing out now or later. And he said he wasn't sure but would get back to me. The following week I signed up for yoga."

The wisdom of the ancients and Adriana's reluctance notwithstanding, Montecatini has recently moved an inch towards modernity with the addition of an outdoor jogging track. "The director of the spa thought it might appeal to a somewhat younger generation," Adriana explained. "But Tuscan women generally don't use it, preferring their local health club instead."

"Why is that?"

"Because coming here is about beauty and elegance, not about lashing sneakers to your feet and covering your body in sweat."

She caps her answer with a self-deprecating laugh—a laugh that says she, in some way, understands the futility of assuming one cannot be beautiful while sweating. And yet, she would sooner forego pasta forever than accompany me this afternoon when I go running. Not because she herself doesn't run. Actually, Adriana is quite the athlete, although she would be very hesitant to use that particular term. A swimmer and occasional runner, she exercises three or four times a week. But always and exclusively at her health club, which, having been created for just that purpose, confers order and propriety to the sweaty business of working out.

Order and propriety are very important where Tuscans are concerned, not only because they serve as a counterbalance to the rampant drama and anarchism that so define the society, but because they are the underpinnings for a very clearly defined sense of style and elegance. Elegance, in fact, suffuses the Tuscan landscape, whether in language, architectural detail, or dress. Its corner-stone is, of course, tradition, which confers a rich, dignified opulence. But it also confers a certain ponderous restraint which makes it impossible to make a move without the blessing of the ancients.

"Well, at the risk of offending your elegant sensibilities, I am going running on the new track," I tell her. "Sure you won't join me?"

"No, thank you. I have an appointment for a mud treatment," she says and saunters off towards the rotunda.

The track is, in fact, deserted, and, by the third lap, I find myself focusing al-most exclusively on Adriana's definition of beauty and elegance, of her appear-ance with respect to grooming and style, of the general ways in which Tuscan women differ from American women when it comes to the concept of "femi-ninity."

"Americans have yet to come to terms with their womanhood," she once told me after hearing a New York friend recount how offended she had felt when a man at a dinner party complimented her figure. "Any woman I know would have been thrilled to receive such praise."

In truth, Adriana is much more beautiful than I will ever be. But she also works harder at it. Although, to her, it is not work but merely an effortless part of her daily grooming schedule. When we have talked about these things, it is clear that our concepts of womanhood are very different. My idea of beauty is a more natural, quasi-androgynous, from-the-inside-out sort of conceptualiza-tion. Adriana, on the other hand, travels with an entire bag full of creams and lo-tions and special scrub stones. She would no sooner think of going to get the morning paper before first applying makeup than she would of going on the same errand naked.

"Tuscans feel very connected, one to the other," she says when I question that aspect of her behavior. "The people you see when you walk down the street are part of your larger family, and good grooming is simply a respectful part of the social contract—not only for women, but men also."

"But wouldn't you say it is more *expected* of women here?"

"No. Absolutely not. Furthermore, I would cut through the veneer of this dis-cussion and say that American women's incessant drive towards sexual equality has poisoned the air. It is one thing to say, 'We are equal,' and another to resent any sexual awareness of ourselves as women. It used to be called Puritanism; now you call it political correctness, but it is still the same thing."

These debates are not new for us; rather they form the nucleus of our relationship. If we are not arguing about whether it is better to jog than take a nap, we are locked into combat about the social and physical implications of using Retin-A to retard the aging process. But regardless of the actual topic, the underlying question is always the same: how important is tradition and how much should we allow it to guide our present-day behavior. In her mind, tradition is the quintessential determinant—always practical, always right, always applicable. To me, tradition is one very important factor, but only one.

We end our stay at Montecatini and continue on to Colognora, where I have an appointment with the caretaker of the world's only museum devoted exclusively to chestnuts. Adriana has said she will go with me both because she, too, has never seen it and because, afterwards, we're having dinner with a mutual friend who recently opened a wonderful new restaurant in Ghivizzano. Also, what could be more fascinating than meeting a man whose job it is to document a way of life dating back to 820?

We get on the road fairly early and wind our way through the Lucchesia, zigzagging through villages whose entire population could fit into a minivan. Along the way, we pass numerous cyclists decked out in skintight shirts and shorts bearing advertisements of some sort or other. "Now, *that's* a good form of exercise," says Adriana. "At least if you sweat, the air removes all trace."

It is chestnut season in Tuscany, and the chestnuts are starting to fall from the trees; in certain places, you can see men and women surreptitiously entering the forest carrying straw baskets and pointed sticks—*bastoni*—used to ferret the chestnuts from their spiky shells. When we get close to Colognora, the road is literally blanketed with chestnuts, prompting Adriana to wonder why people just don't come here and pick them off the road.

"Tradition," I tease her. "They've been going to the same forest site since the 1100s and it doesn't matter that they would find more chestnuts here."

"Very funny," she replies.

You cannot drive a car into Colognora. For one thing, the streets are too narrow. For another, they are made of large, rounded stones arranged in subtly gradated steps undulating over the hilly topography. The stonework pavements were laid over 500 years ago by what was called *i militari zoppi*—the army of the lame, dozens of one-legged men who could no longer participate in the ongoing wars against the Ghibelline invaders. The village itself dates back to 1400, when it was moved to this spot after floods buried the original Colognora (named Castello), located further down the hill.

Il Museo del Castagno is the first thing you see as you round the final bend. A beautifully refurbished stone building, its entryway sports a huge, rounded arch flanked on both sides by enormous stone crocks overflowing with geraniums. But as we get closer to the rough-hewn double green doors, we see that they are locked and that the mailbox has a message tacked to it, saying, *"Sono a casa."* I am at home. Signed: Roberto Fratti.

Before we figured out whether the message means *this* is his home and he is here, or his home is located elsewhere and he is out, an old woman leans out of a nearby window and announces that Roberto's home is *"La."* She points up the street and tells us to follow the chirping of the canaries. "Roberto has six orange *canarini* that do nothing but sing, especially during chestnut season," she says.

Ever the researcher, Adriana asks why canaries sing more now than at any other time.

"Because it is cooler," the woman says in a tone of voice that suggests the question was best left unasked. "Also, with the leaves and the chestnuts having fallen from the trees, you can hear them better."

"Ah," says Adriana, hurrying me along the cobbled street.

Sure enough, when we reach the top of the hill and are standing in what might generously be called the central piazza, we hear a loud chirping. *"La,"* another woman tells us, pointing to the house that caps the adjacent hill. "This caretaker must be a very popular person," says Adriana as we make our way down one hill and up the other.

Roberto Fratti is, in fact, a very popular person. Among other things, he single-handedly divined the idea for the museum and convinced the local church to donate the site, formerly a priest's house. In addition to caring for the more than 300 artifacts housed in the museum's eight rooms, he is also the village historian, a responsibility that has been handed down through the generations of his family since 1687. It is a job he takes seriously, and, to give us an overview of his duties, he hauls out his extensively archived population charts covering Colognora and Castello (the village at the bottom of the hill) from 1687 to the present day.

Among other things, the charts tally the number of both families and individual people living in both places year by year. In 1687, for example, Castello had 36 families and 356 people, and Colognora was not yet occupied. By 1688, Castello had 64 families and 337 individuals, and Colognora, 5 families and 48 individuals. A quick perusal of the chart shows that, today, not much has changed beyond the fact that families are smaller: in 1966, Castello (now just a few agglomerated houses) had 5 families and 21 people; Colognora, 50 families and 233 people.

When we ask Roberto when we can see the museum, he looks at his watch and hesitates for one brief moment before announcing we have exactly 20 minutes. It is almost noontime, he says, and—as anyone who spends even a small amount of time in Tuscany learns—nothing interrupts the mid-day meal. *"Buttala giú al tocco,"* he says to his wife and hurries us out the door. Throw the pasta in on the dot of 12.

The museum is organized according to the different ways in which chestnuts and chestnut trees have historically been utilized. The first room, for example, contains 600-year-old tools for cutting and shaping the trunks, one of which Roberto demonstrates as he recounts the area's history. The second room shows the ways in which tannin was extracted and used to fix leather. "To this day," Roberto says, "fine leather products use chestnut tannin to soften the skins." The remaining rooms highlight the chestnut's importance as a food, a flour, a source of carbon fuel, a dye, and a casking medium for fine wines.

His pride and joy, however, is contained in Room 8, a framed document dating back to August 29 of the year 820 and detailing Colognora's importance as a source of chestnuts. "They wanted to put this in a museum in Lucca," Roberto says proudly. "But when the Culture Minister came to personally make his request, I said this was its home and this is where it would stay."

His account of the man's reaction is interrupted by the chiming of the church bells. *"Beh,"* he says with obvious glee. *"Siamo a mezzogiorno."* Noontime has arrived. He ushers us out and we walk with him towards his house, which is also the path to the village's only restaurant. Along the way, he tells us about the fair he organized this past August. "A medieval festival," he says, chuckling. "Many of the residents dressed in costume and stood in front of their homes demonstrating the old way of doing things." He begins pointing to houses lining the street. "Giovanni over there was the glass blower, and Pietro, the woodcutter. Alessio from down the street set up a blacksmith operation and made plant hangers which he sold for a very nice profit.

"Everybody loved it," he says. "We advertised only in a few local newspapers, but, come that Sunday, there were nine tour buses here. Mainly Germans and Britishers."

The event, he tells us, was a great success, especially monetarily. But there were also problems. It seems the Finance Minister somehow got wind of the festival and has already paid a visit. "According to the regulations he showed us, we are not set up for tourism. The restaurant does not have enough bathrooms and the chestnut products we sold need prior inspection to guarantee their cleanliness. If we want to have another festival, we have to effect some very expensive changes, especially in order to get the proper licenses."

He shakes his head, obviously aware that the problem lies less in the proper number of bathrooms and more in paying off the right person. "In the old days, when we wanted to hold a festival we simply did it. No one knew, and it was, basically, a very local event." He points in the direction of the restaurant where Adriana and I will have lunch. "Now we have the potential to turn our town into a big tourist destination, but we have to first pay the price. And yet, if we pay the price and, for example, send our chestnut honey to a packaging house to be sealed in plastic wrapping, our traditions will have altered beyond recognition."

"Maybe you should keep it a local event," Adriana says. "Then you wouldn't have to worry about anyone finding out."

"I fear those days are over," he says. "With the number of tourists flooding Tuscany on any given day, it has become almost impossible to keep things secret. And besides, those are the people who spend the money!"

We part ways after thanking Roberto effusively and promising to come back soon. "Nice man," Adriana says as we walk towards the tiny trattoria.

"Yes, he was nice," I agreed. "But I feel sorry for him, caught as he is in a web between wanting the money that comes with progress and not wanting to give up anything in exchange."

"I don't," says Adriana. "Feel sorry for him, that is. It's not as if his choices are very complicated. On the one hand, Colognora could stay as it is—as it has been for hundreds of years—with everyone going about their business and living out their life. On the other hand, it could scrap all its traditions and manipulate itself into the narrow mold necessary to turn it into a tourist town. Which would you choose?"

She looks at me and realizes she has framed the argument in too stark a framework to make a decision. "Trust me," she says, pushing open the door to the dining room. "There is no substitute for tradition."

About Pods and Seeds

Tuscany is known for its seasonal cooking—for its tendency to use only the freshest ingredients and only at the height of their season. But what determines the "height of season"? Is it when the vegetables are in their infancy, like baby fava beans eaten right out of their shell? When they achieve full maturation, like sweet, tender peas? Or when they dry on the vine and produce large, bumpy pods filled with perfect, full-flavored *borlotti* beans? The answer is all three, each growth stage offering uniquely different opportunities for culinary experimentation.

No category of vegetables, in fact, demonstrates this multi-stage diversity better than pods and seeds. Unlike corn, which seems to have a 3-hour window in August when it is at its unquestionable best, peas and beans are excellent at many stages throughout their growing cycle. The following recipes encompass all the stages of this unique vegetable group, from a spring salad using the shoots formed by pea plants before any peas are even formed to a hearty winter soup using dried, reconstituted chick-peas.

Beans, Dried *Fagioli Secchi*

Although we cavalierly group them into one class simply labeled "legumes," the bean category encompasses such widely divergent vegetables as limas, green beans, snap beans, cranberry beans, favas, and chick-peas. Belonging to the same botanical family as acacias, garden sweet peas, and orchids, beans, as a class, comprise the most important source of nutrition for the greatest number of the world's people, from Mexico to Mozambique. Dried beans are a fine, fat-free source of protein and one of the least expensive, most versatile vegetables.

Season: Any

To Buy: Avoid batches with great numbers of split, off-color, or slightly faded beans. Also, beans that have been dried for longer than one year tend to lose much of their flavor.

To Prepare: Pick over to remove bad beans and foreign particles. Soak overnight in three times their volume of water. Drain and rinse. To quick-soak, place beans that have been picked over and washed into a pot with three times their volume of water, bring to a boil, and cook uncovered for 2 minutes. Cover the pan and set aside for 1 hour. Drain, rinse, and cook.

NOTE: Many people have difficulty digesting beans and, after eating, develop gas pockets that last anywhere from one to three days. Fortunately, about 80% of the indigestible elements are water soluble, which means that if you throw away the soaking water, you greatly reduce your chances of producing undesirable gas. Another option for reducing gastrointestinal distress is to add a few drops of Beano to the cooking water, a commercially produced liquid sold in pharmacies and health food stores. According to those who use it regularly, Beano completely eliminates the possibility of intestinal rebellion.

Beans, Fresh Fava *Fave*

Called broad beans in England and heralded in Mediterranean countries since the Bronze Age, fava beans have only recently become widely available in the U.S. Favas have large pods 6 to 8 inches long; the beans nestled inside are about the size of a quarter and, when mature, have tough outer skins that are peeled before eating. Tuscans especially prize very young favas which are shelled but not skinned and eaten raw as an appetizer with shavings of *pecorino* cheese.

Season: Early spring

To Buy: Look for bright green, velvety pods. A little bronzing on the pods is all right but avoid beans that look wrinkled and dry.

To Prepare: Young favas can simply be shelled and eaten raw. Pop open each pod by pressing the seam near the stem end. Then run your thumbnail down the seam to split it open and expose the beans. When you have removed the beans, again use your thumbnail to split the protective skin on each fava bean lengthwise so you can pull away the skin in one piece. Mature ones require a little more work. String the pods if necessary (remove the cap at the top of the pod, pull it back and downward; if the cap is no longer there, locate any string and pull down) and remove the beans, then blanch in boiling water for a minute. Slip off the skins and cook the beans in boiling salted water for 10 to 15 minutes. One pound unshelled equals about 1 cup shelled.

NOTE: Fava beans are also available dried and can be purchased at Italian markets and specialty stores.

Beans, Fresh Shell *Fagioli Freschi*

Most people have eaten dried beans in one form or another without ever realizing that those beans were once fresh. Fresh shell beans are simply snap beans whose seeds were allowed to ripen. Although greenmarkets currently offer only a few varieties—at mine, I can buy wide and flat-podded limas, spotted cranberries, fat white runners, and long thin-podded black-eyed peas—I predict the demand will soon result in a far greater supply.

Borlotti shell beans.

Season: Late summer and fall

To Buy: Look for pods with many uniform bulges. Avoid any overlarge beans or excessive black mottling. Pods should be fresh and crisp.

To Prepare: Peel back and pop out the beans, discarding the pod.

Beans, Green *Fagiolini*

Botanically, green beans are referred to as *Phaseolus vulgaris* and include tiny *fagiolini* as well as wide-pod Romano beans, yellow wax beans, the French *haricots verts,* burgundy runner beans, and any other variety with edible pods eaten before the beans inside mature. Known to the ancient Egyptians and mentioned by Roman agronomist Pliny the Elder in his diaries, green beans are easy to prepare, although they must be carefully watched to avoid overcooking.

Season: June through October

To Buy: Select beans that are firm and straight, even in color, without blemishes, and with few shrivelled ends. Beans should be tender and crisp enough to break when bent to a 45-degree angle. The freshest have slightly fuzzy skins. Enclosed seeds should be small, not large and bulging.

To Prepare: Wash, cut or snap off ends. Remove any spots. Leave whole or cut into desired lengths.

Chick-Peas Ceci

Chick-peas (*Cicer atietinum*) are legumes grown since the time of antiquity. In their native Mediterranean, fresh chick-peas come in white, black, and red and are eaten raw as they come from the pod or roasted and used as snacks. The whites are the only variety currently available to us and they come dried, canned, ground into flour, or—with prior roasting—ground into a coffee substitute. High in protein and devoid of fat, chick-peas, or *ceci* in Italian, are a wonderfully versatile food whose American popularity has yet to be established.

Season: Any, since only available dried, canned, or ground.

To Buy: Avoid broken or faded chick-peas since they will cook at different rates.

To Prepare: Dried chick-peas must be soaked for 24 hours in several changes of water. Even so, they will take 2 to 2½ hours to cook (in three times their weight of water).

Lentils Lenticchie

Lentils (*Lens esculenta* or *Ervum lens*) are members of the legume family and one of the most ancient and nutritious of foods. Lentil plants grow about 18 inches high and contain around 50 tiny pods, each enclosing only one or two lentils. Optical lenses were named for this bean because of the marked similarity in shape. A number of lentil types are now available in U.S. markets in addition to the common brown variety which is relatively easy to grow and, because it falls apart when cooked, is excellent for soups. Red lentils are the most widely consumed type outside the U.S. Sold here in both whole and split versions, these slightly sweet kernels are generally used in stews or sauces. Beluga lentils are named for their caviar-like appearance; tiny and aromatic, these work best when used in salads or side dishes. The celebrated Du Puy lentils come from France's Haute Loire region and carry a robust, earthy flavor that makes them perfect for salads. Spanish Pardina lentils grow in the Spanish Pyrenees, where they acquire their nutty flavor and soft texture.

Season: Any

To Buy: Avoid broken, discolored lentils.

To Prepare: Pick over to remove foreign objects or small stones. Soak for 2 hours before using if the dish features lentils; soaking prevents them from disintegrating during cooking. If making soup or a stew, no soaking is necessary. In either case, do not boil, since lentils disintegrate in agitated water.

Peas Piselli

There are three categories of peas (*Pisum sativum*, of the legume family): edible podded (sometimes called snow peas), podded peas (also called English peas), and sugar snap, although, in their young stage, all peas have edible pods. Young pea leaves are wonderful in salads or sautéed with a dash of olive oil (although every pea vine eaten means that many less actual peas). In Tuscany, the arrival of spring peas (by which is meant podded peas which are the only ones generally available) creates a madness not otherwise seen. For weeks, they are used in virtually every form. Last year, I even had a spring pea frittata!

Season: May through June

To Buy: Look for firm, fresh, moderately filled-out pods, or, for edible pods, fresh green color with no black mottling which signifies poor growing conditions.

To Prepare: Podded peas should be shelled and rinsed. Edible pods should have their stem end removed as well as the side strings.

Quick and Easy

Dried Beans

The most basic and basically delicious way to prepare dried beans is simply to boil them and serve drizzled with olive oil and accompanied by crusty bread. If you like, top with sautéed onions, sautéed garlic, or a raw *battuto* (see page 321). Season with salt and pepper and serve over garlic-rubbed bread. Pureed beans also make excellent dips with or without additional flavoring agents.

Fava Beans

As mentioned earlier, one of the best ways to enjoy young favas is to eat them right out of the shell without peeling. Tuscans traditionally add wedges of *pecorino* cheese or simply dip the beans in salt. Older favas can be pureed and served as a dip or spread. Mixed with a little flour and seasoning, the puree can be formed into croquettes and fried. Older favas are also delicious added to stir-fries or steamed and drizzled with butter. Favas cooked in broth makes a simple and delicious soup, especially when sprinkled with Parmesan or *pecorino* cheese.

Fresh Shell Beans

Can be used in all the same ways as dried, but their freshness gives them a unique advantage when served as is, drizzled with very good olive or truffle oil. Fresh shell beans are a natural for late summer cold salads, mixed with chopped onions, tomatoes, greens, lemon zest, and herbs. Toss with a mustard vinaigrette or drizzle with oil and lemon.

Green Beans

To me, there is no better way to eat very young green beans than to boil them in salted water for 3 or 4 minutes, just until tender (but not crunchy), and then simply drizzle with very good olive oil and salt. Mid-life beans can be blanched and braised in a skillet with previously sautéed onions, canned tomatoes, minced black olives, and chopped parsley.

Chick-Peas

Cooked chick-peas are marvelous when combined with minced garlic, chopped parsley, shredded anchovies, olive oil, and salt. Chick-pea puree makes a wonderful thickener for vegetable soups and stews. Mixed with bread crumbs, egg, sautéed onion, parsley, and seasoning, pureed chick-peas can also be rolled into balls and baked or fried until golden brown or braised in broth.

Lentils

What can be better than a simple lentil soup? Cook the lentils in water or broth, add sautéed onions, carrots, and celery, season, and presto! Like beans, lentils are also wonderful simply cooked and drizzled with oil. Like chick-peas, they make very good purees as well as heavenly croquettes.

Peas

There are not many recipes I can offer for peas, because the peas in my garden never make it to the kitchen; I almost exclusively eat them right off the vine, no matter how many I grow. Sorry.

Adriana da Prato: "When people have been doing something for 3,000 years, how can anyone just dismiss it out of hand?"

Insalata di Fave e Pecorino
Fava Bean, Dandelion, and Pecorino Salad

When the first little bumps appear on the fava bean pods, it's time to pick a basketful and organize a picnic. The following recipe aggrandizes the traditional Tuscan method of eating baby favas right from the shell with wedges of soft pecorino cheese (the traditional variety is marzolino, an especially fresh cheese made in early spring, hence its name, which means "March"). Feel free to further aggrandize the salad with green beans or baby turnips or chicory or anything else that finds its way into your harvest basket.

3 pounds baby fava beans, shelled and peeled	½ teaspoon fresh ground white pepper
6 ounces soft *pecorino* cheese, cut into 1-inch cubes	12 ounces dandelion leaves, cleaned and torn
⅓ cup extra-virgin olive oil	1 ounce fresh violets for garnish
½ teaspoon salt	

1. Place the favas in a salad bowl with the cheese, oil, salt, and pepper. Mix well and set aside for 2 hours.

2. Add the dandelion and toss to blend all ingredients. Serve garnished with violets and accompanied by dense, crusty bread.

SERVES 4   TIME: 20 minutes in addition to the 2 hours for marinating.

LEVEL OF DIFFICULTY: Easy

VARIATIONS: 1 tablespoon balsamic or other vinegar can also be added.

Fagiolata
Pasta Dumplings and Fresh Borlotti Beans

Whenever we make this dish at the cooking school, it never fails to garner rave reviews. A wonderful first course, the tiny, gnocchi-like dumplings are a unique blend of flour and bread crumbs that are tossed with a bean and tomato sauce flavored with the basic Tuscan soffritto of celery, carrot, and onion.

The Dumplings

2 cups unflavored bread crumbs
1 cup unbleached white flour, plus
    additional flour for kneading
1 cup boiling water
1 egg, lightly beaten
Salt to taste

The Sauce

3 tablespoons extra-virgin olive oil
1 medium carrot, peeled and diced
1 medium onion, minced
1 celery stalk, diced

3 very ripe Italian plum tomatoes,
    diced
1 small potato, diced
¼ pound fresh shelled Borlotti
    (cranberry) beans
1 teaspoon fresh chopped oregano
¾ cup Basic Vegetable Broth (see
    page 308)
1 tablespoon unsalted butter
Salt and freshly ground black
    pepper
¼ cup fresh grated Parmigiano-
    Reggiano

1. Place the bread crumbs and flour in a large bowl. Add ½ the boiling water, the egg, and the salt and stir to blend. Keep adding water, 1 tablespoon at a time, stirring constantly until a thick paste has formed. Place the remaining flour in a heap on a pastry board and set the dumpling dough on top of it. Knead thoroughly until the mixture is well blended, smooth, soft, dry, and elastic.

2. Roll the dough into strips about ¼ inch in diameter. Cut into pieces ¼ inch wide, sprinkle with flour, and transfer to a floured board.

3. Meanwhile, make the sauce. Heat the oil in a large skillet. Sauté the carrot, onion, and celery for 7 minutes over low heat or until translucent. Add the tomatoes, potato, beans, oregano, and broth and stir to mix. Cook for 40 minutes, stirring occasionally.

4. Drop the dumplings into a large pot of boiling salted water and cook for about 3 minutes, during which time they will rise to the surface. Drain and add to the sauce along with the butter, salt, pepper, and cheese. Gently stir to blend all ingredients and serve immediately.

SERVES 4   TIME: 90 minutes   LEVEL OF DIFFICULTY: Advanced

MAKE AHEAD: The dumplings can be made up to Step 2, up to 1 day in advance and either refrigerated, wrapped in plastic wrap or frozen. The sauce can be made up to 1 day in advance and refrigerated or frozen.

Fagiolini Fritti
Fried Green Beans

There's an old Tuscan saying: Un gusto solo no far sapore. *One flavor alone does not make a meal. True in most cases. But I have no trouble making a meal out of early green beans fried to golden perfection and served with wedges of lemon.*

1 pound baby green beans (no
    longer than 4 inches), trimmed
Unbleached flour for dredging

Olive oil for frying
Salt
Lemon wedges

1. Parboil the beans and drain. Immediately (before they dry) roll them in flour, shaking off any excess.

2. Heat ½ inch oil in a large skillet over medium heat. Place the beans, one at a time, in the hot oil and cook over medium heat for 3–5 minutes or until lightly browned. Do not crowd the skillet or you will lower the temperature of the oil. Drain on paper towels, salt, and serve immediately on a platter surrounded by lemon wedges.

SERVES 4   TIME: 25 minutes   LEVEL OF DIFFICULTY: Easy

VARIATIONS: The beans can also be served at room temperature with a dipping sauce.

MAKE AHEAD: The beans can be parboiled 4 hours in advance and refrigerated. Refresh the beans under running cold water before storing.

Tagliatelle di Ceci con Pesto di Prezzemolo
Chick-Pea Pasta with Parsley Pesto

Chick-peas are almost a religion in Tuscany. There are chick-pea salads, entrées, dips and spreads, soups, pizzas, polentas, and—one of my favorite uses for this ubiquitous little legume—pasta made with chick-pea flour. Normally served with a simple tomato sauce, I have varied the recipe by adding a creamy parsley pesto.

The Pasta

3 tablespoons extra-virgin olive oil
2 cloves garlic, minced
1 teaspoon fresh chopped
    rosemary
2 cups unbleached flour
½ cup chick-pea flour*
3 eggs, lightly beaten
1 teaspoon salt
Freshly ground black pepper

The Pesto

2 cups packed parsley leaves (dis-
    card stems)
½ cup extra-virgin olive oil
½ cup walnut pieces
2 cloves garlic, peeled and halved
Salt and freshly ground black
    pepper
½ cup fresh grated Parmigiano-
    Reggiano

1. Heat the oil in a small skillet and sauté the garlic over low heat for 3 minutes. Add the rosemary and sauté for 30 seconds more.

2. Meanwhile, combine the flours in a heap on a pastry board. Make a well in the center and add the eggs, salt, and pepper. Pour the garlic, rosemary, and oil into the well. Proceed making the pasta according to the directions on page 312, steps 1 to 8.

3. When the pasta sheet is ready for cutting, run it through the widest set of cutting blades.

4. To make the pesto. Place all ingredients in the bowl of a food processor. Process until smooth. Place in a large pasta bowl.

5. Cook the pasta for 5 minutes in boiling salted water, drain, and place in the bowl with the pesto. Toss until all the strands are well coated, sprinkle with cheese, and serve immediately.

SERVES 4   TIME: 75 minutes   LEVEL OF DIFFICULTY: Advanced

VARIATIONS: Pasta machines only allow two basic variations with respect to noodle width (although extra rollers can be purchased that create anything from angel hair to pappardelle). For additional variety, lay the final sheet on a floured board and cut into creative shapes—squares, rectangles, hearts, diamonds—your choice.

MAKE AHEAD: The pasta can be made up to 1 day in advance and refrigerated or frozen. The pesto can be made up to 10 days in advance, stored in a container with a substantial layer of olive oil coating the top, refrigerated.

*Chick-pea flour can be purchased in Italian specialty stores.

Favetta

Traditional Fava Purée with Escarole

I ate this when I was young, and so did my grandparents and their grandparents before them. A highly nutritious winter dish, Favetta makes a perfect one-dish meal when served with garlic-rubbed bread and a full-bodied Chianti Riserva.

1 pound dried fava beans, soaked overnight and drained
½ cup extra-virgin olive oil
1 medium onion, minced
Salt and freshly ground black pepper
2 pounds escarole, stems removed
3 cloves garlic, minced

1. Place the beans in a heavy-gauge soup pot with enough water to cover by 2 inches. Bring to a boil, decrease the heat to low, cover, and cook for 90 minutes or until tender.

2. While the beans are cooking, heat 2 tablespoons of the oil in a skillet and sauté the onion over low heat for 5 minutes or until soft. Add the onion and oil to the soup pot.

3. When the beans have cooked for 60 minutes, add ½ teaspoon salt and a few grindings of pepper.

4. Meanwhile, wash the escarole very thoroughly in several changes of water. Roughly chop the leaves and parboil in salted water until just wilted. Drain.

5. Heat another 2 tablespoons of the oil in a large skillet. Sauté the garlic for 5 minutes over low heat until soft. Increase the heat to medium high. Add the escarole and sauté for 3 minutes, stirring constantly. Season with salt and pepper.

6. While the escarole is sautéeing, pass the cooked beans and their liquid through a food mill. Divide the purée among 4 plates, spreading the purée to cover the entire center of the dish. Top with the sautéed escarole, drizzle with the remaining oil, and serve.

SERVES 4   TIME: 2 hours   LEVEL OF DIFFICULTY: Moderate

MAKE AHEAD: The fava purée can be made up to 2 days in advance and reheated in a double-boiler before assembly.

Frittelle di Lenticchie all'Aceto Balsamico
Lentil Fritters on a Bed of Wilted Beet Greens Drizzled with Balsamic Vinaigrette

Tuscan schools break in midmorning for merenda, *a snack so broad in spirit that it might include anything from bread with ricotta to a slice of pound cake to the following fritters made from lentils and grated potatoes and flavored with dill (sans the beet green bed, of course). At one time, mothers and nannies would deliver the* merenda *fresh from the kitchen. Nowadays, those poor Tuscan lads and lassies have to make do with cold leftovers.*

¼ pound red lentils, picked over, soaked for 1 hour and drained
1 tablespoon fresh chopped dill
1 teaspoon paprika
½ teaspoon salt
¾ pound red potatoes, peeled
Olive oil for frying

1 pound beet greens, stems removed
1 tablespoon balsamic vinegar
½ teaspoon stone-ground mustard
½ teaspoon capers
Salt and freshly ground black pepper
3 tablespoons extra-virgin olive oil

1. Place the lentils in a soup pot with enough water to cover by 2 inches. Cook over medium heat for 20 minutes or until tender. Drain and force through a food mill. Place the mash in a bowl, stir in the dill, paprika, and ½ teaspoon salt. Grate the potatoes into the bowl and stir to blend.

2. Form the lentil mixture into half-dollar-sized fritters and fry in a thin layer of oil until browned, about 4 minutes. Turn and brown on the other side. Drain on paper towels.

3. To make the dressing place the vinegar, mustard, capers, salt, and pepper in a small bowl. Whisk in the olive oil until blended.

4. Parboil the beet greens in salted water until wilted. Drain and divide among four plates. Arrange 4 or 5 fritters over the greens. Drizzle with dressing and serve.

SERVES 4   TIME: 60–70 minutes   LEVEL OF DIFFICULTY: Moderate

VARIATIONS: The fritters and greens can also be dressed with a simple drizzle of olive oil and lemon.

SOLO VERDURA

Orecchietti con Rampolli
Orecchiette with Pea Shoots

When I first saw my cousin Mauro picking pea shoots off the vine, I thought he was crazy. "Those are all potential peas," I told him, wondering why anyone would voluntarily limit their future harvest. "Hai ragione," he said. You are right. "But wait until you taste these with pasta and then let me know what you think." Not only have I since become somewhat of a pea shoot addict, but I was also informed by a gardening friend that the peas simply grow more shoots to make up for what was lost.

5 tablespoons extra-virgin olive oil
1 clove garlic, mashed
¼ cup fresh chopped chives
½ pound fresh pea shoots*

Salt and freshly ground black
    pepper
1 pound *orecchiette* (ear-shaped pasta)
Baby chives for garnish

1. Heat the oil in a large skillet. Sauté the garlic for 1 minute over medium heat. Remove the garlic and discard.

Colognora, a fifteenth-century village where all the streets are made of stones.

2. Add the chives and the pea shoots. Sauté for 2–3 minutes, stirring constantly. Add salt.

3. Cook the pasta in a large quantity of boiling salted water until it is almost done. Drain, reserving 1 cup of the pasta water. Add the pasta to the skillet and toss until coated with oil and greens. Add the reserved pasta water, ¼ cup at a time, stirring constantly, until the pasta is creamy and *al dente*. Serve immediately, dusted with black pepper and garnished with the chives.

SERVES 4   TIME: 20 minutes

LEVEL OF DIFFICULTY: Easy

VARIATIONS: In place of pea shoots, use snow pea pods.

*The pods, flowers, and tendrils of sweet pea flower plants (*Lathyrus odoratus*) are poisonous and should not be confused with edible peas (*Pisum sativum*).

Tortelli di Piselli con Burro e Salvia
Green Pea Tortelli with Brown Butter and Sage

This is a dish for mid-season pea harvests, when the peas are no longer young enough to be featured on their own, but not yet the big starchy legumes that make such wonderful soup. I first ate a variation of these tortelli *at Oliveto's in Oakland while listening to chef Paul Bertolli explain how he had bought the peas just that morning expecting to use them as a vegetable side dish. "But in the last few days, peas have moved into middle age, and sometimes I feel it's happening that quickly with me too."*

2 pounds unshelled peas
3 tablespoons extra-virgin
    olive oil
1 medium onion, minced
Salt and freshly ground black
    pepper
1 recipe Basic Pasta Dough (see
    page 312) rolled to the thinnest
    setting

3 dozen plucked parsley leaves,
    washed and dried
Flour
8 tablespoons unsalted butter
2 cloves garlic, mashed
8 leaves fresh sage
¼ cup freshly grated Parmigiano-
    Reggiano
4 sprigs fresh sage for garnish

1. Shell the peas by removing the cap at the top of the pea pod and yanking it back and downward. If there is no cap, feel the tip of the pod's seam, locate any string, and pull down. Plunge the peas into salted boiling water for 3 minutes. Drain and place in the bowl of a food processor.

2. Heat the oil in a small skillet. Sauté the onion for 5 minutes over low heat until soft. Add the onion and oil to the food processor and purée. Season with salt and pepper, remove to a bowl, and set aside.

3. Meanwhile, make the ravioli. Sprinkle half the total length of the sheet of dough with the parsley leaves. Fold the other half over, adjust the pasta machine to the next thinnest setting and roll the entire folded length through the machine. Decrease the setting to the thinnest and re-roll the dough which will come out silhouetted with parsley leaves.

4. Place the pasta on a floured surface and cut into two sections. On one section, distribute the pureed peas in nickel-sized mounds spaced roughly 1 inch apart. Using a slightly damp pastry brush, moisten the edges around the mounds. Cover with the other sheet of dough and gently press with your fingers

between the mounds so that the dough looks like an even series of hills and valleys. Using a ravioli wheel, cut the dough into 2 × 2-inch squares.

5. To make the sauce, heat the butter in a skillet and when it is frothy, sauté the garlic for 2 minutes over low heat. Remove the garlic and discard. Add the sage leaves and cook for 5 minutes. Remove and discard. Continue to cook the butter until it turns light brown and gives off a nutty aroma. Be careful not to burn the butter. Season with salt and pepper.

6. Bring to boil a large quantity of salted water. Drop in the *tortelli* and cook for 5 minutes, during which time they will rise to the top. Drain and place in a large bowl. Drizzle with the butter sauce and add the cheese, tossing gently until the *tortelli* are well coated. Garnish with the sprigs of sage and serve.

SERVES 4   TIME: 2 hours   LEVEL OF DIFFICULTY: Advanced

Bruschette con Pure di Fagioli
Garlic Toasts with Puréed Shell Beans

Bruschetta is generally thought of as a summer food, pulled off the grill and slathered with chopped fresh tomatoes and leaves of fragrant basil. But it is just as wonderful in fall or winter, topped with a bean spread and served with a bowl of hearty soup or salad.

½ pound fresh shelled cranberry or
    lima beans
1 bay leaf
½ teaspoon dried crumbled sage
¼ cup heavy cream

Salt and freshly ground black
    pepper
8 ¾-inch-thick slices day-old
    peasant bread
2 cloves garlic, halved
2 tablespoons extra-virgin olive oil

1. Place the beans in a pot with the bay leaf, sage, and enough water to cover by 2 inches. Cover and cook for 15 minutes or until tender. Force the beans and their cooking liquid through a food mill and place the mash in a bowl. Stir in the cream and season with salt and pepper. Keep warm.

2. Toast the bread on both sides and immediately rub tops and bottoms with garlic. Baste one side of each slice with oil, top with bean purée, and serve.

SERVES 4   TIME: 30 minutes

LEVEL OF DIFFICULTY: Easy

VARIATIONS: A food processor can be substituted for the food mill.

MAKE AHEAD: The bean purée can be made up to 2 days in advance and refrigerated. Bring the purée to room temperature or reheat before serving.

Insalata di Lenticchie e Cannelini
White Bean and Lentil Salad

When summer comes, I like to be in my garden. Period. And I don't like to be interrupted just because my stomach signals it is time for lunch. So, more often than not, I make large quantities of bean salad and eat it a few days in a row. Like many foods with peasant origins, it gets better as it sits.

½ pound dried *cannelini* beans,
  soaked for 12 hours and drained
1 medium onion, peeled
2 bay leaves
½ pound small green (French)
  lentils
1 large onion, minced
2 carrots, shredded
2 tablespoons chopped lovage
Grated zest of 1 lemon

4 tablespoons extra-virgin olive oil
1 tablespoon balsamic vinegar or
  raspberry vinegar
Salt and freshly ground black
  pepper
½ pound assorted greens (chicory,
  arugula, romaine, amaranth,
  mustard, dandelion, sorrel,
  or watercress), washed and
  spun dry

1. Place the *cannelini* in a heavy-gauge pot with the onion, one bay leaf, and enough water to cover by 2 inches. Cook over low heat for 90 minutes or until tender. Salt at the 60-minute mark.

2. Place the lentils in another pot with the remaining bay leaf and enough water to cover by 2 inches. Cook over low heat for 20 minutes or until tender.

3. Drain the *cannelini*, discarding the onion and bay leaf. Place in a large bowl and cool to room temperature.

4. Drain the lentils, discarding the bay leaf, and add to the bowl with the *cannelini*.

SOLO VERDURA

5. Add the minced onion, carrots, lovage, and lemon to the bowl with the beans and mix well. Toss with the oil and vinegar, season with salt and pepper, and serve on a bed of greens.

SERVES 6–8   TIME: 1¾ hours plus additional time for cooling

LEVEL OF DIFFICULTY: Moderate

VARIATIONS: Any chopped herb can be used in place of lovage; try parsley, basil, dill, or a combination of herbs.

Piselli con Salsa di Noce
Green Peas Steamed in Lettuce Leaves with Walnut Sauce

One of the best ways to cook young green peas is to steam them in lettuce leaves. Upon contact with heat, the leaves release moisture and, when they are completely wilted, after about 10 minutes, their rendered moisture will have steamed the peas to perfection. Topped with the following nut sauce and served with rice, the peas make a perfect entrée.

2 or 3 large lettuce leaves
2 cups fresh shelled young peas
¼ pound shelled walnuts, crushed
   to a paste
1 small garlic clove, crushed

¼ cup heavy cream
2 tablespoons extra-virgin olive oil
Salt to taste
¼ pound arugula for bedding

1. Rinse the lettuce leaves and arrange them to cover the bottom of a saucepan, extending part way up the sides. Place the peas in the center of the leaves, leaving a ½-inch margin so they do not spill out as the leaves shrink during cooking. Cover with more leaves. Cover the pan tightly and place it over low heat. When the leaves are completely wilted, about 10 minutes, the peas are done. Remove the peas to a bowl and discard the lettuce.

2. Meanwhile, make the sauce. Place the nuts and garlic in a small bowl. Stir in the cream, oil and salt until well blended.

3. Divide the arugula among 4 plates, cover with peas, top with sauce, and serve.

SERVES 4   TIME: 30 minutes   LEVEL OF DIFFICULTY: Easy

VARIATIONS: Bed the peas on rice instead of arugula.

MAKE AHEAD: The sauce can be made 4 hours in advance and refrigerated. Reheat before serving.

Sformati di Fagiolini e Lenticchie
Individual Green Bean and Lentil Molds

This is as delicious a dish as it is lovely to behold. Young, vividly green beans are laid one on top of the other to form the outside walls of individual ramekin molds. The walls are then filled with a creamy lentil puree and the dish is served cold, dressed with a final drizzle of lemon and olive oil.

½ pound young green beans, trimmed

4 tablespoons extra-virgin olive oil

1 medium onion, minced

1½ cups cooked lentils

¼ cup Basic Vegetable Broth (see page 308)

1 very ripe Italian plum tomato, peeled and seeded

1 clove garlic, mashed

1 teaspoon fresh chopped lemon thyme

⅛ teaspoon fresh chopped rosemary

Juice of ½ lemon

8 very thin lemon slices, for garnish

20–25 chives divided into 4 bundles and tied with a chive, for garnish

1. Grease the sides and bottoms of 4 ramekins or custard cups with olive oil. Boil the beans in salted water until tender, about 5 minutes. The beans should be soft and pliable. Drain. Line the bottom and sides of the ramekins or custard cups with beans laid on top of each other. Set aside.

2. Heat 2 tablespoons of oil in a skillet. Sauté the onion for 5 minutes over low heat and transfer to the bowl of a food processor. Add the lentils, broth, tomato, garlic, thyme, and rosemary and purée until smooth and creamy.

3. Fill the ramekins with the lentil purée and refrigerate for 2 hours. Carefully unmold onto small plates, drizzle with the remaining oil and lemon juice, and serve garnished with lemon slices and chive bundles.

SERVES 4   TIME: 45 minutes (plus 2-hour refrigeration)

LEVEL OF DIFFICULTY: Moderate

MAKE AHEAD: The prepared ramekins can be refrigerated for up to 1 day.

Orzo e Ceci
Orzo with Chick-Peas

I am a big fan of the simple peasant dishes still served in modest, working-class restaurants throughout Tuscany. Many are the occasions when I will accompany friends to a fancy eatery and order a basic plate of linguine with tomato sauce. The following dish—a variant on the classic pasta e fagioli—*is simple, hearty, and delicious. What more could one want?*

½ pound chick-peas, soaked for 24 hours and drained

1 large onion

1 medium carrot, scraped

1 bay leaf

2 cloves garlic, halved

Salt and freshly ground black pepper

1 pound orzo

4 tablespoons extra-virgin olive oil

1 clove garlic, minced

3 tablespoons finely chopped fresh parsley

1. Place the chick-peas in a heavy-gauge soup pot with the onion, carrot, bay leaf, and garlic halves. Add enough water to cover by 2 inches, cover, and cook over low heat for 2 hours or until tender. Add ½ teaspoon salt at the 1-hour mark. Drain, discarding the onion, carrot, and bay leaf, and place in a large bowl.

2. Cook the orzo in boiling salted water for 7 minutes or until tender. Drain and add to the bowl with the chick-peas. Stir in the oil, garlic, and parsley, mix well, season with salt and pepper, and serve.

SERVES 4   TIME: 2½ hours   LEVEL OF DIFFICULTY: Easy

VARIATIONS: Can also be served lukewarm, and canned chick-peas can be substituted.

MAKE AHEAD: The chick-peas can be cooked up to 2 days in advance and refrigerated. Return to room temperature before serving.

Fagioli Briachi
Drunken Beans (in Red Wine)

This is the Tuscan version of baked beans (what else would you expect Tuscans to use except wine?). Any full red wine can be used; most of the times I've had this dish, it has been made with home-made Sangiovese.

½ pound red kidney beans, soaked
    for 12 hours and drained
1 medium onion
1 bay leaf
Salt and freshly ground black
    pepper
2 tablespoons extra-virgin olive oil

1 medium onion, minced
2 cloves garlic, minced
1½ cups dry red wine
1 cup canned Italian tomatoes,
    liquid reserved
1 tablespoon unsalted butter

1. Place the beans in a heavy-gauge soup pot with the onion, bay leaf, and enough water to cover by 2 inches. Cover and cook over low heat for 2 hours or until tender. Add ½ teaspoon salt at the 1-hour mark. Drain and set aside.

2. Meanwhile, preheat the oven to 350 degrees. Heat the oil in a skillet. Sauté the onion and garlic for 5 minutes over low heat until soft. When the beans are done, add them to the skillet with the wine and tomatoes. Season with salt and pepper and warm through, stirring to blend all ingredients.

3. Transfer to an ovenproof dish, cover with aluminum foil, and bake for 45 minutes. Stir in the butter and serve hot.

SERVES 4   TIME: 3 hours   LEVEL OF DIFFICULTY: Easy

VARIATIONS: Canned beans can be substituted for the dried variety.

MAKE AHEAD: The beans can be cooked up to 2 days in advance and refrigerated.

Insalata di Fichi, Crescione, Fagiolini, e Ricotta

Fig, Watercress, Green Bean, and Ricotta Salad with Truffle Oil

There are few things in life I love as much as figs. In fact, not only do I manage to clean-sweep my neighbor's two trees, but I scavenge as many as I can find on the ancient wild trees lining my running route. The taking gets noticeably easier as August turns to September because Tuscans only eat figs on those 5 or 6 days when they are deemed to be absolutely "perfect." Beyond that, it's no thank you, which, of course, simply leaves more for me.

¼ pound young green beans, trimmed

½ pound watercress, stems removed

8 ripe figs (either green or purple)

4 ounces sheep's milk ricotta

Salt and freshly ground black pepper

1 teaspoon fresh lemon juice

3 tablespoons white truffle oil

1. Boil the beans in salted water until tender, about 5 minutes. Drain and set aside.

2. Arrange the watercress on 4 salad plates or bowls. Remove the stems from the figs, cut in half, and carefully position 4 halves on each plate. Ring the plates or bowls with green beans.

3. Scoop a dollop of ricotta into the center of each fig. Sprinkle with salt and pepper.

4. Pour the lemon juice into a small bowl. Whisk in the oil until smooth, drizzle over the salads, and serve.

SERVES 4   TIME: 35 minutes   LEVEL OF DIFFICULTY: Easy

Minestrone di Fagioli Bianchi con Pesto di Salvia
Winter White Bean Minestrone with Sage Pesto

White beans and sage are paired together in many Tuscan dishes such as the classic fagioli all'uccelletto. But the following soup, thick, hearty, and comforting, seems to cry out for not only a few leaves of sage, but an entire concentrated dollop of the musky herb.* Serve it with crusty bread and a hearty red wine.

The Soup

½ pound dried *cannelini* beans, soaked for 12 hours and drained
1 onion
1 bay leaf
Salt
2 tablespoons extra-virgin olive oil
1 medium onion, minced
3 cloves garlic, crushed
½ cup canned Italian plum tomatoes and their liquid
2 cups Basic Vegetable Broth (see page 308)

The Pesto

½ cup fresh sage leaves
½ cup parsley leaves (discard stems)
1 clove garlic
3 tablespoons toasted pine nuts
3 tablespoons fresh grated Parmigiano-Reggiano
½ cup extra-virgin olive oil
Salt and freshly ground black pepper

1. Place the beans in a heavy-gauge soup pot with the onion, bay leaf, and enough water to cover by 2 inches. Cover and cook for 1 hour. Add ½ teaspoon salt at the half-hour mark.

2. Meanwhile, heat the oil in a skillet. Sauté the onion and garlic for 5 minutes over low heat, until soft. Transfer to a bowl and stir in the tomatoes (squeeze the tomatoes into the bowl to shred them) and broth. Set aside.

3. When the beans are done, discard the onion and bay leaf. Using a slotted spoon, remove half the beans and force them through a food mill with a ladleful or two of bean liquid. Return to the bean pot and stir to blend.

4. Stir the tomato and broth mixture into the beans, cover, and cook for 15 minutes over medium heat.

5. To make the pesto, place the sage, parsley, garlic, pine nuts, and cheese in the bowl of a food processor. Puree, pouring the oil in a steady stream through the feeding tube, until soft and smooth. Transfer to a small bowl and season with salt and pepper.

6. Ladle the soup into individual bowls, stir a dollop of pesto into each, and serve.

SERVES 4   TIME: 1½ hours   LEVEL OF DIFFICULTY: Moderate

VARIATIONS: Canned beans can be substituted for the dried variety in Step 1. The finished soup can also be placed in a large terrine and all the pesto added before ladling into bowls.

*Because sage leaves are thicker and drier than pesto regulars such as basil and parsley, it may be a little harder to hold the emulsion together; you may have to whisk the sauce again just before serving.

Montecatini Terme: Tuscany's most glamorous thermal spa: host to kings and maharajas, musicians and writers, divas, and the divine.

Vegetable Fruits

They Could Have Lived like Nobles

In Lucca, in the back corner of the Church of San Michele, behind the table of promotional literature and to the left of the statue of St. Teresa, there is a large marble plaque inscribed with this dictum: "Blessed is he who works; let him ask no other blessing than to forever be surrounded with the unbridled joy of his labors." Seeing it through the burnt-sienna glow of the overhead chandelier, one can't help but be impressed with its earnest simplicity—with the fact that every letter was obviously chiselled with care and intent. And yet, at the same time and in the same moment, I can't help but chortle, knowing as I do how thoroughly Tuscans disagree with the very innards of that sentiment.

For those who envision Tuscans largely as whistle-while-working kind of people, let me be somewhat more precise: work is *never* an opportunity for "unbridled joy" where Tuscans are concerned. In fact, one might almost say that the passion and playfulness they exhibit in their off hours vanishes completely when the situation changes to one involving work. *"Accidenti a Eva,"* goes the local grouse. *"Se non fosse per lei, si sarebbo tutti in pensione durevole."* Damn Eve; but for her, we would all be in permanent retirement.

This lack of occupational fervor comes into view most clearly when my Tuscan friends and relatives journey to New York on holiday, especially if they spend time at my apartment. I live in Soho, you see, and in Soho few topics of conversation generate more enthusiasm than the passion for one's work. Let me add, as an aside but also by way of amplification, that most of the area's residents are artists of one kind or another, so that the work in question is more a matter of either *trying* to get work or *dreaming* about getting work than any actual work. Since nothing generates passion more than the quest for a dream, however, it makes perfect sense that Soho-ites would talk about their work with a feverishness approaching the fanatic. But not to Tuscans.

"Siete sempre a parlare di lavoro"—you are always talking about work—my friend Erico from Lucca chastised me after yet another Soho dinner party which started casually with a simple conversational exchange: two people discussing their discovery of Amazon.com, a bookstore located on the Internet. But before we had even reached the main course, everyone was passionately cerebrating over the pros and cons of using cyberspace as a vehicle for self-promotion. By evening's end, poor Erico had been reduced to washing the dishes as a means of keeping himself from falling asleep.

Which brings me to the story of my Tuscan cousins, Alfredo and Morena Bicicchi, who, eight years ago, sold a chain of successful coffee bars and retired while still in their early forties. Six months later, while driving through the countryside in search of chestnuts, they spotted the crumbling remains of a tiny stone house last used as a shelter for grazing sheep. Located at the summit of a hillside blanketed with hundreds of severely neglected olive trees, the house had neither running water nor electricity. But it looked out over a spectacular valley beyond which one could see the Tyrrhenian Sea and, on very clear days, the Gorgone Islands.

"Non c'era altro da fare," says Alfredo. *"S'e' capito subito che, propio, dovevamo comprarla."* There was nothing else to do. We knew immediately that we just had to have it.

As I have surely mentioned elsewhere, building permits are impossibly hard to come by in Tuscany. But Alfredo and Morena persevered and, in the process, traded a life that was the envy of all their friends for one filled with jackhammers, plumb lines, scaffolding, and mason's trowels. They did all the work themselves, this despite the fact that they had never previously wielded anything more work-intensive than a calculator.

Moreover, between waiting for each series of permits (sometimes for years), they worked on the olive trees, cutting dead specimens, restructuring the hillside terraces, pruning dead limbs, and spreading fertilizer. It took six years to fully rejuvenate the grove, but at the end of that time, every tree was once again producing barrels of fat, purple olives. Which is when they got the Big Idea that—depending on who tells the story—either infused their life with purpose or ruined it.

Alfredo and Morena have gone into the business of making olive oil. From spreading the nets to gathering up the olives to separating the fruit from the leaves to hauling the fruit to the press to designing the labels and affixing them to the bottles, their lives now almost completely revolve around the production of an end product considered by Tuscans to be liquid gold. As Morena tells the story, every facet of the process fills them with patent ecstasy. Even when the *tramontana* threatens to stage an early appearance and decimate the orchard with its hurricane-like winds. Even when she and Alfredo are forced into spending 12-hour days on bended knee scooping the olives by hand because animals chewed holes into the nets and the olives all fell through. Even when they wake up in the morning with the standard aches and pains of those who are almost fifty.

"Siamo matti," says Alfredo, throwing his hands into the air and grinning conspiratorially at his wife. We are crazy.

She grins back. "The truth is, we have never been happier. But we knew from the start that that would be the case. What we didn't know was that, in the process, we would lose all our friends."

Her story carries a minimum of resentment. They-must-not-really-have-been-friends-in-the-first-place and other such rationales.

But the underlying truth is very clear: Morena is hurt that her friends opted out of the relationship because she and Alfredo were no longer "familiar."

"As long as we were all living the same kinds of lives, everything was fine," she says. "But then Alfredo and I made a change that was alien to their experience and it simply became easier for them to forego the friendship than stretch to encompass our new reality."

Her words do not come as a great surprise. Let's face it, for all intents and purposes and in spite of Tuscany's reputation for being "different" from the rest of Italy, Tuscans lead fairly uniform lives and demonstrate little enthusiasm for making any great lifestyle changes. Their families all live close by (if not in the same house), they eat formal meals at formally set tables with all family members in attendance, they take holidays each year in August, and they generally try to do as little work as possible so that there is plenty of time for evening *passeggiate*, visits with friends, and Sunday outings.

Alfredo and Morena strike out on all counts. Their house is now in a remote area on top of a hill that is very difficult to climb unless one has 4-wheel drive. They eat random meals in random fashion and often while pruning the trees. They have not taken a holiday in eight years because they are either busy working on the house or busy tending to the olives. And they have no time for anything, much less an evening stroll around the piazza.

"But it is not just that we scare people because our lives are so different from theirs," Morena says, "it is also that people look down on us for having made what they consider a shockingly bad choice." She brushes back her hair and struggles to synthesize what is obviously a complicated sentiment. "It really happened in two stages. At first, there was distance because our friends reacted in that jealous way that Tuscans have. . . . "

"A genetic legacy," teases Alfredo. "The Florentines and the Lucchese even fought over who made the best *ragu*."

"They would call us and fish for details about how much money we'd made," Morena continues. "But, underneath it all, we knew they, at least, were paying us a compliment. In their eyes, what we had done was good, even if we thought there was something wrong with their definition of 'good.'"

Alfredo takes over. "When we bought the land and came to live here, however, everything changed. Overnight we went from being *birbanti* [sly rogues] to *cretini*. And the amazing thing was, it didn't matter that we were clearly ecstatic.

"Tuscans are very rigid in their idea of what constitutes happiness," he continues. "Class is crucial, although, like you *Americani*, we too are starting to view it as more a question of money than of ancestry." He shakes his head in obvious disagreement with that trend. "Nevertheless, if Tuscans have status and/or money, they demonstrate it in a way that is largely fixed—by dressing well, driving an expensive car, living in a noticeably expensive house, eating at all the right restaurants, and never *ever* engaging in any form of manual labor. Well . . . ," he spreads his arms to take in their tiny, hilltop house and slightly dilapidated pickup, "by those standards, we must be absolute *miserabili*. After all, we love work!"

His eyes stray to the front door of the house. "*Ciao, Mamma*," he cries, greeting his mother who has just walked out onto the terrace bearing a large platter covered with a white linen towel. We—she and I and twelve other family members—have journeyed today to this mountaintop aerie to celebrate the annual harvesting of the olives. All of us have worked at least half a day for the past week picking olives in the final crunch. Now that it is over, we will feast from just after the sun goes down until the early hours of tomorrow morning on a magnificent assortment of dishes, all featuring newly pressed extra-virgin oil as the main ingredient. The first course consists of pizzas and *focaccias* cooked in the outdoor pizza oven.

The oven is another of Alfredo and Morena's building projects, completed just this past summer. With a large convex dome made of mineral-rich *cotto,* the oven is heated with olive branches placed in a knee-high concrete compartment. When the ceramic floor is hot enough (as measured by the sacrificial *focaccia* now being placed on its surface) the individual pizzas will be inserted using a long-handled wooden peel—side by side, four at a time—and cooked until the dough begins to bubble. Toppings range from the simple—tomatoes, anchovies, and fresh bufala mozzarella—to the intricate—prosciutto, capers, roasted peppers, marinated mushrooms, and quartered artichoke hearts—to the sophisticated—shrimp, scallops, mussels, *mascarpone,* and leeks.

My aunt Tina has been asked to bestow that final drizzle of oil that will elevate the flavor of these pizzas from the spectacular to the sublime. The job had initially been mine, but I was judged, in advance of my having done even one pizza, to be too light of hand. Truth be told, if I had to single out just one factor that makes Tuscan cooking better than any of its competitors, I would pinpoint the liberal use of *olio extra virgine.*

Having surrendered the oil can, I move towards Alfredo who is now serving Bellinis on the terrace. As I pass behind Tina, I overhear her talking to Signora Nilda, Morena's mother. *"Potevano fare quello che volevano,"* she is saying, her voice heavy with disappointment. They could have done whatever they wanted. The Signora, who is the same age as Tina and lives around the corner from her in Piano di Mommio, obviously agrees. *"Che sciupio,"* she laments in return. *"Potevano essere signori,"*—essentially, they could have lived like nobles.

I'm not sure about Signora Nilda; my aunt, on the other hand, misses no opportunity to lament over her children and their families. In fact, her laments not only pour forth whenever anyone mentions either Alfredo or Morena's name, but cover a territory so vast as to leave no room for remediation.

Alfredo is the oldest of Tina's four sons and, therefore, the one on which she had pinned her most grandiose hopes. Until eight years ago, he had not disappointed her, marrying well, producing a bright and beautiful daughter, emerging as a successful businessman, and making daily trips to his mother's house for a bowl of noonday pasta. But that was then, and this is now, and what I've come to realize is that it does no good to lecture my aunt—to either suggest she is forcing her lifestyle choices on him or to hint that the problem may be less his and more hers. Like all Tuscan women of a certain age and class, she is immune to psychological arguments.

Pizzas consumed, sixteen of us greet the setting of the sun by gathering around a beautifully set table whose center sports an enormous white porcelain soup terrine. The first "real" course is, naturally, the traditional *zuppa alla frantoiana* (olive harvest soup) which contains over a dozen autumn vegetables including fresh *borlotti* beans. Thick enough to eat with a fork, the *zuppa* has been cooking over a low flame since early morning. Morena uses the age-old technique of placing the pot over two thick bricks which, in turn, are placed directly on the burner; the job of the bricks is to keep the heat evenly distributed.

Before eating, we cover the soup with a hefty dollop of newly pressed oil, pouring from a large stone pitcher that has been in Morena's family for 100 years and always used for exactly this purpose. Traditionally, people celebrating an olive harvest did so right in the *frantoio*, the olive-pressing room. When I was young, every estate had their own press; hence the celebrations were strictly family affairs. After the oil had been tested for flavor, body, and acidity, 30 or 40 family members would gather at long wooden tables to eat, drink, and breathe in the heady aroma of newly pressed oil.

Nowadays, one *frantoio* services two or three villages, the residents being granted appointments based on how many olives they have. Those with the largest numbers receive the best time slots; the rest, Alfredo and Morena included, have to make do with middle-of-the-night appointments. "But that's the best time to go," argues Alfredo when he overhears his mother carping about the 3:00 A.M. appointment they received. "Morena and I pack a basket with bread and *biroldo* (blood sausage) and a bottle or two of *spumante* (sparkling wine) and spend a wonderful two or three hours celebrating the end of another year's work."

"Different from everybody else, these two," his mother responds, passing the pitcher of thick, new oil. "Everybody else complains about having to go at 3:00 A.M.; these two *snaturati* have the wonderful gift of turning everything in their lives into a *festa*. True, they could have lived like nobles, but how can you fault two people who are so happy?"

As the evening progresses and the courses move from *tagliatelle con funghi porcini*—broad noodles with *porcini* mushrooms—to *branzino alla griglia con peperonata*—grilled sea bass with roasted red pepper salad—to *arista di maiale con purea di finocchio e castagne*—oven-roasted pork loin with pureed fennel and chestnuts— to salad and numerous *dolci* and coffee and liqueurs, I am made more and more aware not only of how different Alfredo and Morena are from everyone else at the table, but of how often the topic of their difference surfaces in general conversation. In fact, the conversation seems almost dominated by differences of one sort or another.

"What do you think of Miss Italia?" asks my cousin Iliano between pasta courses. His question revives a topic that has, this past week, captivated Italians everywhere: the crowning of Deny Mendez, a black woman originally from Santo Domingo, as this year's Miss Italia. She entered the contest as a representative from Tuscany where she has lived for the past four years (in Italy, four years are enough to constitute citizenship). For days prior to the event, news stations had hinted at the possibility of her victory, a circumstance that later fueled suspicions as to whether the selection process had been tainted in order to make a statement.

Not that anyone thought Deny was lacking in either beauty or talent. Quite the contrary. "She was clearly the most glamorous of the finalists," said Bob Freger, an Italian journalist opining on Raiuno's TG1. His sentiment was widely echoed, many interviewees taking the occasion to also declare that they were neither *rassisti*—racists—nor opposed to "a different kind of woman" representing Italy. The headlines in Italy's three major papers—*La Stampa, La Nazione* and *Il Corriere Della Sera*—all trumpeted a variation on the same theme: Italy Has Taken a Step Forward.

But there was also an undercurrent of concern. "What does it mean to be Italian?" asked an article in *Epoca*, a weekly news magazine. "Gone are the days when everyone descended from peoples who had always lived in Italy. Today, Italy— like every other nation in the western world—has a resident population representing many countries: Tunisia, Morocco, Senegal, Eritrea, the Cape Verde Islands, China, the Philippines. These people have learned our language and are, in most cases, legal citizens. But are they Italians?"

"It is a good question," says Iliano when I tell him about *Epoca*'s article. "Just because they are citizens does not mean they're Italians. 'Italian' connotes heritage, not merely residence."

"So are you saying that Deny Mendez should not have been selected?"

"In one sense, yes, that is what I am saying."

He hastens to explain. "It is not that we must always choose a woman of Italian heritage. Just that we are not yet ready to define ourselves by our differences."

I hold back from sarcastic comments about how patrician timetables always seem to vary from those envisioned by the masses. "Who is this 'we'?" I ask. "Obviously, a great number of people were, in fact, ready. That's why Deny won, no?"

"No. She won because Italy decided to placate its foreigners with an insignificant token of acceptance. The Italian government is not stupid. They see the problems experienced by France and Great Britain with respect to their Third World populations. This is our way of avoiding conflict."

His words cause me to stop and think, particularly in light of the "Extracommunitarian Festival" he and I and Alfredo and Morena attended together last week. "Extracommunitarian" is Italy's official name for Third World immigrants, the majority of whom make their living selling tissues, cigarette lighters, or cheap beaded necklaces. *"Vu compra?"* they say whenever they catch you looking in their direction. Want to buy? Consequently, they're referred to as *vu compras* by both those who would use the term in a derogatory manner and those who merely repeat what they have heard.

The Extracommunitarian Festival took place in Piano di Mommio's central piazza and featured music, crafts, and a photographic exhibition entitled "From Macaroni to *Vu Compra*: A Historical Look at Those Who Left Italy and Those Who Have Come." It was sponsored by the local church whose pastor, Don Michele, has often been known to sermonize about "the need to embrace diversity."

"Our people have always embraced diversity," I heard him joking to a local reporter. "Just look at the way they switch political alliances—from communist one day to Forza Italia (the right-wing party led by Silvio Berlusconi) the next."

Iliano's friend, Sergio, provided the music for the festival. When we arrived a Paraguayan band was doing a wonderful rendition of *"Oye Como Va."* At one point, a woman complained that she couldn't understand any of the words. *"Che razza di musica é questa?"* she asked Sergio. *"Almeno se ogni tanto sonassero un valzerino."* What kind of music is this? At least, every so often, they could play a little waltz.

There were also supposed to be two other bands, Sergio told us, one Senegalese and one from the Cape Verde Islands.

"They went instead to play in Lucca," he explained after the Paraguayans had played for over an hour. "It's the third day of Lucca's annual *Santa Croce* celebration, an event that draws thousands. Obviously, there is more money to be made there than here." He heaved a sigh of exasperation. "But they had told me they would play!"

His lament was overheard by Mario, the village grocer, who edged his way through a group of dancing teenagers to join our circle. I had seen him earlier, clapping his hands and swaying in time to the music. "What can you expect," he said by way of comfort. "These people just don't have that same sense of *integrita*." It was the very tone he might use to describe thieves robbing his store.

I had wanted to say something; all of us had wanted to say something. But instead we just slowly edged away. "The problem," Iliano later concluded, "is that if you brought to his attention the racism implicit in that statement, he would vehemently deny it. To him, it's a fact, and facts are above labels."

My attention is hauled back to the moment by the sight of Morena about to serve the first *secondo*: the grilled sea bass. "*Dai*," she says, noting that I had hardly touched my pasta. "*O mangi, o vai a casa.*" Either you eat, or you go home.

"But I'm full," I tell her, pleading my case.

"You can't be full. We haven't even started eating."

"And what if I am?"

"Then I told you," she says, laughing, "you go home."

"You mean there's no room at this table for someone who is different?"

She thrusts her hands onto her hips and breaks into a wide grin. "Not here," she says sarcastically. "Here we all march in absolute lockstep."

About Vegetable Fruits

The very mention of the word "tomato" conjures up images of sunshine and warmth and bounty. And, in fact, tomatoes serve as a harbinger of just those very things as well as of long afternoon lunches at outdoor tables spread with crusty *bruschettas* and achingly fresh salads. Likewise for the tomato's cousins: eggplant, peppers, cucumbers, and squash. Who can even *think* of ripe red peppers without feeling their nose begin to tan?

In botanical terms, tomatoes, eggplants, and peppers are fruits. Cucumbers, on the other hand, are squashes which, in turn, are gourds. Chestnuts are, of course, nuts, but since they are used by Tuscans largely as a vegetable, I have stretched the definition of "fruits" to include the fruits of trees.

Chestnuts *Castagne*

There are several different kinds of chestnuts *(Castanea)*, at least three of which have edible fruits. These members of the oak family are very important to Tuscans, who use them as a vegetable as well as in the form of ground flour from which they make cakes, bread, polenta, and crepes.

Season: October through January

To Buy: Chestnuts should be firm, smooth, full, shiny, and vividly brown.

To Prepare: Make a cross on the flat side of each nut with a sharp knife. Roast, boil, or bake until flesh is tender. To peel, parboil for 10 minutes, remove inner and outer skin.

Zucca.

Cucumbers *Cetrioli*

Generally thought of as a "raw" food to be included in salads, cucumbers *(Cucumis sativus)* are one of the very oldest vegetables. They are mentioned in the Old Testament and were cultivated in China over 3,000 years ago. Tuscans use these prized cucurbits in everything from risotto to a mixed vegetable braise.

Season: June through September

To Buy: The best cucumbers are firm, crisp, vividly green, and well-shaped. Yellow coloring means the vegetable is overmature.

To Prepare: Wash, trim ends, and peel if the skin is tough or waxed.

Eggplant *Melanzane*

A member of the nightshade family *(Solanum melongina)*, eggplant is part of a varied household whose members include cherished relatives (tomatoes and potatoes) as well as deadly ones (belladonna and tobacco). Tuscan eggplants are smaller, thinner, and sweeter—like the Asian varieties—than our roundish bulbous types. In this country, many types are now readily available: pale green striped, bright orange, lavender and white, pure white, and elongated green. In general, smaller versions are sweeter and have fewer seeds, making them an ideal choice for grilling, sautéeing, or broiling. Larger ones are good choices for roasting, stuffing, or baking.

Season: July through October

To Buy: Whether you buy the large or small variety, select only spherically shaped globes, heavy for their size (light eggplants indicates pulpy or immature flesh), with firm, taut exteriors and no blemishes or soft spots.

To Prepare: Trim off stem end. Peel if skin is tough, cut just before use, and immediately dip in lemon water. Larger eggplants should be salted and placed in a colander for an hour to release bitterness. Rinse and drain before using.

Peppers *Peperoni*

Peppers are generally divided into two rather vague categories: sweet and hot. Both are members of the nightshade family *(Capsicum annuum)* and come in a variety of ever-expanding colors. Green peppers are merely unripe peppers; given time, all green peppers mature into yellow, red, or orange. Brown or purple peppers mature into dark red, and whites into ivory.

Season: Summer

To Buy: Select only well-shaped peppers with shiny coats and fresh-looking stems. Avoid those with soft spots or shriveling.

To Prepare: Wash, cut in half lengthwise, and remove core, seeds, and white membranes. Or leave whole (as for stuffing) and cut out core from end. When handling hot peppers, use gloves or wash hands immediately afterwards.

Tomatoes *Pomodori*

The history of the tomato *(Lycopersicon esculentum)* is among the most fascinating of any vegetable's. Cultivated by Peruvian Indians long before the arrival of Columbus, it eventually made its way northward; our word "tomato" is, in fact, derived from the Aztec *"zitomate."* The fruit—for tomatoes are really fruits—reached Italy in the early 16th century, where they were long thought to be deadly poisonous. In this country, the first tomatoes came from Thomas Jefferson's garden.

Season: Summer

To Buy: Should be firm but not hard, with little or no green core. Should also be smooth, without bruises, blemishes, cracks, or discoloration. If underripe, let stand 2 to 3 days at room temperature. Never refrigerate.

To Prepare: For use with skins on, remove core. To peel, score the bottoms with a small "x" and plunge into boiling water for 5 to 15 seconds (do not listen to those who advocate 30 to 60 seconds; you'll wind up with mush). Cool immediately in ice water. Slip skins off and remove core. Even better than a water bath, which slightly dilutes the flavor, is to char the skins over an open burner. Stick the tomato on the tines of a fork and twist the fork quickly so that the flesh doesn't cook. Cool and strip away the skin.

Zucchini *Zucchini*

While there is much confusion about the names and origins of squashes in general, all belong to the cucurbit family and are variants of the common pumpkin. Zucchini (*Cucurbita pepo*) is also known as vegetable marrow, Italian squash, green squash, and *cocozelle*. Adopted by Italians as their own, zucchini is prized for both its flesh and its blossoms which are generally served either stuffed or sautéed.

Season: Summer

To Buy: Try to find the smallest, youngest specimens possible. When only 3 or 4 inches in length, zucchini have a delicate, almost ambrosial flavor. They should be firm, heavy for their size, and crisp.

To Prepare: Young zucchini do not need peeling. Wash or scrub well and trim ends.

Quick and Easy

Chestnuts

Fresh chestnuts can be boiled, roasted (stovetop or oven), or grilled (place in aluminum foil packets) and consumed with *vin santo* or any other dessert wine. Chestnut meats can be combined with vegetable broth and baked until soft, then blended with bechamel and served as a side dish. Dried chestnuts can be boiled until soft, puréed, and plated with sautéed greens.

Cucumbers

Apart from the traditional salads and sandwiches, cucumbers are very good cut into 1-inch-thick slices, steamed, and topped with olive oil and a heavy dusting of black pepper. One easy Tuscan method of preparation is to stuff the halves with a parsley, bread crumb, garlic, and Parmesan filling and broil for 10 minutes. They are also good on the grill, cut into thick slices and brushed with oil.

Eggplants

Baby eggplants can be steamed whole and eaten with a drizzle of lemon. Older ones can be baked and the flesh mashed with garlic, parsley, lemon, and oil to make a spread. Brush thick slices with olive oil and grill over an open flame.

Grilled slices can also form the "bread" for a tomato sandwich. Cubed and sautéed, eggplant makes a wonderful topping for pizza or pasta—just add garlic, olive oil, and salt.

Peppers

Roasted peppers are everybody's favorite. For directions on roasting, see page 218. For a wonderful sandwich, layer strips of roasted pepper with buffalo mozzarella and slather with basil mayonnaise. To preserve roasted peppers, pack them in olive oil with a little vinegar; properly sealed, they will last for up to two months. Fresh peppers, julienned, make a wonderfully colorful salad when combined with carrot curls and radicchio leaves. Alternated with cherry tomatoes and vinaigrette-soaked bread cubes, they can be threaded onto skewers and grilled.

Tomatoes

There are many Tuscans who feel that, short of eating tomatoes directly off the vine, there is no better preparation than to line a platter with slices of tomato alternating with slices of fresh bufala mozzarella, sprinkle with basil chiffonade, and drizzle with oil and balsamic vinegar. Of course, you also need lots of bread and wine. . . .

Tomatoes can also be chopped raw and added to cooked pasta with olive oil, a handful of chopped basil, some minced garlic, and fresh grated cheese.

Sun-dried tomatoes can be turned into a luscious appetizer by boiling them until soft and packing them in olive oil with some garlic and fresh rosemary. Refrigerated, they will keep this way for months.

To make cold tomato soup, place in a blender with cucumbers, a chili pepper, and vegetable broth. Pour the puréed soup into a bowl and top with chopped onions.

Zucchini

Cut into thin strips and sauté in garlic and olive oil. Or sauté with eggplant, garlic, and tomatoes and use as a topping for pasta, pizza, or polenta. Baby zucchini are excellent simply sprinkled with oil and cheese and roasted for 20 minutes. Larger ones can be cut into 1-inch-thick slices, basted with olive oil and lemon thyme, and grilled.

Pomodori Saltati con Gremolata
Sautéed Tomatoes with Lemon Gremolata

In my family, this is a very popular picnic dish. For one thing, it almost begs to be eaten outdoors; for another, it is quick and simple to make and works well hot, lukewarm, or even chilled. Regardless of which of those temperatures you choose, add the gremolata *just before serving to preserve the very freshest flavor, and don't even think of using out-of-season tomatoes.* Per l'amor di Dio!

The Tomatoes

2 tablespoons extra-virgin olive oil
4 very ripe medium tomatoes, peeled and cut into wedges
1 tablespoon fresh lemon juice
Salt and freshly ground black pepper
16 wedges rosemary *focaccia*, lightly toasted
10–15 nasturtium flowers

The Gremolata

3 tablespoons finely minced fresh parsley
1 tablespoon finely minced fresh mint
1 clove garlic, finely minced
3 tablespoons crushed walnuts
⅛ teaspoon salt
1 teaspoon lemon zest

1. To prepare the tomatoes, heat the olive oil in a large skillet. Sauté the tomatoes over medium heat for approximately 2 minutes per side. Add the lemon juice, salt, and pepper, toss to blend, and transfer to a serving platter. Surround the tomatoes with the *focaccia* wedges and scatter the nasturtium flowers around the perimeter.

2. For the *gremolata,* place all the ingredients in a small bowl and mix well. Sprinkle over the tomatoes just before serving.

SERVES 4   TIME: 20 minutes   LEVEL OF DIFFICULTY: Easy

VARIATIONS: Polenta wedges or garlic-rubbed bread slices can be substituted for the *focaccia.* The entire recipe can also be used as a topping for pasta or grilled pizza.

MAKE AHEAD: The *gremolata* can be made 8 hours before serving and refrigerated.

Bastoncini di Melanzana al Balsamico
Roasted Eggplant Batons with Balsamic Sauce

This is a dish from my childhood, although, at that time, the eggplant batons were fried in olive oil instead of broiled. I remember loving the crispy texture but wishing that the flavor of the eggplants were more noticeable. The following recipe is my solution to that dilemma as well as another excuse for using balsamic vinegar.

The Batons

3 small, thin eggplants, about ½ pound each, stems removed
¾ cup unflavored bread crumbs
½ cup freshly grated Parmigiano-Reggiano
⅛ teaspoon dried crumbled sage
½ teaspoon freshly ground black pepper
¾ cup unbleached flour
2 eggs, lightly beaten

The Sauce

3 tablespoons extra-virgin olive oil
1 tablespoon balsamic vinegar
1 tablespoon fresh chopped parsley
1 clove garlic, crushed
⅛ teaspoon salt
½ pound arugula, cleaned and stems removed for garnish

1. Preheat the broiler. Cut each eggplant into ½-inch-thick slices. Cut each slice into ½-inch sticks. Place the bread crumbs in a bowl with the cheese, sage, and black pepper. Stir to mix. Place the flour and the eggs in separate bowls.

2. Dip each eggplant stick first into the flour, shaking off any excess, then into the eggs, and, finally, into the bread crumbs. Place on a greased baking sheet and broil about 4 inches from the heat, for 5 minutes. Turn and broil 2 minutes longer or until golden.

3. Meanwhile, place all the sauce ingredients in a small, nonreactive saucepan and cook over low heat for 5 minutes, stirring constantly until thickened. Remove from heat and cool to room temperature.

4. Place the sauce in a serving bowl and center on a platter. Surround with arugula, cover with eggplant batons arranged in a star pattern, and serve.

SERVES 4   TIME: 45–60 minutes   LEVEL OF DIFFICULTY: Moderate

MAKE AHEAD: The batons can be breaded 4 hours in advance and refrigerated. In fact, it is usually better to let breaded foods dry for an hour or so before cooking. They brown up better and the breading adheres well.

Fiori di Zucca Ripieni
Stuffed Zucchini Blossoms

This is as beautiful a dish as it is delectable. It requires your finding very young zucchini with blossoms still attached, a task made increasingly easier by the proliferation of farmers markets. The blossoms are stuffed and the entire zucchini braised in a light sauce made from stock and beer. Wonderful as an appetizer or as a first course in place of pasta.

12 baby zucchini, no longer than 3–4 inches and with blossoms attached
3 tablespoons Basic Vegetable Broth (see page 308)
2 tablespoons amber beer
2 tablespoons extra-virgin olive oil
1 clove garlic, minced

3 tablespoons finely minced shallots
½ cup unflavored fresh bread crumbs
2 tablespoons freshly grated Parmigiano-Reggiano
Salt and freshly ground black pepper
Sprigs of fresh rosemary

1. Clean and dry the zucchini. Cut each zucchini off 3 inches below the flower. Shave the remaining part so that the end farthest from the flower is narrower, like a carrot. Leave a collar of green at the flower end. Place the trimmings in a saucepan with the broth and beer and simmer for 10 minutes over medium heat. Strain and reserve the liquid. Mince the trimmings.

2. Meanwhile, heat the oil in a skillet. Sauté the garlic and shallots over low heat for 5 minutes until soft. Increase the heat to high, add the minced zucchini trimmings, and sauté for 5 minutes, stirring constantly. Remove from heat, add the bread crumbs, cheese, salt, and pepper and mix well.

3. Divide the stuffing into 12 portions. Slit each flower blossom on one side and insert the stuffing with a spoon. Fold the flower around it.

4. Place the zucchini in a skillet in one layer. Pour the reserved liquid over and cook for 5 minutes over medium heat. Transfer the zucchini to a heated platter.

5. Boil the juices until syrupy. Pour over the zucchini and serve garnished with the rosemary sprigs.

SERVES 4   TIME: 45–60 minutes   LEVEL OF DIFFICULTY: Easy

MAKE AHEAD: The zucchini can be stuffed 6 hours in advance and refrigerated until braising time.

Peperonata Cruda con Lenticchie Verde
Roasted Red and Gold Peppers with Green Lentils

The traditional peperonata *consists of roasted peppers sautéed with onions and garlic and served either as a side dish or as a topping for pasta. The following version is my variation on that theme: roasted peppers tossed with an anchovy-caper sauce and served on a bed of savory green lentils. Make sure to provide plenty of crusty bread.*

The Lentils

½ pound small green (French) lentils, picked over, rinsed, and soaked for 2 hours
1 medium onion, peeled and halved
1 medium carrot, scraped and cut into thirds
½ teaspoon salt
4 cups Basic Vegetable Broth (see page 308)

The Peppers

3 large red peppers
3 large yellow peppers
4 anchovy fillets, drained and minced
3 tablespoons basil chiffonade*
2 tablespoons capers, drained, rinsed, and drained again
1 garlic clove, minced
¼ cup extra-virgin olive oil
1 tablespoon good quality red wine vinegar (or use balsamic)
Salt and freshly ground black pepper

1. Drain the lentils and place them in a heavy-gauge pot with the onion, carrot, salt, and broth. Cover and bring to a boil. Reduce heat to low and simmer for 30–40 minutes or until tender. Remove the carrot and onion and discard. Cool to room temperature.

2. Meanwhile, roast the peppers. Hold each over an open flame, using tongs, and turn until blackened on all sides. Place in a paper or plastic bag for 15 minutes. Remove from the bag, pull out the cores, seeds, and inner fibers. Rub off the black-

Alfredo and Morena Bicicchi: "Siamo matti!" We are crazy.

ened skin and cut into slivers. Place in a large bowl. Add the remainder of the ingredients to the bowl and toss to blend.

3. Arrange the lentils on a serving platter. Top with the roasted peppers, spooning any sauce remaining in the bowl over the lentils, and serve.

SERVES 4   TIME: 60 minutes   LEVEL OF DIFFICULTY: Moderate

VARIATIONS: The roasted peppers can also be used as a pasta or pizza topping or added to a salad made of greens.

MAKE AHEAD: The lentils and the pepper mixture can be made 1 day in advance and refrigerated. For maximum flavor, return to room temperature before serving.

*To make basil chiffonade, place 5 or 6 basil leaves on top of one another and then roll from the long end into a tight cylinder. Using a sharp knife, cut the cylinder into thin slivers.

Gnocchetti di Zucca Gialla
Yellow Squash Gnocchi
with Smoked Tomato Sauce

Having recently discovered gnocchi, Americans tend to think of them as simply potato dump-lings or, at best, potato dumplings with spinach added. To Tuscans, however, gnocchi are as ver-satile as pasta and can be made with an infinite number of ingredients. The following version uses baby yellow squash as the main ingredient in a hearty dish of thimble-sized gnocchetti topped with a sauce made of tomatoes smoked on an outdoor barbecue.

The Sauce

2 pounds Italian plum tomatoes
   (Roma)
2 tablespoons extra-virgin olive oil
2 cloves garlic, minced
3 leaves fresh basil
Salt and freshly ground black
   pepper

The Gnocchi

¼ pound new red potatoes, peeled
½ pound baby yellow squash
½ cup unbleached flour
Freshly grated Parmigiano-Reggiano

1. To smoke the tomatoes, make a fire and burn until the coals have turned completely to white ash. Toss in a handful of wet wood chips (hickory work nicely) and set an oiled grill over the coals. Place the tomatoes on the grill, cover, and cook for 30–45 minutes. When done, the tomatoes will be slightly shriveled and beginning to crack. Remove them and pass through a food mill. Season with salt and pepper.

2. Heat the oil in a skillet and sauté the garlic for 5 minutes over low heat. Add the tomatoes and basil and cook for 15–20 minutes, stirring frequently.

3. Meanwhile, make the *gnocchi*. Boil the potatoes in salted water until very soft. Boil the squash separately until it, too, is soft. Pass them together through a food mill.

4. Put the flour in a heap on a pastry board and add the potato and squash mash. Knead thoroughly until the mixture is well blended, smooth, soft, and elastic.

5. Roll the mixture into strips about ¾ of an inch in diameter. Cut into pieces ¾-inch long. Press your thumb into the middle of each piece.

6. Drop them into a generous amount of salted boiling water and stir gently with a wooden spoon. Cook for about 3 minutes, during which time they will rise to the surface. Remove with a slotted spoon and add to the sauce. Lightly sauté for 1 minute, tossing gently, and serve hot, sprinkled with cheese.

SERVES 4   TIME: 75–90 minutes   LEVEL OF DIFFICULTY: Advanced

VARIATIONS: Simple tomato sauce can be used in place of smoked. The tomatoes can also be smoked on an indoor wok. Place them on a rack over a bed of rice kernels mixed with black tea. Seal the wok with foil and place over low heat for approximately 45 minutes.

MAKE AHEAD: The smoked tomatoes can be frozen or canned in advance. The *gnocchi* can be frozen for up to 1 week before serving.

Melanzana Ripiena
Eggplant Boats Stuffed with Gorgonzola Polenta

I thought I had tasted just about every variation of stuffed eggplant there was to taste. And then I was invited for dinner at my friend's house and she served the most inventive, the most savory, the most wonderful stuffed eggplant I have ever eaten. Here it is, courtesy of Adriana da Prato.

2 eggplants (about ¾ pounds each)	¼ pound Kalamata olives, pitted and finely chopped
Salt and freshly ground black pepper	¼ pound Gorgonzola cheese
6 tablespoons extra-virgin olive oil	1 medium onion, minced
4 cups Basic Vegetable Broth (see page 308)	1 tablespoon fresh chopped lemon thyme (or combine regular thyme with lemon zest)
1 cup coarse-grind polenta	

1. Preheat the oven to 400 degrees. Cut the tips from the eggplants, wash, and slice in half lengthwise. Make little crosscuts in the pulp, sprinkle with salt and pepper, and drizzle with 2 tablespoons of the oil. Place on a baking sheet, cut side up, and roast for 20 minutes.

2. Meanwhile, heat 3 cups of the broth to boiling in a large saucepan. Reduce the heat to low and add the polenta in a steady stream, whisking constantly

until thickened. Cook for 25 minutes, stirring frequently and adding additional broth if necessary. The finished polenta will have a thick, creamy consistency.

3. Rinse a 14 × 16-inch metal pan with cold water. Shake off the excess water but do not dry. Stir the olives and cheese into the polenta and pour into the pan. Cool to room temperature.

4. Remove the eggplants from the oven and carefully scoop out the pulp, leaving about ¼ inch of pulp around the edges. Chop finely. Heat 2 tablespoons oil in a skillet and sauté the onion over low heat for 5 minutes or until soft. Add the eggplant pulp and sauté for another 5 minutes, stirring constantly.

5. Using your hands, crumble the cooled polenta into the eggplant mixture and mix well.

6. Fill the eggplant boats with the polenta and eggplant. Place in an ovenproof pan. Drizzle the boats with the remaining oil, sprinkle with lemon thyme, and bake in a 450-degree oven for approximately 20 minutes. Serve at room temperature.

SERVES 4   TIME: 90 minutes   LEVEL OF DIFFICULTY: Moderate

VARIATIONS: For a creamier filling, add ¼ cup cream at the end of Step 5.

MAKE AHEAD: The polenta can be made up to 1 day in advance and refrigerated. Bring to room temperature before assembling the eggplant boats.

Pasta con Burro Rosso
Pasta with Red Butter

Every so often I come across a recipe technique so simple and delicious that I wonder why I never thought of it before. Red butter is one of those—a quick and elegant solution to what to serve for dinner when you have very little time but still want a certain complexity of flavors.

4 red peppers, seeded and coarsely chopped
4 tablespoons unsalted butter, softened
½ cup heavy cream
¼ cup Basic Vegetable Broth (see page 308)

Salt and freshly ground white pepper
1 pound dried linguine
¼ cup freshly grated Parmigiano-Reggiano

1. Put the peppers in a food processor with the butter, cream, and broth. Purée until smooth. Season with salt and pepper.

2. Cook the pasta in a large quantity of boiling salted water. Drain and place in a bowl. Toss with the butter sauce and cheese and serve.

SERVES 4   TIME: 20 minutes   LEVEL OF DIFFICULTY: Easy
VARIATIONS: Fresh pasta can be substituted for dried.

Timballo di Melanzana
Eggplant Timballo

Timballi are old-fashioned festival pies whose ingredients include pasta, vegetables, cheese, and sometimes meat, all folded into a luscious pastry crust cooked to a perfect golden brown and sliced at the table. Recently popularized by the movie Big Night, *timballi were also featured in Luchino Visconti's 1963 movie* The Leopard, *when Burt Lancaster as the Prince made the ceremonial cut. According to Pellegrino Artusi, they originated in northern Italy where cooks "are generally skilled in making this costly and most complicated dish." The following recipe is my version—neither overly complicated nor as costly or laden with fat as the Big Night version.*

The Crust

3 cups unbleached flour
8 tablespoons unsalted butter at room temperature
2 large eggs
¼ teaspoon salt
½ cup dry white wine, cold
1 large egg white, lightly beaten (for brushing over pastry shell)

The Filling

1 large eggplant, peeled and cut into 1-inch cubes
⅓ cup extra-virgin olive oil

4 anchovy fillets, drained and finely chopped
3 garlic cloves, minced
3 tablespoons fresh chopped parsley
Salt and freshly ground black pepper
2 eggs, lightly beaten
2 cups cooked orzo
¾ cup freshly grated Parmigiano-Reggiano
Pickled baby vegetables for garnish

1. Place the flour and butter in a food processor and blend until crumbly. Add the eggs, salt, and wine and mix until the dough forms a smooth, elastic ball. Remove to a counter and divide in half. Wrap both halves in plastic and refrigerate for 1 hour.

2. Put the eggplant cubes in a colander, sprinkle with salt, cover with a weighted plate, and leave for about 30 minutes until the eggplant discharges its bitter juices. Pat dry with paper towels.

3. Heat the oil in a large skillet. Add the anchovies and garlic and cook over medium heat for 3 minutes. Add the eggplant and cook for 8–10 minutes, stirring frequently. Add the parsley, salt, and pepper and cook for an additional 1 minute. Transfer the mixture to a bowl and cool to room temperature.

4. Add the eggs, cooked orzo, and cheese to the eggplant and mix well.

5. Preheat the oven to 350 degrees. On a lightly floured surface, roll out half the dough to a 12-inch circle. Fit into a 10-inch springform pan. Fill with the eggplant mixture.

6. Roll the remaining dough into a 12-inch circle and place on top of the eggplant. Seal the edges and form into a rolled crust. Brush the top with the egg white and bake for 45 minutes or until the top is golden brown and a knife inserted into the middle comes out dry.

7. Cool for 30 minutes before serving. Garnish with pickled baby vegetables.

SERVES 6–8   TIME: 2 hours (not including cooling time)

LEVEL OF DIFFICULTY: Advanced

MAKE AHEAD: The dough can be made 1 day in advance, wrapped in plastic and refrigerated. The eggplant mixture can be made through Step 3 and refrigerated, up to 1 day in advance.

Pappa al Pomodoro con Battuto di Arugula
Tomato Bread Soup with Arugula Battuto

Like all Tuscans, I grew up eating tomato bread soup. Not only is it easy to make and a perfect use for sweet, late-season tomatoes, but it takes all your stale bread and converts it to a light, one-dish meal fit for royalty. Because I am a great fan of soups that have a final raw flavoring stirred into the broth, I have added an arugula battuto. *Make sure to use only very good bread whose texture is coarse enough to stand up to being cooked in broth—the older the better.*

VEGETABLE FRUITS

¼ cup extra-virgin olive oil

8 cloves garlic, thinly sliced

2½ pounds very ripe Roma tomatoes, peeled, seeded, and roughly chopped

½ pound stale country-style bread, ripped into rough chunks

5 cups Basic Vegetable Broth (see page 308)

Salt and freshly ground black pepper

½ pound arugula, stems removed and finely minced

10 leaves basil, finely minced

1 clove garlic, finely minced

⅛ teaspoon salt

1. Heat the oil in a large, heavy-gauge soup pot. Add the garlic and cook over medium heat for 1 minute. Add the tomatoes and bread and cook for 5–10 minutes or until the bread begins to fall apart.

2. Increase the heat to high. Add the broth, salt, and pepper and bring to a boil. Immediately reduce the heat to low and simmer for 10 minutes, stirring occasionally. Remove from heat and let sit for 5 minutes.

3. Meanwhile make the *battuto*. Place the arugula, basil, garlic, and salt in a small bowl. Mix well.

4. Pour the soup into individual bowls. Stir 1 tablespoon of *battuto* into each bowl and serve.

SERVES 4   TIME: 45 minutes

LEVEL OF DIFFICULTY: Easy

VARIATIONS: For additional flavor, drizzle an extra tablespoon oil over the soup before serving.

The Chestnut Museum at Colognora. Curator Roberto Fratti demonstrating how chestnut furniture was made 400 years ago.

Souflé di Castagne
Chestnut Soufflé

As Americans are only beginning to discover, chestnuts can be used in infinite ways—and that's not counting what can be done with chestnut flour. The following soufflé can be served as an appetizer or—because chestnuts are so intrinsically sweet—as a dessert. Of course, if you like chestnuts as much as I do, you might even pair it with a large salad of wild greens and serve it as an entrée.

1 pound chestnuts
⅛ teaspoon salt
2 tablespoons unsalted butter
2½ cups Basic Vegetable Broth (see
  page 308)

3 egg whites, beaten to stiff peaks
8 sprigs fresh rosemary, for garnish
8 thin slices lemon, for garnish

1. Place the chestnuts in a saucepan with enough water to cover. Boil for 5 minutes. Drain and peel, taking care to remove all the inner skin.

2. Place the peeled chestnuts in another saucepan, cover with water, and cook over medium heat until tender, approximately 30 minutes. Drain and force through a food mill.

3. Place the chestnut puree in a saucepan with the salt, butter, and broth. Cook over medium heat, stirring constantly, until the stock has been completely absorbed, about 10 minutes. Cool to room temperature.

4. Preheat the oven to 350 degrees. Gently fold the egg whites into the chestnuts. Pour into a greased soufflé bowl and bake for 30 minutes. Serve garnished with the lemon slices and rosemary sprigs.

SERVES 4   TIME: 90 minutes   LEVEL OF DIFFICULTY: Moderate
MAKE AHEAD: The chestnuts can be peeled and skinned 1 day in advance.

Cetrioli Fritti con Riso al Limone
Fried Cucumbers with Lemon Rice

Cucumbers are one of the most underused of vegetables in this country, restricted as they are to either being pickled or eaten raw as part of a salad. And yet, Tuscans use this tangy squash in mak-

ing everything from risotto to ravioli to the following dish, which makes a perfect appetizer when sprinkled with lemon thyme and served with little timbales of lemon-scented rice.

1½ cups short grain white rice
2 cups Basic Vegetable Broth (see page 308)
1 cup sorrel, roughly chopped
2 tablespoons fresh chopped lemon thyme
2 cucumbers, peeled and sliced into ¼-inch rounds

Salt and freshly ground black pepper
2 cloves garlic, finely minced
Unbleached flour for dredging
Olive oil for frying
Violets for garnish

1. Cook the rice in the broth for 20 minutes or until tender. Cool to room temperature.

2. Preheat the oven to 350 degrees. Puree the sorrel in a food processor. Add half the lemon thyme and fold the mixture into the rice. Place the rice in 4 greased timbale rings and bake for 25 minutes or until solid.

3. Meanwhile, place the cucumber slices in a colander, salt well, and let drain for 30 minutes. Rinse and pat dry.

4. Toss the slices with the garlic and a large amount of freshly ground black pepper. Dredge in flour and fry in ⅛ of an inch oil for about 3 minutes per side, making sure not to crowd the pan. Drain on paper towels.

5. To serve, place one rice timbale in the center of each plate. Surround with fried cucumber slices sprinkled with the remainder of the lemon thyme and garnish with the violets.

SERVES 4   TIME: 60 minutes
LEVEL OF DIFFICULTY: Moderate

One small section of Alfredo and Morena's olive orchard.

VARIATIONS: The cucumber can also be served without the rice on a bed of sorrel leaves.

MAKE AHEAD: The rice timbales can be made 6 hours in advance and reheated.

Zuppa di Peperoni Gialli
Golden Pepper Soup

Peppers are one of my favorite crops to grow. The plants are neat and compact, and until the peppers are large enough to topple the central stem, they require very little care save for heat and water. When I first started planting sweet peppers, my plot was fairly small and accommodated maybe 15 specimens. But then came the explosion of colored peppers—chocolate, white, orange, yellow—and I just had to have some of each. Now I devote 3 entire plots to the enterprise just so I can indulge myself and try every recipe that comes to mind.

3 tablespoons extra-virgin olive oil
1 medium onion, minced
2 cloves garlic, minced
4 golden peppers, seeded and
   coarsely chopped
Juice and zest of 1 orange
6 cups Basic Vegetable Broth (see
   page 308)

3 tablespoons dry sherry
Salt and freshly ground black
   pepper
4 ¾-inch-thick slices coarse
   country bread, stale
2 garlic cloves, halved
Sprigs of fresh rosemary for garnish

1. Heat the oil in a heavy saucepan. Add the onion and garlic and cook over low heat for 5–7 minutes or until translucent. Increase the heat to high. Add the peppers, juice, and zest and cook for 5 minutes, stirring frequently, until the peppers are soft.

2. Add the broth, reduce the heat to low, and simmer for 15–20 minutes. Puree the soup in a food mill and return to the pot. Add the sherry, salt, and pepper and heat until warm.

3. Meanwhile, toast the bread on both sides and rub with garlic. Place the bread in individual soup bowls, top with soup, garnish with the rosemary, and serve.

SERVES 4   TIME: 45–60 minutes   LEVEL OF DIFFICULTY: Easy

MAKE AHEAD: The soup can be prepared 1 day in advance and reheated.

Crespelle con Ricotta
Chestnut Crepes with Sheep's Milk Ricotta

When you say "ricotta" in Tuscany, you can only mean sheep's milk ricotta, which is to the cow's milk variety as pecorino is to Parmesan—everything from flavor to texture is different. Until recently, it was impossible to purchase sheep's milk ricotta in this country, and, even now, it is only carried by a very few specialty stores (in New York, I buy it at Alleva Dairy on Grand Street). If you ever see some, buy it. Eat it plain, as a topping for bread—sprinkled with sugar or ground espresso—or wrapped into these sweet, light, chestnut crespelle.

1½ cups chestnut flour	1 tablespoon extra-virgin olive oil or
Water	extra-virgin spray
	½ pound fresh sheep's milk ricotta

1. Place the flour in a bowl. Add water, 1 tablespoon at a time, until the texture is liquid and syrupy.

2. Heat a slope-sided skillet and brush (or spray) with oil. Pour ¼ of batter into the skillet and swirl around to create a thin, even layer. Cook for 2 minutes on each side or until the crepe is dry and smooth.

3. Place 3 or 4 tablespoons ricotta in the center of the crepe, roll into a cylinder, and serve.

SERVES 4   TIME: 20 minutes   LEVEL OF DIFFICULTY: Easy

VARIATIONS: For zestier *crespelle*, grate a teaspoon or two of lemon rind into the batter. If you like, you can also add ⅛ teaspoon fresh minced rosemary leaves.

Melanzane Sott'Olio
Eggplant Marinated in Olive Oil

An avid gardener, I am always as excited about the arrival of a new season as I am sorry to see the previous one go. One way I've found to extend the seasons is by canning the produce from my garden. The canning process itself is a pleasure, but much more pleasurable is the sensation of reclaiming the memory of that particular crop whenever I want. It certainly is an equitable return for all the digging and composting and manuring.

2 pounds long, thin eggplants
Salt
2 fresh red chili peppers, stems
   removed and halved
2 tablespoons fresh chopped
   rosemary

4 garlic cloves, minced
1 cup red wine vinegar
Extra-virgin olive oil
1 wide-mouthed quart canning jar
   with lid and safety seal

1. Wash the eggplants and remove the stems. Cut into 4-inch pieces and then cut those into very thin (½-inch) slices. Place in a colander, salt thoroughly, weigh down with a heavy plate, and let drain for 30 minutes. Rinse and pat dry with paper towels.

2. Place the eggplant in a bowl and toss with the peppers, rosemary, garlic, and vinegar. Place the eggplant in the jar, laying the pieces horizontally with long ends curling up along the sides. Pour any liquid from the bowl over the top and use a spoon or pestle to push the eggplant down a little. Cover with a solid layer of oil.

3. Seal and refrigerate. The eggplant will be ready to eat in three weeks but will keep up to four months and get better with age. Always return to room temperature before eating. Make sure to replace the solid covering of oil whenever removing pieces of eggplant.

Alfredo Bicicchi—The Lord of the Manor.

MAKES 1 QUART

TIME: 60 minutes

LEVEL OF DIFFICULTY: Easy

VARIATIONS: Eggplant can also be pickled before canning. For this method, place the colander with the salted eggplant in a larger bowl filled with water to which 2 cups red wine vinegar have been added. Drain, rinse, pat dry with paper towels, and proceed from Step 2.

Insalata di Zucchini e Pomodori con Taleggio e Salsa di Noce

Zucchini and Tomato Salad with Taleggio and Walnut Vinaigrette

Tuscan families almost always have three-course meals, even today. Not for them a quick sandwich eaten at one's desk while teleconferencing with clients. At the very least, they will sit down to a grain, an entree with side dishes, and a fruit and cheese course. In summers, one of those courses generally consists of a somewhat elaborate salad, often including cheese or meat. The following is one of my favorites; note that the nuts are preboiled to soften them and restore the delicate fruitiness of fresh green walnuts.

¼ pound walnuts, shelled and cut
    into ¼-inch pieces
2 tablespoons lemon juice
1 teaspoon grated lemon rind
4 tablespoons extra-virgin olive oil
½ teaspoon salt
½ teaspoon freshly ground black
    pepper

1 pound zucchini, trimmed
1 tablespoon fresh chopped dill
¼ cup finely chopped scallions
1 cup sliced white mushrooms
¼ pound Taleggio cheese, cut into
    1-inch cubes
¼ pound arugula, stems removed

1. Bring 2 cups water to boil in a small saucepan. Add the walnuts and bring the water back to a boil. Boil for 30 seconds and drain. Combine the walnuts in a bowl with the lemon juice, lemon rind, oil, salt, and pepper. Mix well and set aside.

2. Using a mandoline or a knife, julienne the zucchini. Blanch in 3 quarts salted water for 30 seconds, drain, and transfer to a bowl. Add the dill, scallions, mushrooms, and Taleggio. Toss with the walnut sauce.

3. Arrange the arugula on a platter. Top with the zucchini salad and serve.

SERVES 4   TIME: **30 minutes**   LEVEL OF DIFFICULTY: Easy

Torta di Zucchini con Salsa di Pomodori Arrostiti

Zucchini Tart with Slow-Roasted Tomatoes

Three summers ago, the weather was so cold and rainy that many of my tomatoes caught a disease called blossom end rot. Beyond the tragedy of watching those defenseless little fruits be eaten by an unscrupulous fungus was the even greater misfortune of having only a limited number of tomatoes and, hence, none to spare for such luxuries as oven roasting. The zucchini tart in the following recipe is not a tart at all, in that it has no crust. Made simply of zucchini, flour, and eggs, it forms a light but sturdy crust for the summery topping that I did not get to eat at all that long-ago summer.

The Sauce

1½ pounds very ripe tomatoes (not plums), cored and cut in half horizontally
2 garlic cloves, minced
5 tablespoons extra-virgin olive oil
Salt and freshly ground black pepper
10 basil leaves, shredded
¼ cup fresh grated Parmigiano-Reggiano

The Tart

4 tablespoons extra-virgin olive oil
2 pounds baby zucchini, trimmed and cut into thin rounds
1 medium onion, minced
½ cup unbleached flour
2 eggs, lightly beaten
Salt and freshly ground black pepper

1. Preheat the oven to 300 degrees. Arrange the tomatoes, cut side up, in a baking dish. Sprinkle garlic over the top and drizzle with oil. Season with salt and pepper and bake, uncovered, for 2 hours, basting once or twice with oil from the bottom of the dish.

2. Meanwhile, make the tart. Heat 3 tablespoons of the oil in a large skillet. Sauté the zucchini and onion over medium heat for 20 minutes, stirring frequently, until tender and light brown. Transfer to a large bowl and bring to room temperature. Stir in flour, eggs, salt, and pepper.

3. Brush a nonstick skillet with the remaining oil. Pour in the zucchini batter and cook over medium heat for 5 minutes or until the bottom is brown. Using

a spatula, turn and cook until the second side is brown. Transfer to a plate and keep warm.

4. When the tomatoes are cooked, force them through a food mill along with all the juices and oil. Add the basil and cheese, spoon over the zucchini tart, and serve.

SERVES 4   TIME: 2¼ hours   LEVEL OF DIFFICULTY: Moderate

MAKE AHEAD: The tomato sauce can be made 1 day in advance and reheated before serving.

Insalata d'Estate
Summer Farro and Tomato Salad

Because farro is such a nutty grain, it works perfectly in summer salads, especially when paired with the sweetness of tomatoes. I first tasted the following salad at a restaurant in Viareggio called Buonamico. It is the oldest restaurant in this seaside town, and its current proprietor—the grandson of the original—thinks it very funny indeed that, when his grandfather first opened the trattoria, farro was considered too much of a peasant dish to be included on the menu. "Now it is all the rage," he says, laughing.

½ pound *farro*, cooked according to package directions and cooled to room temperature

6 very ripe Roma tomatoes, cut into small cubes

15 Gaeta or other black olives, pitted and minced

3 tablespoons fresh basil chiffonade

4 cloves garlic, crushed

¼ cup extra-virgin olive oil

½ teaspoon salt

1 small dried red chili pepper, crushed

Mix of dandelions, chicory, watercress, and arugula, cleaned and with stems removed

1. Place all ingredients save for the *farro* in a large bowl, mix well, and let sit for 30 minutes.

2. When the *farro* is cooked and cooled, add to the salad, toss to blend, and serve on a bed of greens.

SERVES 4

TIME: Approximately 1 hour depending on cooking directions for *farro*

LEVEL OF DIFFICULTY: Easy

VARIATIONS: Barley, rice, bulghur, or millet can be used in place of *farro*.

MAKE AHEAD: The grain can be cooked 1 day in advance, refrigerated, and returned to room temperature before use.

Alfredo's mother Tina: "Yes, they could have lived like nobles. But how can you fault two people who are so happy?"

VEGETABLE
FRUITS

233

CHAPTER EIGHT

Mushrooms and Truffles

He Who Has the Spoon Stirs the Polenta

There exists in Tuscany an entire generation of middle-class men and women in their late forties and early fifties who spend much of their time bemoaning the fact that, as children, they were very rich. Once, they will tell you, their families had their own vineyards worked by *contadini*—peasant farmers—who did everything from harvesting the grapes to arranging the bottled wine so as to be easily accessible to the master of the house. They had their own olive orchards as well as their own *frantoii* (olive presses), their own sheep from which workers made cheese, their own fruit orchards, vegetable gardens, barnyard animals, and wheat fields to supply the grain for bread.

In summer, they would travel to their beach houses where, at night before going to sleep, their mothers would instruct the cooks as to the following day's lunch. The cooks would then pass the "shopping list" on to fishermen who would leave in their wooden boats when the moon was high and return the next morning with the shrimp or sea bass or whatever had been ordered. At 1:00 P.M., these privileged mortals would walk from the sand to their cabanas and sit down to lunch at outdoor tables shaded by striped canopies.

235

In August, when the sun and the sea became too much, beach houses would be abandoned for country homes where the air was pure and the nights reserved for sitting in front of the fire. Sunday lunch would always be served outdoors, at long, rustic tables set in meadows with panoramic views of the Apuan Alps. Towards the end of the season, when the ground began yielding plump *porcini* mushrooms, kitchen workers would journey daily into the woods, frequently accompanied by the master's children and hordes of visiting cousins.

Facilitating this existence required a diversified staff; there were maids and gardeners and chauffeurs and a constant stream of peasants bearing baskets filled with seasonal produce. The first few pews in church and at local concerts were always reserved for the use of certain families, and in midmorning and late afternoon during school season, *babinaie* (nannies) would arrive in classrooms bearing *merende,* thick slices of bread or chestnut fritters spread with ricotta.

But then it ended, and at this point in the chronicle, listeners may note a shifting of mood on the part of the narrator. Anger surfaces from the depths of idyllic reminiscence, an unmistakable anger felt by people who had never imagined—and were unprepared to negotiate—a life any different from what they had known.

"It happened almost from one day to the next," says Paolo Gori, whose parents, the Marchese Carlo and his wife, the Marchioness Lidia, sold their land in 1963 and frittered away the money. "Now that I am out on my own and have read and studied and interacted with different kinds of people, now I can see we were living in a dream world, that anyone could have predicted what, in fact, did happen." He shakes his head as if still trying to understand. "But I guess I continue to harbor a great deal of anger towards my parents who, in my opinion, just threw up their hands and gave up and in doing so, robbed me of my rightful heritage."

Paolo is not exactly correct when he says that *it* happened almost from one day to the next. In fact, the Agrarian Reforms that changed his life as well as that of an entire social class took place during a period spanning more than thirty years, from the 1930s to the late 1960s when the final and definitive sharecropper laws were passed. Before then, much of Tuscany's land had been held by a limited number of people. In some cases, the land had been in the family for generations; in others, it was given as a reward to loyal supporters of the Fascist party.

As with any other country operating under a feudal system, the large estates were controlled by one family and worked by large numbers of peasants who received, in return, great security but little money. While not slaves in any connotation of the word, the *contadini* were, nonetheless, tied to the estates in a way that dominated their lives.

"Yes, their lives were hard," Paolo admits, "but not without a certain measure of the limited joy that comes from having more than enough to eat and drink, a roof over one's head, a defined responsibility, and an intact family. I personally don't think they missed what they didn't have, namely property of their own. It sounds cruel—especially coming from someone on the privileged side of the divide—but I truly believe they never stopped to examine the 'why' of their lives. They simply accepted the fact that God and God alone determined whether one was born to the manor or the wooden shack."

Paolo's beliefs notwithstanding, the range of attitudes surrounding the lives of *contadini* is best conveyed by the proverbs emanating from that period, from the self-serving *chi pane mi da, mi é padrone* (he who gives me bread is my master) to the realistic *chi ha il mestolo in mano sminestra a modo suo* (he with the wooden spoon in hand stirs the soup according to his own tastes) to the resentful *il pane degli altri ha sette croste* (bread that belongs to others has seven crusts, meaning it is hard to swallow).

According to Paolo, the real changes started in the early 1950s. "The Italian Communist party had gained a foothold in regional politics, and they began organizing the *contadini* into union-type groups who mounted increasingly aggressive campaigns for the right to own their own property. Strikes became the order of the day, as did the sight of grapes withering on the vine and crops rotting in the field. In 1968, Italy passed the most stringent of the sharecropper laws. From then on, workers were owed a certain percentage of the land they worked, a certain percentage of the produce they generated, and a wage that corresponded to the amount of work they did rather than to the importance attached to that work by the landowner."

This, he points out, effectively spelled the end of the large estates, in that landowners had the bulk of their worth tied up in dirt and trees and bushes and vines and not a great deal of available currency. "To be forced to concede not only land but an hourly wage was more than we could financially bear," he says. "But we also could no longer count on the loyalty of our workers who were partially working for themselves and getting paid for the first time in their lives. Suddenly they could go on trips, eat in restaurants, send their children to school, and even drink enough *grappa* to not care whether our olives were har-vested on time. My parents became increasingly unwilling to deal with both the hostility and the sense of having been betrayed by those whose families had lived alongside us for generations." And so, he says, they sold.

Since his parents knew nothing other than life as coddled landowners, how-ever, they mainly frittered the money away, leaving Paolo—now approaching middle age and dreaming of retirement—embittered that his parents failed to provide.

Vera, Paolo's cousin and my friend from childhood, is another perfect case in point. "When it came time for my family to sell," she says, "my father was ap-proached by a representative of the Interior Ministry who wanted to buy the land in order to build what subsequently became the A-11 [an *autostrada*]. The amount he offered was not as great as the sum total of what might have been possible if we had sold the land in plots. But my father argued in its favor be-cause we would receive the money immediately and thus be spared the agony of watching our land be parcelled out."

It was not, she explains, the right decision. "Not only did my father facilitate the construction of an elevated roadway that bisects one of the most spectacu-lar valleys in the Lucchesia, but . . . " she shakes her head in bewilderment, "he then bought a ridiculously inappropriate house right in the central piazza of our village and donated a large part of what was left to the church across the way. The only explanation I can come up with is that he hoped the Church would take care of him and my mother if they ran out of money and contracted a seri-ous illness.

"How could it never have occurred to them that the best thing was to invest the money and live off the interest?" she asks, before answering her own ques-tion. "I guess all they knew was that, in fall, the workers would pick the olives and deliver the first pressing to their door."

Now an art historian involved in the restoration of the frescoes in Lucca's Chiesa di San Michele, Vera concedes the difficulty of generating even a gram of sympathy for her situation. "Most people who listen to my laments about how I went from rich girl to public school student throw the argument right back in my face," she admits. "'You're doing the same thing you're damning your parents for having done,' they say. 'Avoiding responsibility. Their money was, after all, theirs. If they spent it irresponsibly, it was their right to make that choice.'

"I disagree," she says. "What they had was inherited from their parents. It was a gift with which they were entrusted, a gift that was supposed to be handed down through the generations. But, instead, they gave it away."

Paolo and Vera's grumbling aside, the sharecropper laws passed in 1968 laid the groundwork for Italy's transformation from a land controlled by the rich to one that is increasingly middle class. But only the northern part of the country. Because the same laws that created a window of opportunity for northern peasant farmers to move into more lucrative jobs generated by the economic boom of the last few decades also reduced the less industrial South into a ragtag collection of small landowners unable to make it on their own.

"The North and the South are further apart every day in terms of lifestyle and economic possibilities," says Paolo. "In a way, the situation is very similar to that in America after the Civil War. We even have our own version of the carpetbaggers who flocked to the South to take advantage of the newly freed slaves. Here, though, we call them mafiosi."

His point is well taken. There is no question—regardless of source—that the Mafia controls the South. There is also no question that the North has been pushed to its absolute limit with respect to lining the Mafia's bottomless pockets. Says Paolo, "There are bridges in Apulia that were bombed during World War II and have still not been rebuilt despite the North having appropriated the money fifteen times." When I teasingly observe that he seems to draw no distinction between the northern part of the country and the national government at large, as in "The North appropriated the money fifteen times," he explodes with passionate righteousness: "Eighty percent of the government's money comes from the North! In the South, the money goes instead to the local Mafia don!"

Whether Paolo is totally right or only partially right, the fact remains that an increasing number of northerners share his conviction. In many cases, the antipathy is indeed based on money—on the fact that the North, itself buffeted by a diminishing economic return, can simply no longer allocate as much of its resources to solving the South's problems. But snobbism also plays a part. *"Quelli del sud sono tutti cafoni"* (Southerners are all rustic boors), Northerners are fond of declaiming, especially Tuscans, who imagine themselves to be Italy's foremost intellectuals.

Vera tells a funny story of an incident that transpired many years ago while visiting New York with her mother. At one point during their two-week stay, the increasingly homesick woman decided she absolutely had to have an Italian newspaper. Since this was seven years ago and well before the ready availability of international publications, Vera took her mother to a store in Little Italy mentioned in her guidebook as stocking a wide variety of Italian language periodicals.

"Now, you know my mother," she says, "how feisty and bitchy she can be." I nod my head, having known her mother since childhood. "But since we'd set foot in New York, she had become noticeably more docile. I think that not being able to speak the language had left her feeling very much out of control. Well, all that changed once we got into the store."

According to Vera, the shopkeeper heard them speaking Italian and immediately came rushing over. "'*Buon giorno*,' she said in a heavy southern Italian accent, and as soon as my mother heard that, her docility vanished. She threw back her shoulders and demanded a copy of *La Nazione*. '*Questi non valgano nemeno la pena*,' she said haughtily of the handful of tabloid papers the woman had hastened to produce." These are not even worth the effort.

But the story's most astonishing factor, Vera points out, is the way the shopkeeper immediately fell into servility. "She started treating my mother with a deference that was more befitting of a lady in waiting. And the two proceeded like that for the next ten or fifteen minutes, my mother proclaiming and demanding and the shopkeeper hastening to satisfy her needs. "*Si, signora. No, signora*," babbled the woman as she followed my mother around the store. The best part is, my mother ultimately bought nothing!"

Another friend, Giada—a possible rival for Vera's mother in terms of haughtiness—tells of the time she went to Bari (capital of the southern province of Apulia) to collect material for a thesis on Albanian emigration, and supported herself by working in the office of a local shipping agent. "One day a middle-aged woman came in with a large package she had just received from a cousin in Brooklyn," says Giada. "The package had been somewhat ruffled in its journey and a corner of the box was crushed to the point of exhibiting a large hole where the tape had come loose. Well, the woman was furious, claiming that someone had stolen one of the items."

Giada smiles in a way that can only be described as condescending. "I asked the woman what made her think anything had been stolen, and she produced a piece of paper on which her cousin had listed everything that had been packed into the box. '*Questo, questo*,' cried the woman, pointing to the last item on the list. '*Questo non c'era*.' This item wasn't there. I took the paper and looked at the list—at the itemization of dishtowels and blouses and potholders and under-shirts—and, under the last item, in a shaky scrawl, her cousin had written *'that's all.'* 'This item, *that's all*, is not in the box,' the woman kept screaming. 'Somebody stole it and I want it back!'"

Giada folds her hands in a praying position. *"Ma ora ti chiedo,"* she says, lifting her face towards the ceiling. Now I ask you.

"Fortunately," she says, "we had an English-Italian dictionary in the office, be-cause the woman kept insisting that customs agents had stolen an item listed by her cousin. To this day, she probably still thinks we lied to her."

Anecdotes aside, an increasing number of northerners feel a widening gap between themselves and their less-industrialized southern counterparts. "Many," Paolo observes, "have decided to do something about it, recently joining together in support of what is being called *federalismo*, but what summarily amounts to the North's secession from the South. The movement's leader, Um-berto Bossi, is a member of Parliament and the founder of La Lega del Nord, a political party whose platform is dedicated to 'keeping people's money in their *own* pocket.'

"Until recently," he notes, "the Lega's success depended on its ability to form a coalition with the ruling party of the moment. But when the Socialists took con-trol of the government in 1996, Bossi decided to strike out on his own. Last Sep-tember he mounted a three-day manifestation that culminated in the creation of what he calls a 'separate nation,' which he has named Padania. There were banners and t-shirts and registration booths and membership cards and even a national anthem which was played so many times on televised news that, by the end of the weekend, it was more familiar than Italy's own anthem."

"Cu cu cu RU, L'Italia non c'e piu," chanted 100,000 supporters who had formed a human chain along the Po River on the day of Padania's Declaration of Indepen-dence. Italy is no longer.

There was also, I recall, the unveiling of a new constitution, the most trou-bling aspect of which is Article 8, stipulating that registered Padani are fully justi-fied in withholding tax money from the Italian government and rendering it instead to Padania's governing body, headed, of course, by Bossi.

"Can Bossi *do* this?" I ask Paolo, amazed by a behavior that, in many of the world's nations, would be judged treasonous and grounds for immediate exe-cution.

His answer carries the resentment that suffuses most people's voices when talking about either Bossi himself or the Padania movement. "Bossi is a member of Parliament. And as such, he is constitutionally above the law. So there are no legal grounds on behalf of which anyone can block his actions."

"But what's going to happen?" I say, thinking of the former Yugoslavia.

His answer surprises me. "If everything goes as it should, Bossi and his Padania could be the best thing that ever happened to Italy." He sees the look on my face and hastens to explain. "Secession is ridiculous and dangerous, but apart from that, Bossi is right—much as I hate to give that *fanfarone* (braggart) credit for anything. The North *does* send too much of its money to the South without getting anything in return. If at least it went to repair roads and bridges as intended, that would be one thing. Perhaps this will be a wake-up call to the government that it simply has to do something about the Mafia."

According to Paolo, many of our mutual friends are supporting the Lega, among them his cousin Vera, who is the last person I thought he would name.

"Is it true?" I ask her one night over dinner. The Lega's supporters seem to be mostly working-class men, and Vera is probably the most class-conscious person I know.

"I haven't yet sent any money," she says. "But I might."

She gives me a justification based on rights and responsibilities and tax burdens and the fact of how angry she feels at the thought of people—namely southern Italians—not taking responsibility for their own lives.

At this last—the mention of personal responsibility—I realize what she's saying. This is just another vehicle for expressing anger at her parents.

"So, because you aren't living in a palatial villa with servants at your beck and call, you're thinking about sending money to Umberto Bossi? Is that it?" I stare at her over a platter of marinated eggplant.

"Not at all," she says, dipping her bread into a bowl of golden oil. "Despite what you think, I've never really appreciated having my home overrun with servants. For one thing, they're always there, living alongside you, sharing the same house."

"But they certainly come in handy when you want a fresh plate of risotto and don't want to bother making it yourself."

"Yes, but what about if, that night, you prefer having simple steamed greens? You can say, 'I don't want this risotto, make something else,' but once you've had a menu-planning session and stipulated risotto on Tuesday, it's not that easy to change your mind." She breaks into a wide grin. "It's also not that easy to say, 'Make something else.' There's such a thing as mutual respect, and it operates between you and servants in the same way it operates with everyone else.

"My parents had this one kitchen servant, Nadia, who you knew was always watching you behind closed doors," Vera continues. "The minute any of us stopped eating for longer than four minutes, she would breeze into the dining room and whisk away the plate. It got to the point where, even if I had to blow my nose, I kept my fork in hand."

She takes a sip of wine. "Actually, when I think of it now, I realize I could *never* have lived like my parents. Paolo and I complain because we weren't offered that chance. But maybe we're better off. We both have good jobs and make enough money to live well. And we have fun—much more fun than I ever remember anyone having in my old life, when dignity and propriety made it impossible to ever do anything spontaneously.

"What I remember of my parents' life was the conspicuous boredom of never *having* to do anything and, consequently, never having anything to do. Of floating from one day to the next with very little change in routine. Of having to maintain a certain control even when there was nothing that needed controlling. I remember, even then, thinking, how lackluster an existence!"

"So are you saying you're glad things happened the way they did?"

"No. No matter what, I can never forget the horrific effect on my parents of suddenly being tossed to the lions."

I lean across the table. "But wasn't that sort of inevitable?"

"In a way, I guess it was. But that's my rational mind talking. My emotional mind still winces at having to go home tonight and clean my own kitchen." She laughs.

"And Bossi?"

"Well. . . . " She purses her lips and pretends to be agonizing over what decision to make. "Actually I hate Bossi!" She laughs out loud. "But I love being able to say, 'Maybe I'll send him some money.' It makes me feel so . . . so absolutely wild and irresponsible!"

About Mushrooms and Truffles

When summer begins to fall away and the air turns crisp with the fragrance of fennel and chestnuts and new red wine, a particular ritual takes hold through-

Trumpet mushroom.

out Tuscany whereby perfectly rational people routinely traipse through the forest at 4:00 A.M., flashlight in hand, searching for wild mushrooms. "We become maniacal," says my cousin Renza, who, by October of this past year, had already brought home over 120 pounds of assorted *funghi*. What she doesn't eat immediately, she freezes so that, for the next month or two, Renza will spend innumerable evenings with family and friends eating meals whose every course features mushrooms as the main ingredient.

Tuscan forests—a mix of pine, fir, oak, and chestnut trees—generally yield approximately 20 varieties of wild mushrooms, everything from the bulbous *porcini (Boletus edulis, Boletus pinicola* or *Boletus aereus)* to golden *guatelli* (Chanterelles) to the rare and highly prized *ovole (Amanita cesaria)*. Two other commonly found mushrooms prefer meadows to woods: *scaroche (Lepiota procera)* and *pratolini* which are much like our common white mushrooms.

Mushrooms Funghi

There are thousands of different types of *funghi*, the vast category of flowerless plants that include both edible mushrooms and the deadly poisonous creatures known as toadstools. Of the Tuscan varieties, none is as prized as the fat, meaty *porcini (Boletus edulis)* found near pine and chestnut trees. *Porcinis* have rust-brown caps and plum beige stems that flare at the base. They may also be pale or almost white, depending on the sun exposure of the part of the forest where they grew. Dried *porcinis*, while different in character, still have the same wonderful woodsy fragrance. Other commonly available mushrooms include *shiitake, cremini, portobello,* and oyster.

Season: September through December

To Buy: Like all other wild mushrooms, fresh *porcinis* should be springy and resist a firm squeeze. The caps should be firm and dry and look fresh with no bruised spots. Avoid those that appear stringy, mushy, or discolored as well as those with a pronounced smell. Dried specimens should be as light-colored as possible (the lighter, the more expensive) and not too hard.

To Prepare: All mushrooms, wild or otherwise, should be cleaned with a damp cloth or a gentle brushing. Do not rinse under running water or immerse as mushroom caps act like sponges and soak up liquid. In the case of just-picked large, wild mushrooms, you may want to salt the underside of the cap to draw out any worms or insects. Trim off tough stem ends before using. Dried *porcinis* should be soaked in warm water for 30 to 45 minutes. The mushrooms should be rinsed before using and the liquid strained through several layers of cheesecloth to remove grit.

Truffles *Tartufi*

Like mushrooms, truffles are a kind of fungus or, more correctly, the fruit of a fungus; unlike mushrooms, truffles grow completely underground. There are over 70 species but only a few are highly prized:

Black truffles (*Tuber melanosporum*) are found in Tuscany, Umbria, and France from September to December. Dark brown with traces of violet on the outside, black truffles have similarly dark insides with whitish veins running through the flesh. In size they vary from as small as a nut to as large as a fist. The best are moist to the touch and exude a sweetish perfume. Black truffles keep for approximately one week. The best methods for conservation include: submerging them in rice so the fragrance permeates the rice kernels; surrounding them with eggs—the perfume penetrates the shells; or setting them in the refrigerator next to butter which also picks up the fragrance. Black truffles are generally cooked before eating. They are best with eggs or layered under the skins of chickens and turkeys before roasting.

Summer truffles (*Tuber aestivum*) are similar to black truffles on the outside but have light-colored, marbelized interiors. In size, they range from 1½ to 3 inches and are harvested from late summer to early winter. Less expensive than black truffles (although often sold as such), these have a milder, nut-like taste and smell. Cook before eating.

White truffles *(Tuber magnatum)* are found principally in Tuscany and the Piedmont from October to December. Their name is deceptive, since these highly fragrant tubers are really light brown on the outside and yellow-gray inside. For the most part, they grow to various depths at the base of oaks, poplars, willows, or lindens in highly alkaline soil. The best are those uprooted in late season, since earlier ones tend to be immature and less fragrant. Bigger and smoother ones are better (less waste) and more expensive. They can also be purchased canned, although much of the fragrance is lost. White truffles should be kept no longer than one week and, like their black and summer counterparts, can be conserved in rice, among eggs, or refrigerated next to butter. White truffles are generally eaten raw, shaved over pasta, rice, eggs, carpaccio, or raw mushrooms. In most cases they should be sprinkled on top of food rather than stirred into it.

American truffles *(Tuber gibbosum)* are found primarily under evergreen trees along the northern California and southern Oregon coast. Not nearly as prized as the preceding varieties, American truffles have a mild, woodsy flavor that grows slightly stronger with age.

Season: September through December

To Buy: Should be resilient to the touch and very pungent (whites especially). Avoid those with mild odors or spongy textures. The most prized are usually round and uniformly shaped. They are *very expensive.*

To Prepare: Truffles always arrive in this country brushed of surface dirt. Before using, however, brush again using a very soft brush to clear away any remaining dirt and rub with a wet cloth.

"My father facilitated the construction of an elevated roadway that bisects one of the most spectacular valleys in the Lucchesia."

Quick and Easy

Mushrooms

The most versatile of vegetables in terms of basic preparations. Raw, they can be sliced thinly (stems removed and saved for soups) and added to salads, or marinated in either just oil or oil and vinegar for a few hours and then served with thick slices of crusty bread.

For a quick and easy appetizer, slice 1 pound of mushroom caps thinly and add to a sizzlingly hot dry skillet. Cook for 3–5 minutes, stirring constantly, until just before they begin to give up their liquid. Transfer to a bowl, add 2 tablespoons extra-virgin olive oil, salt, and pepper and toss to blend. Serve lukewarm with bread or *focaccia* or wedges of fried polenta. If you like your mushrooms spicy, add a pinch of crushed dried chili.

To make mushroom soup, sauté garlic in olive oil, add sliced mushrooms, and cook until soft. Add Basic Vegetable Broth (see page 308) and a handful of chopped chives.

Stuffed mushrooms are easy and satisfying. Remove stems, dice, and add to a bowl along with diced onion, parsley, bread crumbs, grated Parmesan, salt, and pepper. Place a dollop on each mushroom cap, arrange the caps in a baking pan, and dust the tops with additional grated cheese. Drizzle with white wine and bake until the caps are soft. If you like, you can brown the tops under the broiler before serving.

Grilled mushrooms are everybody's favorite. Remove the stems, brush the caps with extra-virgin oil, sprinkle with salt, and grill. When done on one side, turn with tongs or a spatula and baste the other side. Serve as is or drizzle with a little lemon juice.

Fettucine al Tartufo Bianco
Fettucine with White Truffles

Tuscans have a saying to celebrate autumn: "By St. Martin's Day every must is wine." Which is obviously why God decided that truffles should be unearthed in fall—just in time to be paired with copious quantities of new red wine. The following dish is a heavenly combination of fresh fettucine tossed in butter, dusted with fresh grated Parmesan, and—just before serving—topped with shavings of white truffles.

1 recipe Basic Pasta Dough
    (see page 312)
6 tablespoons unsalted butter

4 ounces fresh grated Parmigiano-
    Reggiano
Fresh ground white pepper
1 ounce white truffles

1. Using a pasta machine, roll the dough through the cutting blades to create fettucine. You can also cut the pasta by hand by rolling the dough into paper-thin sheets, rolling the sheets into scrolls, and then cutting it into narrow ribbons.

2. Cook the pasta in boiling salted water until almost done. Drain and transfer to a skillet containing the hot, melted butter. Toss the pasta with the butter and finish cooking in the skillet. Season with the pepper.

3. Place the pasta on a serving dish and sprinkle with the cheese. At the table, serve the fettucine on individual pasta dishes and, with a truffle slicer, cut fine slices of truffle directly over the fettucine.

SERVES 4   TIME: 75 minutes

LEVEL OF DIFFICULTY: Advanced (because of the pasta making)

MAKE AHEAD: Pasta can be refrigerated for up to 2 days. It can also be frozen for up to 1 month.

Paolo Gori: "If everything goes as it should, Bossi and his Padania could be the best thing that ever happened to Italy."

Guatelli in Pastella con Salsa di Melissa
Fried Chanterelles with Lemon Balm Dip

Tuscans have a way with fried vegetables that makes you feel you could eat infinite quantities and not gain weight. Maybe it's the batter whose last minute addition of beaten egg whites creates a sensation of being lighter than air. Maybe it's the vegetables themselves whose freshness shines through the coating. Or maybe it's just the wine served at every meal. Whatever. This particular recipe takes freshness and lightness to new levels with the addition of a dipping sauce made of lemon balm, garlic, and honey.

The Mushrooms

1 cup unbleached white flour
½ teaspoon salt
2 eggs, separated
¼ cup dark beer
2 tablespoons extra-virgin olive oil
Olive oil for frying
1 pound chanterelles, cleaned and halved

The Dip

2 tablespoons heavy cream
1 tablespoon lemon juice
1 small garlic clove, crushed
1 teaspoon honey
4 tablespoons fresh chopped lemon balm, plus 3 leaves for garnish (available at farmers markets)
Salt and fresh ground black pepper

1. Sift together the flour and salt in a bowl. Add the egg yolks and slowly add the beer, stirring until you have a somewhat thin paste. Stir in the oil and set aside.

2. Meanwhile, make the dip by placing the cream, lemon juice, crushed garlic, honey, chopped lemon balm, and salt and pepper to taste into a blender and blending until smooth. Transfer to a bowl and garnish with the whole leaves.

3. Place 1 inch of oil in a medium-sized skillet and heat to 350 degrees.

4. Beat the egg whites to stiff peaks and fold into the batter. Dip the mushroom pieces in the batter and fry, 4 or 5 at a time, for 2 minutes or until golden. Drain on paper towels and keep warm. Continue until all the mushrooms have been fried. Serve with dip.

SERVES 4   TIME: 45 minutes   LEVEL OF DIFFICULTY: Easy

VARIATION: Any mushroom can be used in place of chanterelle. Mint can be used in place of lemon balm.

Rotolo ai Funghi
Herbed Mushroom Roll

Rolled vegetable breads are very popular with Tuscans and can be made using virtually any single vegetable or vegetable medley. This creamy version, flavored with herbs and Dijon mustard, is served warm, garnished with sprigs of fresh herbs and accompanied by a misticanza—mesclun—*salad.*

½ pound *cremini* mushrooms, minced
1 bay leaf
½ cup milk
4 tablespoons unsalted butter
½ cup unbleached white flour
½ teaspoon Dijon mustard
2 ounces grated Emmenthal cheese

2 eggs, separated
1 tablespoon fresh chopped parsley
1 tablespoon fresh chopped chives
1 tablespoon fresh chopped dill
2 tablespoons heavy cream
Salt and freshly ground black pepper
8 sprigs fresh herbs for garnish

1. Preheat the oven to 375 degrees. Grease an ovenproof 9 × 12-inch pan. Place the mushrooms, bay leaf, and half the milk in a small saucepan and bring to a boil over medium heat. Boil for 2 minutes, remove from heat, cover, and set aside for 10–15 minutes. Discard the bay leaf and drain the mushrooms, reserving the liquid. Add the remaining milk to the reserved liquid.

2. Melt the butter in another pan over medium heat, add the flour, and cook for 1 minute, stirring constantly. Slowly add the reserved milk and continue to cook, stirring until you have a thick paste. Add the mustard and grated cheese, stirring to blend all ingredients. Remove one half to a heated bowl and set aside. Add the reserved mushrooms and egg yolks to the remaining half.

3. Beat the egg whites to stiff peaks. Fold into the mushroom mixture, pour into the baking pan, place in the oven, and cook for 12–15 minutes or until the crust is golden.

4. Meanwhile, add the parsley, chives, and dill to the reserved mustard-cheese mixture along with the cream. Season with salt and pepper and mix well.

5. Remove the mushroom bread from the oven and spread with the mustard-cheese mixture. Starting from the short side, roll into a cylinder, slice, and serve garnished with the herb sprigs.

SERVES 4   TIME: 1 hour   LEVEL OF DIFFICULTY: Advanced

Insalata di Funghi e Riso Selvatico
Wild Rice and Mushroom Salad

With a combination of flavors that includes the sweetness of cherry tomatoes, the pungency of Gorgonzola, the lightness of fresh herbs, the woodsiness of wild mushrooms, and the nutty aroma of wild rice, I could feast on this salad and require nothing more.

½ cup wild rice
½ pound pearled barley or *farro*, soaked for 12 hours
4 ounces Gorgonzola cheese, cubed
15 cherry tomatoes, halved
10 scallions, cleaned and julienned
4 tablespoons extra-virgin olive oil

8 ounces wild mushrooms (*shitake*, chanterelles, or *porcini*), cleaned and thinly sliced
1 clove garlic, minced
2 tablespoons tarragon vinegar
2 tablespoons fresh chopped dill
Salt and freshly ground black pepper
Sprigs of fresh dill for garnish

1. Place the rice and barley or *farro* in a pot with enough salted water to cover by 2 inches. Cook, covered, over medium heat, for 45 minutes or until tender. Drain, rinse, and drain again. Place in a bowl and cool to room temperature.

2. Place the rice and grains in a large salad bowl and add the cheese, tomatoes, and scallions.

3. Heat the oil in a skillet and sauté the mushrooms over medium heat for 3 minutes, stirring constantly. Remove from heat and add the garlic, vinegar, chopped dill, salt, and pepper. Transfer the mushrooms and their liquid to the salad bowl and toss until all ingredients are well blended. Serve immediately garnished with the sprigs of fresh dill.

SERVES 4–6   TIME: 90 minutes   LEVEL OF DIFFICULTY: Easy

VARIATIONS: This salad can also be chilled before serving.

MAKE AHEAD: If serving chilled, the entire salad can be made 6 hours in advance.

Uova Tartufate
Truffled Eggs

There are few more classic things to do with white truffles than to shave them over scrambled eggs and serve as a light entree, perhaps following a bowl of vegetable broth. The only problem is that, once having eaten truffled eggs, the plain version no longer seems acceptable. The secret behind this recipe is to add the truffles to the eggs and then set aside for several hours so that the eggs can absorb the truffles' powerful fragrance.

½ ounce fresh white truffles
6 eggs (that have been stored for 2 days alongside the truffles), lightly beaten
Salt and freshly ground black pepper

6–8 very thin asparagus
2 slices whole wheat bread
3 tablespoons unsalted butter
1 tablespoon heavy cream
8 chives for garnish

1. Cut half the truffles into very thin slices and add them to the eggs. Season with salt and pepper and set aside for 2 hours.

2. Just before the eggs are ready to cook, place the asparagus in boiling salted water and cook for 3–5 minutes or until *al dente*. Drain and keep warm.

3. Toast the bread on both sides, spread with 1 tablespoon of the butter, cut in half diagonally, and keep warm.

4. Melt the remaining butter in a nonreactive pan over low heat. Add the eggs and cook for 3 minutes, gently stirring with a wooden spoon until the eggs begin to thicken. They should have a light, creamy consistency. Add the cream, stir once more, and remove from heat.

5. Divide the eggs between two plates. Lay half the asparagus spears on one side and the toast points on the other. Shave the remaining truffles over the eggs, garnish with the chives, and serve.

SERVES 2   TIME: 2 hours, 15 minutes   LEVEL OF DIFFICULTY: Easy

VARIATIONS: Canned truffles can also be used. Add the liquid to the eggs before cooking.

Fettucine di Farina di Granturco con Porcini Secchi
Corn Flour Fettucine with Dried Porcini Sauce

Yet another variation on the traditional white-flour pasta, these fettucine are made of equal parts fine-ground corn flour and white flour. Their grainy autumnal flavor makes a perfect bed for the woodsiness of a sauce made from dried porcinis and tomatoes.

The Pasta

2 cups fine-ground corn flour
2 cups unbleached white flour
5 eggs
Salt

The Sauce

3 tablespoons extra-virgin olive oil
1 medium onion, diced
1 medium carrot, diced
1 stalk celery, diced

3 ounces dried *porcini* mushrooms, soaked in warm water for 30 minutes
1 32-ounce can Italian peeled tomatoes, shredded and with liquid
½ cup dry white wine
Salt and freshly ground black pepper
3 tablespoons fresh basil chiffonade
¼ cup fresh grated Parmigiano-Reggiano

1. Make the pasta using instructions on page 312. Use the mix of corn flour and white flour in place of simply using white. Cut into fettucine.

2. Heat the oil in a large, nonreactive skillet. Add the onion, carrot, and celery and sauté over low heat for 5–7 minutes, stirring frequently until the vegetables are soft and translucent.

3. Drain and mince the mushrooms, reserving the liquid. Add the mushrooms to the vegetable sauté and cook for another 3 minutes, stirring constantly. Strain the liquid through cheesecloth and add to the skillet along with the tomatoes and the wine. Season with salt and pepper. Cook for 20 minutes, stirring frequently.

4. Meanwhile, cook the pasta in boiling salted water until *al dente*. Drain and place in a pasta bowl. Toss with the mushroom sauce, add the basil chiffonade, and serve dusted with the cheese.

SERVES: 4–6   TIME: 90 minutes   LEVEL OF DIFFICULTY: Advanced

VARIATIONS: Fresh mushrooms can be substituted for dried.

MAKE AHEAD: The pasta dough can be refrigerated for up to 1 week wrapped in plastic wrap, or frozen for up to 1 month. The sauce can be made 1 day in advance and refrigerated.

Budino di Funghi
Wild Mushroom Custard

Tuscan dinner custards are generally molded rounds combining traditional dessert ingredients like eggs and cream with bread or rice and finely chopped vegetables. They can be served as appetizers (placed in the center of a plate and garnished with herbs or bundles of baby vegetables) or, topped with a glistening sauce and served with green salad, as a light and satisfying entrée.

1 cup Basic Vegetable Broth (see
    page 308)
½ cup heavy cream
1 cup milk
2 eggs
1 teaspoon salt
2 tablespoons extra-virgin olive oil
2 tablespoons minced shallots
1 clove garlic, minced
½ teaspoon chopped fresh mint

½ teaspoon chopped fresh thyme
1 pound wild mushrooms, cleaned
    and thinly sliced (can combine
    shitake, chanterelles and *porcini*)
Freshly ground black pepper
Butter
4 ¾-inch-thick slices day-old
    peasant bread, crusts removed
    and roughly chopped
12 sprigs of fresh herbs

1. Place the broth in a saucepan over medium heat and reduce by half. Lower the heat, add the cream, and simmer for 3 minutes. Whisk ½ cup of the milk, the eggs, and salt together in a large bowl. Whisk in the broth and cream mixture and set aside.

2. Heat the oil in a skillet and sauté the shallots and garlic over low heat for 5 minutes or until soft. Add the mint and thyme and sauté for another minute. Add the mushrooms and cook until soft, approximately 10 minutes. Season with salt and pepper.

3. Soak the bread in the remaining milk for 3 minutes. Squeeze "dry" and discard the liquid. Butter 4 individual ramekins (4 inches in diameter) and line the

bottoms with ⅓ of the bread, carefully positioning the pieces to form a solid round. Top with half the mushroom mixture. Repeat the layers, finishing up with a top layer of bread. Pour the cream mixture over the bread. Cover with foil.

4. Preheat the oven to 350 degrees. Place the four custards in a roasting pan and pour enough boiling water into the pan to come halfway up the sides of the ramekins. Bake for 45 minutes, remove the foil, and bake for an additional 15–20 minutes, until the custards are set and the tops are browned. Invert onto individual plates and garnish with the herb sprigs.

SERVES 4   TIME: 2 hours   LEVEL OF DIFFICULTY: Advanced

VARIATIONS: The custard can also be made in a 4 × 4-inch loaf pan and cut into slices before serving.

MAKE AHEAD: Once the custard is wrapped in foil (Step 3), it can be refrigerated up to 1 day in advance.

Pizza di Funghi alla Griglia con Olio Tartufato
Grilled Pizza with Wild Mushrooms and Truffle Oil

Many Tuscan homes have outdoor pizza ovens, and, on any given night, you can probably smell the incomparable aroma of baking bread wafting through the trees. But pizza ovens are not portable, and that, coupled with the popularity of picnics and the importance of bread in making any picnic a success, led to the idea of cooking pizzas on outdoor grills. In general, Tuscans use olive wood when making the fire, but an aromatic hardwood will do, especially if perfumed with dried herb stems or vine trimmings. The grill should be high enough over the flames to create an evenly cooked crust—about 6 inches. After grilling, the individual rounds are topped with a delicious sauté of wild mushrooms perfumed with fresh lemon thyme.

1 recipe Basic Pizza Dough (see page 314)
1 pound assorted wild mushrooms (*porcini, shiitake,* chanterelles, oyster), cleaned and thinly sliced
4 tablespoons extra-virgin olive oil
1 teaspoon balsamic vinegar

1 dried chili pepper
Salt and freshly ground black pepper
3 tablespoons fresh chopped lemon thyme
1 tablespoon white truffle oil*

1. Start the fire about ½ hour before the dough's second rise. When the dough has doubled, punch it down and divide into four equal pieces. Roll each piece into a 10-inch circle and set aside.

2. Meanwhile make the mushroom topping. Place a large skillet over high heat and, when very hot, add the mushrooms and cook for 5 minutes, stirring constantly. When the mushrooms begin to give up their liquid, remove them from the skillet and place in a bowl. Immediately add the oil and vinegar. Crush the chili into the mushrooms, add salt, pepper, and the lemon thyme and mix well.

3. When the coals are white, place as many pizzas onto the grill as possible. Cook for 1 minute or until the surface starts to puff. Turn with a spatula and cook until crisp, about 2 minutes. Watch constantly to make sure the crusts are cooking evenly and not burning.

4. When the crusts are done, immediately top with mushrooms, drizzle with truffle oil, and serve.

SERVES 4   TIME: 60 minutes (not counting rising time)

LEVEL OF DIFFICULTY: Moderate

VARIATIONS: Pizza crusts can be made with aromatics like herbs, grated cheese, or minced olives added to the dough. They can also be topped with any sautéed vegetable or vegetable medley, or even a chopped salad (chicory and tomatoes, for example). Just make sure the topping is dry enough to avoid a soggy pizza. An indoor grill can be substituted.

MAKE AHEAD: The pizza dough can be made up to 2 weeks in advance, rolled into individual portions, wrapped in plastic wrap, and frozen.

*Truffle oil can either be purchased in specialty stores or made by combining 2 cups extra-virgin olive oil with half an ounce of carefully cleaned white truffles in a stoppered bottle. Let steep for at least 3 or 4 days before using. Truffle oil is very good drizzled onto salads, fresh pasta, risotto, polenta, fish, or mashed potatoes.

Farrotto di Porcini
Farro and Porcini Mushrooms

Farro is a highly nutritious barley-like grain whose usage dates back thousands of years. Grown almost exclusively in northern Tuscany (in a rugged mountainous area called the Garfagnana), it has a nutty flavor and somewhat crunchy texture. In recent years, it has become a very fashionable ingredient in soups, salads, baked casseroles, and even desserts. While farro comes in many forms (whole, cracked, in kernels), its availability in this country is limited to specialty stores which generally import one of the cracked versions. In the following recipe, farro is paired with sliced porcini and dry white wine to create a risotto-like dish that makes a perfectly satisfying entree when served with a mixed green salad.

½ pound *farro*, cooked according to package directions

3 tablespoons extra-virgin olive oil

2 cloves garlic, minced

1 pound *porcini* mushrooms, cleaned and thinly sliced

½ cup dry white wine

½ cup Basic Vegetable Broth (see page 308)

Salt and freshly ground black pepper

2 tablespoons fresh chopped parsley

Parsley sprigs for garnish

1. Cook the *farro* according to directions on package.*

2. Meanwhile, heat the oil in a large skillet and sauté the garlic over medium heat until golden. Add the mushrooms and cook for 2 minutes, stirring constantly.

3. Drain the *farro* and add to the mushrooms. Pour the wine over the *farro,* turn the heat to high, and cook until evaporated.

4. Reduce the heat to low, add the broth, season with salt and pepper, and cook for 1 minute, stirring to blend the flavors. When done, the consistency will resemble that of risotto.

5. Stir in the chopped parsley and serve garnished with the whole sprigs.

SERVES 4   TIME: 45 minutes (could be more if *farro* requires advance soaking)

LEVEL OF DIFFICULTY: Easy

VARIATIONS: *Shiitakes,* morels, or chanterelles can be used in place of *porcinis.*

MAKE AHEAD: *Farro* can be cooked up to 1 day in advance and refrigerated. If pre-cooked, add an additional 2 tablespoons of broth in Step 4.

*Some types of *farro* require pre-soaking. Read the package directions carefully.

Gnocchi di Farina alla Griglia con Salsa di Funghi
Grilled Farina Gnocchi with Mushroom Sauce

To most Americans, farina connotes Cream of Wheat and steaming bowls of hot cereal served on frigid winter mornings for breakfast on the prairie. But Tuscans have long used the grain in everything from soups to desserts to gnocchi. The following recipe is my alteration of the standard baked version in which the gnocchi are dotted with butter, baked until bubbling, and then broiled to golden brown.

4 cups water
½ teaspoon salt
1 cup farina
1 cup freshly grated Parmigiano-
 Reggiano
5 tablespoons extra-virgin olive oil
2 cloves garlic, minced
½ pound button mushrooms, diced

½ pound assorted wild
 mushrooms (*shiitake, cremini,
 oyster*), diced
½ cup dark beer
¼ cup heavy cream
1 tablespoon fresh chopped parsley
Parsley sprigs for garnish

1. Bring the water with salt to a boil in a heavy saucepan. Lower the heat and add the farina in a slow stream, whisking constantly for 7 minutes. Remove from heat and stir in the cheese.

2. Rinse a 9-inch square pan with cold water. Shake off excess water (do not dry) and spread farina evenly on the pan. Cool to room temperature and refrigerate for at least 30 minutes.

3. Preheat indoor grill or prepare outdoor fire.

4. Heat 2 tablespoons of the oil in a large skillet. Sauté the garlic for 2 minutes over medium heat. Add both kinds of mushrooms and sauté for 5 minutes, stirring constantly. Add the beer and cook until evaporated. Remove from heat. Add the cream and the parsley, stirring to blend all ingredients.

Vera Gori: "My parents' money was a gift that was supposed to be handed down through the generations, but instead they gave it away."

5. Cut the farina into 3-inch squares, brush both sides with the remaining oil, and place on the grill. Cook for 4 minutes or until lightly toasted, turn with spatula, and cook for another 4–5 minutes.

6. Divide the *gnocchi* among 4 plates, top with mushroom sauce, and serve garnished with sprigs of fresh parsley.

SERVES 4   TIME: 60 minutes
LEVEL OF DIFFICULTY: Moderate
VARIATIONS: *Gnocchi* can be baked as noted in recipe introduction. For an interesting presentation, layer half the *gnocchi* in the baking pan, spread with sauce, and then top with another *gnocchi* layer. Dot with butter, sprinkle with cheese, bake for 15–20 minutes, and boil for 3–5 additional minutes.

MAKE AHEAD: The *gnocchi* can be made up to 1 day in advance and refrigerated.

Torta di Funghi, Aglio Arrostito e Formaggio di Capra
Wild Mushroom Terrine with Roasted Garlic and Goat Cheese

Each bite of this terrine brims with intense flavors. Serve it on a late summer afternoon when the day is winding down and you're sitting outdoors with friends enjoying the last rays of sun. Best accompanied by a salad of mixed wild greens and chilled white wine.

6 cloves garlic, unpeeled
2 tablespoons hazelnut oil
1 clove garlic, minced
2 shallots, minced
½ pound wild mushrooms (*porcini,*
  chanterelles, morels, *shiitake,* and
  oyster), diced
1 teaspoon fresh chopped dill

1 tablespoon fresh chives, chopped
  into approximately 1-inch lengths
Salt and freshly ground black
  pepper
1 pound goat cheese at room
  temperature
2 tablespoons heavy cream
Parchment paper
Assorted baby vegetables, marinated

1. Wrap the unpeeled garlic cloves in a packet of aluminum foil. Place in the center of the oven and roast at 350 degrees for 30–45 minutes or until soft.

2. Heat the oil in a skillet over a low flame. Sauté the minced garlic and shallots for 5 minutes or until soft. Add the mushrooms and sauté for 5 minutes, stirring constantly. Remove from heat, add the dill and chives, transfer to a bowl, and set aside.

3. Place the cheese in a small bowl and whisk in the cream.

4. Remove the garlic cloves from the aluminum packet. Skin the cloves by squeezing from the bottom. Place the skinned garlic in a bowl and mash with a fork. Add the mash to the cheese. Season with salt and pepper.

5. Fold the mushroom mixture into the cheese.

6. Line a 4 × 8-inch loaf pan with oiled parchment. Add the cheese mixture, flattening it with a spoon until shaped to the bowl. Refrigerate for at least 5 hours.

7. Unmold onto a serving platter and remove parchment. Cut into ¾-inch slices and serve, garnished with marinated baby vegetables.

SERVES 4   TIME: 45 minutes (excluding refrigeration time)
LEVEL OF DIFFICULTY: Easy   VARIATIONS: Can also be served with a vinaigrette.
MAKE AHEAD: The assembled terrine can be made up to 1 day in advance.

Ragu di Funghi
Wild Mushroom Ragu

A ragu is a thick stew whose very name conjures up autumn nights, country kitchens, blazing hearths, and carafes of red wine. This particular ragu is made with various wild mushrooms and served with thick slices of toasted bread. It's a perfect one-dish meal whose flavor is almost better the next day.

1 pound mixed wild mushrooms
(hedgehog, *shiitake, porcini,*
chanterelles, black trumpet),
stems removed and saved for
another use
1 tablespoon extra-virgin olive oil
2 shallots, minced
1 clove garlic, minced
1 cup Basic Vegetable Broth (see
page 308)

¼ cup heavy cream
1 teaspoon fresh chopped thyme
1 tablespoon fresh chopped chives
Salt and freshly ground black
pepper
4 ¾-inch-thick slices stale country
bread
2 cloves garlic, halved
4 sprigs fresh thyme
4 sprigs fresh rosemary

1. Slice large mushroom caps into roughly even pieces. Leave smaller caps intact.

2. Heat the oil in a large skillet over low flame. Add the shallots and garlic and sauté for 5 minutes or until soft. Increase heat to medium. Add mushrooms and cook for 5 minutes, stirring frequently until they begin to release their liquid.

3. Add broth and cook for 10 minutes, stirring constantly. Stir in cream and cook for another 5 minutes. Add thyme and chives, season with salt and pepper.

4. Toast bread on both sides and rub with garlic. Divide the slices among 4 plates, top with *ragu*, and serve garnished with herb sprigs.

SERVES 4   TIME: 35–40 minutes   LEVEL OF DIFFICULTY: Easy

VARIATIONS: *Ragu* can also be served over pasta, polenta, or rice.

MAKE AHEAD: The *ragu* can be made up to 1 day in advance, refrigerated and reheated, or it can be frozen for up to 2 weeks.

Frittata d'Erbe Ripiena
Herb Frittata Crepes with Mushroom Filling

Very thin frittatas make excellent crepes when wrapped around soft, bechamel-like fillings. I was first served this particular recipe one day last August after an exhausting—and futile—morning spent in Lucca researching the Etruscan alphabet. I had been routed from one library to another for the better part of three hours and, when I walked through the door of my friend Rosella's kitchen, the fragrance alone almost made me cry. Then when I saw it on my plate . . . well, the frustration just vanished.

The Filling

2 tablespoons extra-virgin olive oil
1 clove garlic, halved
½ pound *cremini* mushrooms, stems
    removed and thinly sliced
1 tablespoon heavy cream
Salt and freshly ground black
    pepper

The Frittata

5 eggs, lightly beaten
2 tablespoons mixed fresh herbs
    (parsley, chervil, chives, dill),
    chopped
3 tablespoons water
3 tablespoons extra-virgin olive oil
Sprigs of fresh dill for garnish

1. For the filling: Heat the oil in a large skillet. Sauté the garlic for 1 minute over medium heat; remove and discard garlic. Increase the heat to high, add the mushrooms, and cook for five minutes, stirring constantly. If the mushrooms emit too much liquid during this period, remove them with a slotted spoon and cook the liquid until reduced by one half before replacing mushrooms.

2. Remove the pan from the heat and add the cream, salt, and pepper. The consistency should be sauce-like. Keep warm.

3. For the frittata: Beat the herbs and water into the eggs. Heat half the oil in an 8-inch, slope-sided skillet. Pour in half the egg mixture, twirl the pan around to spread the mixture evenly over the pan's bottom. Cook until set. Slide onto a plate, cover with another plate, and turn upside down. Remove the top plate and slide frittata back into the pan. Cook for 3 more minutes or until set. Transfer to a hot plate and keep warm. Repeat with the remaining egg mixture.

4. Place half the mushroom mixture onto each frittata. Fold the frittata over the mixture, garnish with the dill sprigs, and serve.

SERVES 2   TIME: 35–45 minutes   LEVEL OF DIFFICULTY: Easy

VARIATIONS: The frittata can also be made in one piece and sliced in half. Each half would then be folded into quarters for serving.

Risotto di Porcini con Tartufi Bianchi
Risotto with *Porcini* Mushrooms and White Truffles

One of the most classic of risotto preparations and, with the addition of truffle oil, a veritable masterpiece.

½ ounce dried *porcini* mushrooms

3 cups Basic Vegetable Broth (see page 308)

1 tablespoon unsalted butter

1 tablespoon extra-virgin olive oil

1 medium onion, minced

1 clove garlic, minced

¼ teaspoon dried sage

1 cup Arborio rice

½ cup dry white wine

½ pound fresh *porcinis*, stems removed

½ cup fresh grated Parmigiano-Reggiano

Salt and freshly ground black pepper

1 ounce fresh white truffles

1. Soak the dried *porcinis* in 1 cup very hot water for 30 minutes. Drain mushrooms, reserving liquid. Chop coarsely and set aside. Filter the mushroom liquid through a coffee filter or cheesecloth and set aside.

2. Place the broth in a saucepan and heat to boiling. Lower the heat and maintain a constant simmer.

3. Heat the butter and oil in a large saucepan. Sauté the onion, garlic, and sage over low heat for 5–7 minutes or until soft. Add the rice and cook, stirring constantly, until lightly toasted and coated with the oil-butter mixture.

4. Add the wine and cook until absorbed, stirring constantly, about 4 minutes. Stir in both the dried and fresh mushrooms, the mushroom liquid, and ½ cup of the broth. Cook, stirring frequently, until most of the liquid has been absorbed.

5. Continue adding broth, about ½ cup at a time, stirring frequently until the rice is tender and creamy but not soupy, about 20–30 minutes.

6. Remove from heat. Stir in the cheese and season with salt and pepper. Pour into bowls or plates and, using a truffle shaver, shave the white truffles directly over each serving.

SERVES 4   TIME: 60–70 minutes   LEVEL OF DIFFICULTY: Easy

VARIATIONS: Can also be prepared without using truffles.

CHAPTER NINE

Vegetable Medleys

What I Have Is Best

The Tuscan year is divided into distinct seasons, each producing its own magnificent contribution to the business of eating and drinking. There's cheesemaking in March, rejoicing over the first wild asparagus in April, and hunting for *porcini* mushrooms in September. October, however, is reserved for *vendemmia*, the annual harvesting of the grapes. For me, it is a time to clear my calendar, to put all pending business on a flexible schedule. My mind is on wine come October, and there is no telling when the call will come.

"*Vendemmiamo stamani*," Aldo says in a breathless tone, conveying the utmost urgency. We are harvesting this morning. There can be no advance planning with respect to when exactly is the best time. For one thing, it depends on the moon which needs to be on the wane. For another, the weather. If the season has been especially wet, as has this one, you want to leave the grapes on the vine as long as possible to concentrate the sugars. On the other hand, one October storm can savage the entire vineyard.

In the Barsotti family, Aldo, the grandfather and patriarch, makes the decision. "*Il naso del nonno non sbaglia mai*," says his granddaughter Anita, oozing obvious adoration. Grandfather's nose never makes mistakes. In fact, in all the years I have known the Barsottis, Aldo has always divined precisely the right day—late enough for the grapes to be at their sweetest but within the fewest possible hours before the Big Storm.

Today is that day, and Aldo's call has pulled me from my bed and sent me hurtling into the kitchen to grab a quick breakfast. From my house, it takes fifteen minutes to get to his farm, fifteen minutes of hairpin curves, mountain greenery, and over-my-shoulder views of the Tyrhennian that can only be described as majestic.

"Anna!" I hear my name as soon as I pull into Corsanico's main piazza. It is Anita, a 21-year-old bundle of indiscriminate excitement. Roused to the point of frenzy by thoughts of the impending harvest, she decided it was either drive her grandparents crazy or drive down and meet me. *"Siamo pronti!"* she says and motions me to follow her lead. We are ready!

Anarosa, Aldo's wife, is already in the kitchen preparing the meal that will feed all 18 of us when we return from the morning's harvest. "Aldo went up ahead," she says, "to the summit. He said to remind you that the figs on the big tree are ready." The reference is to a huge fig tree located across from their house on a spot that gets enough sun to lengthen its growing time beyond that of any other tree in the region. Long after the *de facto* end of fig season, Aldo and Anarosa's tree can be relied on to produce fat, juicy green figs whose flavor warrants nothing short of an operatic aria.

I grab as many as I can possibly handle, pick up my pail and iron clippers, and head off behind Anita to the largest of the four vineyards, which is also the highest in elevation. Aldo's land sits on the very top of a hill and encompasses as far as the eye can see in all directions. In addition to the vineyards, there is also an orchard of olive trees, a *frutteto* (fruit orchard), and a pine forest. It is, truly, one of the most beautiful properties I have ever seen, although that particular choice of words brings out a side of Aldo's personality that can only be described as *ergoglioso*, proudly competitive. "What do you mean, *one* of the most beautiful?" he once stormed at me. "Where have you ever seen a piece of land more spectacular than mine?"

"Finalmente!" he cries when Anita and I sprout over the final hill. He points to the vines immediately next to him, on his right. "This time you work over here, with me," he says, laughing. His statement harks back to last year's harvest, when my clippers got caught in a tangle of stinging nettle vines and I inadvertently fell, full-bodied, into the vines trying to extricate them. The resulting sting is as permanently etched in my memory as the subsequent race back to the house and Anarosa's gentle, soothing body rub.

We—18 members of a crew composed of family, neighbors, and friends—spend the rest of the morning stripping the vines of fruit. There is incessant laughing and talking as we cut the *grappoli* with iron clippers that have been in Aldo's family for over 200 years. The sun is brilliant in the sky and the smell of grapes heavy on the sultry air. Our hands are sticky as we move from the *neri*, the red grapes, to the *bianchi*, the white ones, keeping each separate from the other in large buckets that are then emptied into a central vat. Roberto, Aldo's brother, drives the *furgoncino*, a small three-wheeled truck, that goes back and forth between our harvest and the *cantina* where the grapes will eventually be made into wine.

"Will you do me a favor?" says Anita at one point during the picking. "Will you sing *Silent Night* for me?" Anita is a language student at the University of Pisa and is always asking me to sing or recite what she perceives to be quintessential Americanisms. Once, she wanted me to bring her a copy of "Alice's Restaurant."

At morning's end, we file back to the house and Aldo deposits the grapes in a funnel-shaped pressing mechanism located just outside the *cantina*. Manned by his nephew, Carlo Alberto, the press squeezes the grapes just enough to break the skins and release some of the liquid. The must is then tossed into a deep-walled stone trough where it ferments for 72 hours. During this time, Carlo Alberto will frequently climb into the trough up to his waist and stir the brew with a long pole while Aldo watches to make sure nothing goes wrong. "You can easily become intoxicated by the alcoholic vapors," Aldo explains. "In fact, when I was a little boy, a friend of my father's collapsed into the trough and—because nobody was standing watch—drowned."

"I always drink a quart of milk before I climb in," adds Carlo Alberto who, in real life, plays the saxophone in a Viareggio jazz club. "It's a trick I learned while working in the Chianti," where, he says, he trained for many years with a famous enologist. "But most of what I learned about making wine comes from my uncle," he says, grinning at Aldo.

Our job completed, we troop into the house where Anarosa seats us at two long wooden tables and, together with her sister, ladles out the soup—a wonderfully hearty mix of vegetables, chick-peas and *ditalini* (small, finger-shaped pasta). Next comes *arista di maiale*—pork roast—served with roasted potatoes and sautéed turnip greens. And finally, Anarosa's own *torta di mandorle e cioccolata*, chocolate almond cake.

"*Mangia*," says Aldo when I wave away a second helping of dessert. "*A tavola non s'invecchia*." At the table, you stay perpetually young.

We, of course, consume a great deal of wine—all of it Aldo's own, and quite good (if he *does* say so himself every chance he gets). His whites are basically a mix of *Vermentino, Colombana, Moscatella,* and *Trebbiano* grapes; the reds, blended from *Barbarossa* (otherwise known as Merlot), *Sangiovese,* and *Barbera.* Later, we will head off to another vineyard and pick grapes until 6:00 or 7:00 P.M. But for now, there is the great joy of knowing we have kept alive a tradition that has continued, uninterrupted, in Aldo's family since 1712. There is no weariness in the room, no complaining of the hard work involved in making wine. As Aldo said to me the very first time I offered to help, "The more people, the better the party."

The following week, a number of us reunite to watch as the must is put through its final pressing. Again, we are a crowd, 14 people, although only two of us are actually necessary to the process. For the most part, Aldo and Carlo Alberto do all the work themselves, Aldo pouring the must into the 200-year-old press as Carlo Alberto screws the wooden plates down onto the grapes. Our part is to cheer when the first creamy white liquid oozes out into the wooden bucket. In two months, it will turn into very good white wine, but for now we all hold our glasses under the spout and toast the end of another harvest. *"Per fare un amico, basta un bicchiere,"* says Aldo as he takes the first sip. *"Ma per mantenerlo, non basta una botte."* To make a friend, a glassful is sufficient, but to keep the friendship going, even a barrel is too little.

This being wine season, the opportunities for sampling are many. The following week, I am invited for a private wine tasting at La Tenuta di Forci, a small but noted estate in the Freddiana, west of Lucca. Owned by the 61-year-old Baroness Scola Camerini-Diamantina, who designs all the labels herself, Forci produces 5 reds and 3 whites. Two of the 8 are DOC wines, and one, a 16% alcohol Amarone called Vino del Cardinale, is considered to be among the Lucchesia's best.

Getting to the winery is not easy, located as it is at the end of an insanely winding road emanating from Pieve Santo Stefano and heading towards Vecoli. Along the way, I drive past scores of deserted olive groves, a smattering of villas dating back to the 1700s, and chestnut forests reputed to contain more than their share of *porcini* mushrooms.

At journey's end, I am greeted by my friend, Armando Scaramucci, who is both the caretaker of the Forci estate and a great painter. *"Vieni, vieni,"* he says as soon as he sees my car pulling in the front drive. Hurry! He pulls me into the *cantina* just in time to meet Eugenio Pascheretti, a famous enologist who, as it turns out, has come to Forci to sample the new wines. "Pascheretti *loves* last year's Cardinale," Antonio whispers as we enter through the large wooden doors. "He's going to devote his entire October column to it."

I am happy for Armando and thrilled at this evidence of good taste on Eugenio's part, but their conversational exchange bores me within two minutes of being in their presence. Basically, Armando is puffing up his wines while Eugenio puffs up his great knowledge of all things enological and beyond. It is one of those standard discourses between those who have something to sell and those with the power to sway the vast army of consumeristic forces.

I make my excuses and wander away just in the middle of Armando asserting that this year's Cardinale will be the best ever (an assertion he makes about every year's vintage, although he is generally right). My stated destination is the bathroom, but, along the way, I spot a little old man sitting at a folding table with a carton of wine at his feet and a pot of glue at his right hand. I inch closer to see if he is doing what I think he's doing. Yes. He is gluing labels onto bottles of Cardinale one by one and with such pride and care that it takes him more than 5 minutes per bottle.

First he dips the little brush into the paste pot and dabs it on the front of the glass (sometimes he even removes some of the excess with a small white cloth tethered to the right side of his belt). Then he carefully positions the label (sometimes measuring to make sure it is in the right place) and smooths it lovingly with another cloth attached to the opposite side of his belt. As a finale, he holds the bottle up in front of his face and swivels it side to side to be certain of his achievement. One additional glance for artistic appreciation and back in the carton it goes.

The amazing part of this spectacle is that, while not one of Tuscany's greatest producers, Forci is also not a small local holding. Its annual output of over 25,000 bottles makes it impossible to believe they are all labeled by this one little man. And yet, there he is, and he seems to have the tenor of one who has held his job for a very long time.

When I return from my errand, Pascheretti is thankfully gone. *"Allora?"* I say. What did you accomplish?

"He was very excited about both the Cardinale and the Forciano (a blend of Sangiovese and Cannaiola). Some of the best he has tasted, he said. Of course, he was absolutely right. I just wish this year's was ready, but he promised to come back."

"I'd like to agree with you both," I say with as much regret as I can pack into my voice, "but I really don't feel comfortable commenting, since I have yet to taste even one lowly sip." My shaming works. Armando pulls two clean glasses from the rack and uncorks a fresh bottle.

"Let's take it with us," he says after pouring the Cardinale. "I want to show you something."

We climb the rickety stairs to the building's drying level where the entire 5,000 square feet of floor space is covered with grapes. The grapes are grouped according to the various families who live on the estate and care for each vineyard, the names of the families dating back hundreds of years and carved in stone placards hung above each section.

Armando explains that Cardinale wine is made from both fresh grapes and those that have been air dried for a month to raise their sugar content. "The result is a deep, rich wine with 16% alcohol," he says in what is obviously the verbiage used with tour groups. He also explains that the wine was named after Forci's original owner, Cardinal Buonvisi, whose great diplomatic expertise convinced France to join with Poland and Austria in saving Vienna from an attempted Turkish invasion in 1683. In 1690, he adds, Buonvisi was elected primate of Lucca and twice afterwards was considered for the papacy.

I walk among the grapes, sipping my wine—which is exquisite—and soaking in the sight and smell of a centuries-old tradition. The drying floor has windows on both sides, and there is a soft breeze wafting through the room. No light ever shines on the grapes directly, Armando has said, and, true to his words, the rays of the sun slant across the windows in an almost horizontal direction. Titian should have seen this, I think to myself, remembering the luminosity of *Sacred and Profane Love*. But perhaps he did; after all, these people have been using precisely the same method for over 500 years.

We spend another hour or so tasting wine and then repair to Armando's studio where he shows me his latest paintings and tells me he was recently given a one-man show in Florence's Pitti Gallery. I am impressed and say so, although Armando needs no praise to convince him of his worth.

"Which painting is your favorite?" I ask, glancing at the hundreds of canvases strewn about the room.

"I like them all," he answers and thrusts his nose into the air. His vanity is a constant joke between us.

"No, really," I insist.

"All right then, but I will only answer because you are such a good friend. The truth is, I really do like them all, a statement you interpret to mean I lack personal perspective. My mother would feel the same way. But she comes to that sentiment from a lifetime spent listening to her parish priest sermonize about the evils of pride." He shakes his head. "Pride *is* evil when defined in the way Christ intended, the pride that causes people to think themselves better than others and to think of others as inferior creatures."

He picks up one of his portraits and turns it to face me. "But that's not the same thing as my saying, 'I think this work is good.' The fact is, I work very hard at being good. For whatever reason, and we can discuss that problem later, it is very important to me to be good at what I do. If what I do is not at a certain level of accomplishment, I get rid of it, so that the only things I show you are the things I deem worthy of being shown." He shrugs his shoulders. "And so, why shouldn't I express my opinion?"

I have to admit, he has a point. I also have to admit that I am more drawn to people who feel that way about themselves than to people who recoil from acknowledging their own accomplishments. The problem lies in their voicing that feeling, but why should it? Why should others be the only ones allowed to praise your achievements? *"Per arrivare in paradiso, ci vuole solo l'umiltá,"* my mother used to say in an apparent echo of Armando's own mother's sentiments. To enter Paradise, one needs only to be humble. Maybe.

We wind up spending too much time looking at Armando's paintings and talking about humility. The result is that we are late getting on the road to Camaiore, and I can already hear Tiziano carping about how the dinner he cooked for us is now worthy of the garbage.

I'm not sure how this evening came together in the way it has, but I generally like all my friends to know and like one another, and sometimes I fail to think through the implications of certain social configurations. I initially made a date with my friend Tiziano Francesconi to have dinner together at his place, the Enoteca Nebraska, one of the Lucchesia's most famous wine bars. Then my other friend called—Emiliana Lucchese, who is probably Tuscany's most noted enologist—and I asked her to join us. Then I went to Aldo's to help him harvest his grapes and I thought, why not invite him? And finally, I asked Armando because I thought he would like to meet Emiliana and also because Tiziano is a great cook and nobody appreciates food more than Armando.

So here we are, although, as predicted, Tiziano is carrying on about our being late.

"A questo punto, nemmeno i maiali mangerebbero questa pasta." At this point, even the pigs wouldn't eat this pasta.

"I told you not to throw it in until they got here," says Emiliana, who is sitting at the end of the table drinking wine with Aldo.

"She said 8:30, and I took her at her word."

"Just serve it," I say, knowing Tiziano's penchant for exaggeration.

In truth, the pasta is a bit overdone, but the tripe and the stuffed artichokes and the red cabbage terrine and the cardoon salad are works of art. We eat for two hours, drinking various wines brought by Aldo, Emiliana, Armando, and, of course, Tiziano whose collection boggles the mind.

Among his most valued vintages are an 1892 Chianti Selvapiana, a 1964 Sassicaia (the first Sassicaia ever made, in fact), a 1926 Pomerol, a 1942 Barolo, a 1962 Montrachet, and a 1930 Carmignani. But his greatest pride is a 12-bottle collection of Marie Jeanne Grand Cru Bordeaux, spanning the years between 1963 and 1975 and housed in bottles that were hand-blown in the 1700s. Only 12 such collections exist in the world.

In all, he owns 30,000 bottles, and they are all squeezed into three seductive rooms whose walls are covered floor to ceiling with bottles of wine which, in turn, are covered with various levels of dust. "Never," Tiziano answered when I asked if he ever dusted. "It would be a desecration of the ambience."

He started this *enoteca* with his equally flamboyant friend, Giovanni Bonuccelli, in 1959; originally it was "simply an excuse to drink wine." Eventually, others began stopping by, and Tiziano would cook meals specifically paired with his growing cache of prestigious wines. Along the way, he schooled himself on the theory and practice of winemaking and consumption and began structuring his vacations around places known for the excellence of their vintages. "Little by little, it became my life," he says. "And why not? After all, drinking wine is the most beautiful thing in the world."

By 1980, he was writing wine articles for *Time Off* magazine and, by 1985, had joined a number of prestigious French and Italian wine-tasting societies. In 1991, he bought out his partner and, soon afterwards, began appearing in magazine articles and international guide books that touted both his establishment as "one of Tuscany's most serious wine bars" and Tiziano himself as "infinitely knowledgeable about wines and wine production."

Taking nothing away from either Nebraska's "seriousness" or Tiziano's "infinite knowledge," I have always thought such evaluations missed the point. You come to Nebraska to drink good wine, yes. But you come more to hear Tiziano rant and rail and hold court on everything from the crookedness of Italian wine evaluators ("In France, every village has its own appellation; here, we have 500 evaluators for the entire country, and vintners seeking DOC accreditation bring their bottles to the central office rather than that lazy bastard going out to check the vineyard itself.") to Camaiore's penchant for handing out parking tickets ("I'm the only one in this town actively involved in promoting tourism, so what do the *carabinieri* do? They wait until my place is crowded and then ticket every car parked one inch to the left of the approved area.").

Tonight, however, he has met his match in Aldo, Armando, and Emiliana who has brought her snippety dachshund which she wears draped on her shoulder like a fur. Only ten minutes into the evening, I realize what a masterful stroke it was on my part in having brought these four divas together. Not only is each convinced they know more than anybody about wine, but they are all so verbally opinionated that all I have to do for enjoyment is sit back and listen.

"What we're missing in Italy is the legislative process," says Armando, referring to the laws passed in the '60s and '70s that forced producers to include at least 10% of the white grapes Malvasia and Trebbiano in their red wine. Anyone who wanted to make a wine entirely from Sangiovese, Tuscany's best grape, had to label it as a table wine. "Our laws have forced us to take our best vintages and label them *vino da tavola.*"

"You don't know what you're talking about," Aldo retorts. "That is our strength. Look at all those DOC French wines that aren't worth the glass they're bottled in. Here, we put wine on the table and drink it with no fuss. It is part of our meal, not something to worship in front of."

"But we continue to lose out in the world market," says Emiliana, stroking her beloved Cici. "Our wines consistently get less attention than those of France."

"And it's a shame, because there's really no comparison," adds Tiziano.

"Who *cares* about what the world thinks?" shrieks Aldo. "Are we talking about drinking wine or selling it?"

"Both!" yells Armando.

"Well, maybe that's the problem," Aldo retorts. "I don't give *un cazzo* what anybody thinks. I drink my wine because it's the best."

"Come on Aldo," says Armando, pouring some 1992 Cardinale. "Your wine is good enough to go with a simple pasta. But you can't tell me it's better than that Vino Nobile Tiziano just poured ten minutes ago."

"It's better," Aldo says, taking a huge gulp of the Cardinale. "This wine, you can only drink a little bit. It's too strong. Mine, you can drink as much as you want."

By now we are on our sixth bottle and, despite the fact that you will rarely see Tuscans drunk, there are five people here approaching incoherence.

"Maybe we should think about heading home," I say to Armando because I have—unwisely, I now realize—driven him here and need to return him to Forci before heading back to Massarosa.

"One more before everybody goes," says Tiziano, always reluctant to move towards closure. "Let's try this '92 Morellino—truly the best wine Tuscany produced that year."

"Not in my book," says Aldo.

Armando, I know, will be next.

"I know that Morellino," he says, contemplatively. "And it's good. Very good, actually. But that year's Cardinale was exceptional. *No no no,* there is no comparison."

I settle back into my chair. So I *won't* be getting home any time soon. So I *might* have to call my cousin Santi to come and get me. So I *have* cast my lot this evening with four egomaniacs intent on verbally bludgeoning each other before the first rays of dawn. What is that alongside my stunning brilliance in having brought these people together? *No no no,* the true master here is me.

About Vegetable Medleys

Our cooking school students generally arrive on Sunday. They are picked up at 1:25 P.M. at Pisa Airport and delivered to Camporomano at approximately 2:00. By 2:30, they are settled into their rooms and ready for lunch which is served on the main lawn.

The menu varies according to season and the whims of my partner, Sandra Lotti, who prepares that initial meal. But a few items are fixed (besides, of course, large loaves of peasant bread, extra-virgin oil, local cheeses, and dozens of bottles of wine). Sandra always includes a wonderful soup made from whatever vegetables looked best at the market that morning, and a huge platter of grilled or roasted vegetables garnished with sprigs of fresh herbs.

As my mother points out, first impressions are lasting. Which is why Sandra

Vegetable medley.

structures that first meal around vegetables, lots of vegetables, vegetables of every size and shape and color. The effect is mesmerizing, and neither she nor I can ever get enough of those initial *oohs* and *aahs*, those smiles and the looks of absolute delight as students first encounter the unparalleled bounty that is Tuscany.

The following recipes explore that bounty in all its splendor, from soups bursting with a springtime riot of baby leaves and roots to risotto filled with multicolored vegetables. One thing I know about working with vegetables is that there are almost no rules regarding which go best with what. Tomatoes can be paired with beans and mushrooms, or potatoes and rutabagas, or onions and truffles, or fennel and cardoons. It is purely up to the method of preparation and your taste buds.

Bollito Misto di Verdura con Salsa Verde
Mixed Boiled Vegetables with Green Sauce

Most days I cook a big dinner, either because I'm testing recipes or because I generally like to choose how my food is prepared. There are times, however, when I want to eat at home but don't have a great deal of time to spend in the kitchen. On those occasions, I make a simple boiled dinner of whatever vegetables I have on hand and drizzle over them a basic parsley vinaigrette. Easy, satisfying, and delicious. But don't limit this recipe to bouts of laziness; a few years ago, I began serving it to dinner guests as an entree and, without exception, it has always been a great success.

The Vegetables

4 cups Basic Vegetable Broth (see page 308)
4 new red potatoes, scrubbed and quartered
4 medium onions, peeled and halved
4 carrots, scraped and halved
2 small turnips, trimmed and quartered
2 stalks celery, fibrous strings removed and cut into fourths
1 medium head broccoli, cut into florets (stems reserved for another use)

1 fennel bulb, feathery fronds removed, cored and cut into eighths
12–16 stalks thin asparagus, trimmed and with stems peeled
2 small zucchini, cut into 1-inch chunks

The Sauce

1½ cups fresh parsley, stems removed
½ cup extra-virgin olive oil
2 tablespoons Basic Vegetable Broth
1 clove garlic, peeled
Salt and freshly ground black pepper

1. Heat the broth to boiling in a large heavy-gauge soup pot. Add the potatoes, onions, carrots, turnips, and celery. Cover and cook for 15 minutes or until tender. Remove with tongs and arrange on a heated platter.

2. Add the broccoli and fennel to the same broth. Cook, uncovered, for 10 minutes or until tender. Remove with tongs and add to the other vegetables.

3. Boil the asparagus and zucchini for 5 minutes, remove, and arrange on the platter. Reserve the broth for another use.

4. Meanwhile, make the sauce. Place the parsley, oil, broth, and garlic in the bowl of a food processor. Purée until smooth and remove to a bowl. Season with salt and pepper. Drizzle the sauce over the vegetables and serve immediately.

SERVES 4   TIME: 45 minutes   LEVEL OF DIFFICULTY: Easy

VARIATIONS: The vegetables can also be steamed over water. See Chapter 1, pages 35–37 for steaming times.

MAKE AHEAD: The sauce can be made up to 2 days in advance and refrigerated.

Ribollita Lucchese
Ribollita, Lucca-Style

Ribollita is a traditional Tuscan soup made with leftover vegetables reboiled (hence the name) with beans and bread, and drizzled with olive oil just before serving. In most cases, the soup is thick enough to be eaten with a fork; its usage dates back to the days of poor peasant farmers who could only afford one-dish meals. This particular recipe is prepared in the style of Lucca, an 11th-century walled city on the road between Florence and Viareggio. It is made with a combination of beans instead of just cannellini, *and is more tomato-y than the Florentine version. I have substituted kale for the* braschette *(black cabbage) used by Tuscans and not available in this country.*

¼ pound dried *cannellini* beans, soaked for 12 hours and drained

2 bay leaves

2 medium onions, peeled

¼ pound dried cranberry beans, soaked for 12 hours and drained

8 tablespoons extra-virgin olive oil

1 medium onion, minced

1 carrot, minced

1 stalk celery, diced

1 leek, cleaned and diced

1 pound kale, cleaned and roughly chopped

8 cups Basic Vegetable Broth (see page 308)

¼ teaspoon dried sage

¼ teaspoon dried thyme

12 ounces canned Italian tomatoes, with liquid

4 ¾-inch-thick slices day-old peasant bread, roughly chopped

Salt and freshly ground black pepper

¼ cup fresh grated Parmigiano-Reggiano

1. Place the *cannellini* beans in a soup pot with 1 bay leaf, 1 of the whole onions, and enough water to cover by 2 inches. Cook, covered, over low heat for 45 minutes. Salt at the 30-minute mark.

2. Place the cranberry beans in another pot with the remaining onion and bay leaf and enough water to cover by 2 inches. Cover and cook over low heat for 60 minutes, salting at the 45-minute mark.

3. Meanwhile, heat 4 tablespoons of the oil in a large soup pot. Sauté the onion, carrot, and celery for 5 minutes over low heat until soft. Add the leek and kale and sauté 2 minutes more, stirring constantly. Stir in the broth, the sage and thyme, and the tomatoes and mix well.

4. When the beans are cooked, remove half of each and force through a food mill with some liquid. Place the mash in the pot with the vegetables. Add the remaining *cannellini* and cranberry beans and all the bean liquid. Cover and cook over low heat for 30 minutes.

5. When the beans and vegetables are tender, stir in the bread. Season with salt and pepper and remove from heat. Cool to room temperature or let sit overnight.

6. Just before serving, bring to a boil and immediately remove from heat. Ladle into individual bowls or a soup terrine. Drizzle with remaining oil and sprinkle with cheese.

SERVES 4 (with leftovers)   TIME: 2½ hours   LEVEL OF DIFFICULTY: Moderate
VARIATIONS: Canned beans can be substituted.
MAKE AHEAD: Up to Step 6, the soup can be made up to 3–4 days in advance and refrigerated.

Ricotta Fatta in Casa Saltata in Padella con Verdura
Homemade Ricotta Sautéed with Fresh Vegetables

In the old days, true ricotta was not really a cheese, in that it was made from whey instead of from milk. Therefore, the following version should always have been called not ricotta but "fresh cow's milk coagulated with acid." But why parse words? It's fairly easy to make, attractive, and, above all, good.

3 quarts milk

1 teaspoon powdered citric acid

4 tablespoons extra-virgin olive oil

1 medium onion, very thinly sliced

2 cloves garlic, thinly sliced

1 stalk celery, thinly sliced

6 black olives, pitted and halved

1 dried chili pepper, crushed

½ teaspoon fresh chopped marjoram

½ teaspoon fresh chopped sage

Salt and freshly ground black pepper

4 ¾-inch-thick slices crusty peasant bread, toasted

4 tips fresh marjoram sprigs (reserve the rest of the sprigs for another use)

8 large leaves chicory, for garnish

1. Place the milk in a saucepan over low flame and, using a thermometer, heat to 220 degrees. Stir in the citric acid and continue to stir until the milk begins to curdle. Remove from heat and cool for 45 minutes.

2. Drain the ricotta in a colander lined with cheesecloth, place the colander over a large bowl to catch the drips, and refrigerate for 12 hours or overnight.

Labeling Cardinale wine. One additional glance for artistic appreciation.

3. Heat 2 tablespoons of the oil in a skillet and sauté the onion, garlic, and celery for 3 minutes over medium heat. Add the olives and chili and sauté for 1 more minute, stirring constantly. Stir in the ricotta and cook for 30 seconds longer. Season with marjoram, sage, salt, and pepper.

4. Drizzle the remaining oil over the bread rounds and place one round on each plate. Top with a dollop of the ricotta and vegetables, drizzling the oil in the pan over the bread and placing a marjoram sprig in the center of the ricotta. Arrange the chicory alongside and serve.

SERVES 4

TIME: 90 minutes (not counting the overnight setting of the ricotta)

LEVEL OF DIFFICULTY: Advanced

VARIATIONS: Good store-bought ricotta can be substituted for homemade.

MAKE AHEAD: The ricotta can be made up to 2 days in advance and refrigerated.

Taglierini con Patate e Crescione
Taglierini with Potatoes and Watercress

"Pasta with potatoes?" said the incredulous potato vendor. "Too much starch . . . use turnips instead." But I held my ground and when it was finally on the table with everyone complimenting its "unique flavor," I made a mental note to keep some in reserve and deliver it to Mr. Doubtful the very next day.

½ pound small new red potatoes, very thinly sliced
6 tablespoons extra-virgin olive oil
Salt and freshly ground black pepper to taste
1 recipe Basic Pasta Dough (see page 312)
1 medium red onion, thinly sliced

2 garlic cloves, thinly sliced
2 tablespoons Basic Vegetable Broth (see page 308)
2 tablespoons basil chiffonade
1 tablespoon lemon zest
1 pound watercress, stems removed
¼ cup fresh grated Parmigiano-Reggiano

1. Preheat the oven to 350 degrees. Soak the potatoes in cold water for 20 minutes. Drain, pat dry, and toss with 2 tablespoons of the oil, salt, and pepper. Place in an ovenproof pan and bake for 20 minutes, stirring once or twice.

2. Meanwhile, roll the pasta dough into a long sheet and cut into small, irregular rectangles approximately ¾ x 2 inches. Bring a large pot of water to boil.

3. Heat 2 tablespoons oil in a skillet. Sauté the onion and garlic for 5 minutes over low heat. When the potatoes are slightly browned, remove them from the oven and add them to the skillet, tossing to blend. Add the broth, basil, and lemon zest and simmer for 1 minute.

4. Drop the pasta into the boiling water and cook for 5 minutes or until *al dente*. Drain and add to the vegetables, along with the watercress and the remaining oil. Toss to blend and serve, sprinkled with cheese.

SERVES 4   TIME: 1 hour   LEVEL OF DIFFICULTY: Moderate

VARIATIONS: Store-bought pasta can be substituted.

Insalata di Verdura, Erbe e Riso Selvatico
Roasted Vegetable, Herb, and Wild Rice Salad

As colorful as it is delicious, this salad's ingredients can be altered to accommodate the seasons as well as the mood. There are no rules as to what works and what doesn't; the only constant is that the vegetables should create a riotous palette of colors and be arranged in a way that showcases their fanfare. Make believe you're a florist and the vegetables are your wildflowers.

2 medium zucchini, sliced into ½-inch rounds

1 thin, long eggplant, sliced diagonally into ½-inch pieces

8 tablespoons extra-virgin olive oil

Salt and freshly ground black pepper

16 baby icicle radishes with a 1-inch section of green stem left attached

16 baby carrots, with a 2-inch section of green stem left attached

8 small new red potatoes, halved

½ head cauliflower, cut into florets

16 Brussels sprouts

¼ pound broccoli rabe, stems removed

12 leaves Belgian endive

½ pound mixed greens (Red Russian kale, beet greens, mustard, amaranth, chicory, radicchio)

16 cherry tomatoes, 8 red and 8 gold, halved

1 red pepper, seeded, cored, and cut into thin rings

2 cups cooked wild rice

24 sprigs fresh herbs (rosemary, sage, thyme, marjoram, savory, dill)

1 tablespoon balsamic vinegar

Freshly ground green pepper

1. Baste the zucchini and eggplant with 1 tablespoon oil, season with salt and black pepper, and grill for 2 minutes per side on an outdoor barbecue or indoor electric model.

2. Place the radishes, carrots, and potatoes in a bowl. Toss with 2 tablespoons oil, salt, and black pepper, place in an ovenproof baking pan, and roast in a 350-degree oven for 20 minutes or until tender, turning once or twice.

3. Parboil the cauliflower and brussels sprouts in boiling salted water for 4 minutes or until tender. Add the broccoli rabe at the 2-minute mark. Drain.

4. Arrange the ingredients on a large platter in a helter-skelter star pattern with vegetables emanating from the center. Use the shape and color of each to deter-

mine where it will be placed. Lay some over others, stand some leaves up as if they were flowers, and scatter the wild rice around the perimeter.

5. When all the ingredients have been placed, drizzle with oil and vinegar, dust with salt and green pepper, and present at the table.

SERVES 4   TIME: 90 minutes   LEVEL OF DIFFICULTY: Moderate
VARIATIONS: Any vegetable can be used and, instead of arranging, the salad can be tossed in a large bowl.

Caponata di Bozzano
Bozzano-Style Marinated Vegetable Salad

There are as many versions of caponata *as there are bean soups. I love them all. This recipe came to me from a 94-year-old woman in Bozzano, a tiny village 2 miles from my home in Massarosa. She made it for an outdoor church fair held to raise money for African immigrants. When I tasted it, I just knew I had to track her down and find out her exact ingredients.*

8 tablespoons extra-virgin olive oil
2 cloves garlic, crushed
5 long, thin eggplants (about
   1½ pounds total), trimmed and
   cut into 1-inch cubes
3 stalks celery, fibrous string
   removed and cut into a 2-inch
   julienne
2 medium onions, cut into thin
   (⅛ inch) slices

5 ripe Italian plum tomatoes,
   seeded and cut into small cubes
2 tablespoons red wine vinegar
2 teaspoon balsamic vinegar
½ teaspoon granulated sugar
3 tablespoons capers
1 cup oil-cured olives, pitted
Salt
Juice of ½ lemon

1. Heat 4 tablespoons oil in a large skillet. Sauté the garlic over medium heat for 1 minute. Add the eggplant and stir-fry for 10 minutes, until lightly browned. Using a slotted spoon, remove the eggplant and drain on paper towels. Remove and discard the garlic.

2. Add 2 more tablespoons oil to the skillet. Stir-fry the celery for 5 minutes, until translucent. Remove the celery and place in a bowl.

3. Add the remaining oil to the skillet. Stir-fry the onions until soft. Remove the onions with a slotted spoon and add to the bowl with the celery.

4. Add the tomatoes to the skillet and stir-fry for 3 minutes. Return all the vegetables to the skillet and stir-fry for 3 more minutes. Add both the vinegars, the sugar, capers, olives, and salt. Cook for an additional 5 minutes, stirring constantly. Transfer the vegetables to a serving platter and cool to room temperature. Drizzle with lemon and serve.

SERVES 4   TIME: 45 minutes   LEVEL OF DIFFICULTY: Moderate

MAKE AHEAD: The *caponata* can be made up to 5 days in advance and refrigerated. Return to room temperature before serving.

Teglia di Pomodori, Cipolle e Patate
Baked Casserole with Tomatoes, Potatoes, and Onions

A simple dish with peasant origins, its lack of pretension shines through in both the ease with which it is prepared and its clean, uncomplicated flavors. Make sure to use medium-starch boiling potatoes such as Eastern, Yukon Gold, Red Pontiac, or Peruvian Blue. High-starch potatoes will crumble when you try to slice, and low-starch varieties are too small.

1 pound boiled Eastern-type potatoes, peeled and cut into ½-inch slices

1 pound ripe Italian plum tomatoes, peeled, and cut into ¼-inch slices

1 large onion, diced

3 tablespoons unflavored bread crumbs

Salt and freshly ground black pepper

3 tablespoons fresh chopped parsley

4 tablespoons extra-virgin olive oil

1. Preheat the oven to 350 degrees. In an oiled baking pan, alternate layers of potatoes and tomatoes, ending with tomatoes. Cover with chopped onion and sprinkle with bread crumbs, salt, pepper, and parsley.

2. Drizzle the oil over the top and bake for 15 minutes or until the crumbs have browned and the dish is heated through. Serve hot.

SERVES 4   TIME: 35 minutes   LEVEL OF DIFFICULTY: Easy

Crespelle di Patate alla Parmigiana
Sautéed Asparagus with
Parmesan Sauce Wrapped in Potato Wafers

This dish is the result of two separate experiments: one with making flour crepes to wrap around sautéed tomatoes topped with a parmesan sauce; the other with making scalloped potatoes and wondering whether the thin potato slices might not make wonderful crepe wrappers. Allora, I put the two together, and ecco!

3 large baking potatoes, peeled
36 thin asparagus spears

The Parmesan Sauce

10 tablespoons unsalted butter
¾ cup unbleached flour
½ teaspoon salt

¼ teaspoon fresh grated white
    pepper
3 cups milk
1 cup fresh grated Parmigiano-
    Reggiano
½ pound spinach, washed and
    patted dry
2 tablespoons heavy cream

1. Slice the potatoes lengthwise as thinly as possible into 48 slices. Soak the slices in ice water for 20 minutes. Drain and pat dry.

2. Boil the asparagus in salted water for 5 minutes or until tender. Drain and refresh in cold water.

3. To make the sauce, melt 6 tablespoons of the butter in a saucepan over low heat and whisk in the flour. Do not brown. Add salt and pepper and gradually whisk in the milk. Add the cheese, whisking constantly until the sauce begins to boil. Reduce heat even further and simmer for 5 minutes.

4. Divide the asparagus into bundles of three. Wrap 4 potato slices widthwise around each asparagus bundle, making sure to overlap each slice. Melt the remaining butter in a skillet, and sauté the packages over low heat. As the packages brown, the potatoes will stick together and create a solid wrapping.

5. Meanwhile, place the spinach in the bowl of a food processor with the cream. Puree until smooth.

6. To assemble, cover the bottom of 4 plates with spinach cream. Arrange 3 packages on each plate, top with Parmesan sauce, and serve.

SERVES 4   TIME: 50 minutes   LEVEL OF DIFFICULTY: Advanced

VARIATIONS: Flour crepes can be substituted for potatoes.

MAKE AHEAD: The asparagus can be boiled 6 hours in advance and refrigerated. The Parmesan sauce can also be made 6 hours in advance and refrigerated.

Risotto Primaverile con Pure di Porri
Spring Vegetable Risotto with Leek Purée

Risotto is generally thought of as a dish unto itself, one that takes center stage on a plate with no supporting characters. But it can also be layered upon a bed of vegetables—in this case, puréed leeks—and dipped into the purée as one might do with Asian rice and hoisin sauce.

6 cups Basic Vegetable Broth (see page 308)	2 very ripe Italian plum tomatoes, diced
2 ounces dried *porcini* mushrooms	Salt and freshly ground black pepper
5 tablespoons extra-virgin olive oil	2 baby zucchini, sliced into thin rounds
1 medium onion, minced	4 ounces fresh mixed wild mushrooms (*porcini*, chanterelles, and morels), sliced thinly
1 medium carrot, diced	
3 leeks, cleaned and diced	
2 cups Arborio rice	
1 cup dry white wine	⅓ cup fresh grated Parmigiano-Reggiano
1 leek, cleaned	

1. Place the broth in a saucepan and heat to boiling. Reduce the heat and maintain at a simmer.

2. Soak the dried mushrooms in boiling water for 20 minutes. Drain, rinse, and mince. Pour the liquid through a coffee filter or cheesecloth and reserve.

3. Heat 3 tablespoons of the oil in a heavy-gauge pot. Sauté the onion, carrot, mushrooms, and leeks for 10 minutes over low heat. Do not brown. Add the rice and sauté for another 2 minutes, stirring constantly until the kernels are well coated.

285

4. Increase the heat to medium low. Pour the wine over the rice and cook until evaporated. Stir in ½ cup broth and cook until the rice has absorbed most of the liquid. Continue adding broth, ½ cupful at a time, stirring occasionally until it has been almost completely absorbed before adding more.

5. Meanwhile, cut off the green part of the leeks and reserve for another use. Slice the white part into a fine julienne.

6. Place the remaining oil in a skillet and sauté the leek for 2 minutes over low heat. Add ¼ cup broth and the tomatoes, cover, and cook for 5 minutes or until wilted. Purée in a food processor, season with salt and pepper and keep warm.

7. When the rice has cooked for 15 minutes, add the zucchini and fresh mushrooms. Continue to cook, adding broth and stirring occasionally, until the rice is tender and on the dry side of soupy. Stir in half the cheese and season with salt and pepper.

8. Divide the leek mixture among 4 plates and arrange into a bed. Top with a round of risotto, sprinkle with the remaining cheese, and serve.

SERVES 6   TIME: 60 minutes   LEVEL OF DIFFICULTY: Advanced

MAKE AHEAD: While restaurants routinely cook risotto to the halfway point and finish cooking on order, I do not advise this practice for anything other than an absolute absence of time. Risotto can be reheated in a double boiler. Make sure to add some additional liquid, as the risotto will have absorbed all the liquid and be quite dry.

Pecorino con Verdure Miste e Acetosella
Sliced Pecorino with Mixed Vegetable Dice and Sautéed Sorrel

While there is only one Parmigiano-Reggiano, there are dozens of different kinds of pecorino *cheese. Made from sheep's milk (*pecora *means "sheep"), pecorino can be as relatively soft as Gouda or as hard as Parmesan; the difference lies in how long it is stored. Its flavor, of course, corresponds directly to its age: the older the cheese, the sharper the flavor. This delicate blend of sautéed vegetables in a lemon-caper sauce works best with a very young cheese, one whose texture is only slightly denser than that of ricotta.*

6 tablespoons extra-virgin olive oil

1 medium onion, minced

2 carrots, diced

1 stalk celery, fibrous string removed and diced

3 baby zucchini, diced

1 small yellow squash, diced

½ pound sorrel

4 tablespoons fresh lemon juice

3 hardboiled egg yolks

2 teaspoons capers, drained and rinsed

Salt and freshly ground black pepper

½ pound young *pecorino* cheese (*marzolino* or *cacciotta*), cut into 8 ½-inch slices

1. Place 3 tablespoons oil in a heavy skillet. Sauté the onion, carrots, and celery for 10 minutes over low heat, until soft. Add the zucchini and squash and cook for another 4 minutes, stirring constantly.

2. Meanwhile, steam the sorrel over boiling water for 2 minutes or until slightly wilted.

3. Place the lemon, egg yolks, and capers in the bowl of a food processor and puree until smooth. Season with salt and pepper.

4. Add all but 3 tablespoons of the sauce to the sautéed vegetables and stir to blend. Cook for 3 minutes.

5. Divide the sautéed vegetables among 4 plates, creating a foundation bed. Arrange the sorrel over the vegetables and top with the *pecorino*, 2 slices on each plate. Spoon the remaining sauce over the cheese and serve.

SERVES 4   TIME: 35–45 minutes   LEVEL OF DIFFICULTY: Moderate

VARIATIONS: For a spicier flavor, add 1 crushed dried chili pepper to the initial vegetable sauté.

MAKE AHEAD: The sauce can be made up to 2 days in advance and refrigerated.

Fettucine alla Crudaiola
Fettucine with Raw Vegetables

There is nothing quite like those wonderful days in August when it seems as though the days could go on forever. The vines are heavy with ripe red tomatoes and the scent of basil clings to your skin long after you have left the garden and are lying on a striped chaise, dreaming. This is a dish expressly made for just one of those days. Fresh, fragrant, and delicious.

½ pound ripe Italian tomatoes,
  cored and diced
10–15 leaves fresh basil
1 cucumber, peeled, seeded, and
  diced
2 baby zucchini, diced
4 cloves garlic, crushed

¼ pound arugula, roughly chopped
½ cup extra-virgin olive oil
⅔ cup fresh grated *pecorino*
Salt and freshly ground black
  pepper
1 pound dried fettucine

1. Combine all the ingredients save for the fettucine in a large bowl. Season with salt and pepper, mix well, and set aside for 30 minutes. Toss once or twice during this time.

2. Cook the fettucine in boiling salted water for 7 minutes or until *al dente*. Drain and add to the bowl. Toss to blend all ingredients and serve.

SERVES 4–6   TIME: 35–45 minutes   LEVEL OF DIFFICULTY: Easy
VARIATIONS: Parmesan can be substituted for *pecorino*.

Tortelli di Castagne Tartuffati
Chestnut Tortelli with Mushroom Wine Sauce and Truffles

The inherent sweetness of chestnuts blends particularly well with pungent truffles, especially when accompanied by a smooth, rich mushroom-and-red-wine sauce. The overall effect is somewhat akin to lying on a sheepskin rug in front of a crackling hearth and listening to Luciano sing Turandot.

The Tortelli

1 recipe Basic Pasta Dough
  (see page 312)
¾ pound chestnuts, peeled and
  boiled (see "Chestnuts," page 210,
  for directions on peeling)

½ cup heavy cream
1 tablespoon white truffle oil

1. Pass the pasta dough through the narrowest rollers, cut the resulting sheet into four equal sections, and place on a flat surface.

2. To make the filling, place the chestnuts, cream, and oil in the bowl of a food processor and puree to a smooth paste. Distribute teaspoons of filling over 2 sheets of the dough at 2-inch intervals. Using a pastry brush, moisten the space around the mounds. Cover with the remaining 2 sheets and press gently between the rows of filling to seal. Using a ravioli cutter, cut into 2-inch rounds and set aside on a lightly floured surface. Bring a large pot of water to boil.

The Sauce

1 tablespoon extra-virgin olive oil
4 shallots, minced
2 cloves garlic, minced
1 pound fresh *porcini* mushrooms,
   stems removed and thinly sliced
1½ cups dry red wine

1 cup Basic Vegetable Broth (see
   page 308)
2 tablespoons unsalted butter
2 tablespoons unbleached flour
Salt and freshly ground black
   pepper
2 ounces fresh white truffle

3. To make the sauce, heat the oil in a large skillet. Sauté the shallots and garlic for 5 minutes over low heat. Increase the heat to medium, add the mushrooms, and sauté for another 3 minutes, stirring constantly. Deglaze the pan with the wine and cook, stirring constantly, until the liquid has reduced by half.

4. Stir the broth into the sauce and keep warm.

5. Melt the butter in a skillet over medium heat. Whisk in the flour until a thick paste has been created. Stir the paste into the sauce and cook for 3–4 minutes, until the sauce has thickened. Season with salt and pepper.

6. Cook the *tortelli* in the boiling water for 5 minutes, during which time they will rise to the surface. Drain, add to the wine sauce, and gently stir until well coated. Shave the truffle over the *tortelli* and serve hot.

SERVES 4   TIME: 75–90 minutes   LEVEL OF DIFFICULTY: Advanced

VARIATIONS: Dried chestnuts can be used in place of fresh. Soak for 12 hours and boil for 1½ hours or until tender.

MAKE AHEAD: The uncooked *tortelli* can be made 1 day in advance, wrapped in plastic and refrigerated, or frozen.

Lasagne alla Bandiera
Tricolor Lasagna with Wild Mushrooms and Greens

Whenever I serve this dish, my guests all ooh and aah over the colorfully striped lasagna. They love the flavor too—the creamy mushroom bechamel layered with mixed greens—but, somehow, that always seems to be a secondary reaction.

1 recipe Basic Pasta Dough, colored (see page 313) divided into ½ portion white, ¼ portion red, and ¼ portion green
6 tablespoons extra-virgin olive oil
6 cloves garlic, minced
1 pound mixed wild mushrooms (*porcini, shiitake,* chanterelles, oyster, black trumpets), chopped, stems reserved for another use

Salt and freshly ground black pepper
7 tablespoons unsalted butter
3 tablespoons unbleached flour
½ cup heavy cream
1 cup Basic Vegetable Broth (see page 308)
1 pound mixed greens (kale, mustard, beet, amaranth), cleaned and chopped
¼ cup freshly grated Parmigiano-Reggiano

1. Pinch off ⅓ of the white dough and set aside. Pass the remaining dough through the narrowest roller on the pasta machine and place the resulting sheet on a floured board. Now pass the softball-sized white dough through the rollers and, finally, the red and green dough. Place all the flattened rectangles on a floured board.

2. Cut the red, green, and small white rectangles into strips that are ⅓ as wide as the large white sheet. Carefully arrange the strips on the large white sheet in a red, white, and green pattern so that they resemble the Italian flag. Cut the double-layered sheet into 4 smaller, more manageable pieces and pass each through the pasta machine's narrowest rollers. The double layer should now be fused into one tricolor sheet. Repeat with the remaining 3 pieces of dough. Cut into 6-inch rectangles and set aside. Place a large pot of salted water on to boil.

3. Heat 3 tablespoons of the oil in a skillet. Add the garlic and sauté over low heat for 3 minutes. Add the mushrooms and sauté for 7–10 minutes, stirring constantly, until soft. Season with salt and pepper, transfer to a bowl, and set aside.

4. Melt 3 tablespoons of the butter in the same skillet over low heat. Whisk in the flour and cook until you have a thick paste. Add the cream and broth and continue to whisk until the sauce is thickened. Replace the mushrooms and heat through. Cool to room temperature.

5. Heat the remaining oil in another skillet. Sauté the remaining garlic over medium heat for 3 minutes. Add the mixed greens and sauté for 5 minutes, stirring constantly, until wilted. Season with salt and pepper and cool to room temperature.

6. Butter an ovenproof baking dish. Spoon a layer of sauce across the bottom of the dish. Now make alternating layers of pasta, greens, and mushroom sauce. Finish with a layer of pasta, dot with the remaining butter, sprinkle with cheese, and bake for 25 minutes or until the top is lightly browned.

SERVES 4   TIME: 2 hours   LEVEL OF DIFFICULTY: Advanced

MAKE AHEAD: The basic pasta can be made up to 2 days in advance, wrapped in plastic wrap and refrigerated, or frozen.

The contadini who tended our vines also shared our chapel.

Misticanza con Verdura e Scamorza

Mesclun with Roasted Vegetables and *Scamorza* Cheese

Misticanza is the Italian way of saying "mesclun." The greens are somewhat different because, while arugula is native to many countries, certain greens are only grown or favored by individual cultures. Scamorza is a soft, delicate, melting cheese that is often used by Tuscans in place of mozzarella.

2 red and 2 yellow peppers, seeded, cored, and cut into thick slices
2 long, thin eggplants, trimmed and cut into thick lengthwise slices
4 baby zucchini, trimmed and cut into thick rounds
2 purple onions, peeled, trimmed, and cut into 1½-inch-thick slices

1 pound mixed *misticanza* (mesclun), washed and spun dry
½ pound *scamorza* cheese, thinly sliced
4 tablespoons extra-virgin olive oil
Salt and freshly ground green pepper

1. Grill the vegetables on an outdoor barbecue or indoor electric grill, or cook them in a nonstick skillet over high heat. Turn the vegetables once during the cooking so that both sides are thoroughly grilled.

2. Meanwhile, arrange the *misticanza* on individual plates. Top with grilled vegetables and immediately place a slice or two of cheese over the hot vegetables. Drizzle with oil, season with salt and pepper, and serve.

SERVES 4   TIME: 25–30 minutes
LEVEL OF DIFFICULTY: Easy

VARIATIONS: Smoked mozzarella can be substituted for *scamorza*.

Armando Scaramucci — Winemaker Extraordinaire.

Arrotolata di Verdura
Vegetable Bread Roll

This is a wonderful bread to make for parties, not only because you can include whatever vegeta-bles are in season, but because it takes relatively little time to make while giving the impression that you worked all day. I always make 3 or 4 different ones and serve them in overlapping slices arranged on beautiful platters.

3 tablespoons extra-virgin olive oil
2 cloves garlic, minced
1 pound kale, washed, spun dry, and
    roughly chopped
Salt and freshly ground black
    pepper

1 recipe Basic Pizza Dough
    (see page 314)
1 cup black olive paste
    (store-bought or homemade)
1 cup roasted red peppers packed in
    oil
½ pound smoked mozzarella,
    shredded

1. Head the oil in a large skillet. Sauté the garlic for 3 minutes over low heat. Add the kale and sauté for 5 minutes, stirring constantly, until wilted. Season with salt and pepper and cool to room temperature.

2. Preheat the oven to 350 degrees. Place the the dough on a floured surface and roll into a 16 × 20-inch rectangle.

3. Spread the olive paste evenly over the surface of the dough, leaving a 1-inch margin all around. Cut the peppers into small pieces and arrange over the olive paste. Top with kale, sprinkle with mozzarella, and roll up from the short side, being careful to keep all the vegetables in place.

4. Place the roll seam side down in an ovenproof baking pan and bake for 35–45 minutes or until the top is lightly browned. Cool to room temperature, cut into 1-inch-thick slices and serve.

SERVES 4   TIME: 60–75 minutes (not including dough preparation)

LEVEL OF DIFFICULTY: Moderate

VARIATIONS: Any green can be substituted for kale. Try using other kinds of cheese such as Fontina, Gouda, Emmenthal, or Taleggio.

Tiziano Francesconi in the "Cavern" of his Enoteca Nebraska: "Drinking wine is the most beautiful thing in the world."

MAKE AHEAD: The kale can be prepared 1 day in advance, refrigerated, and used chilled. The dough can be prepared up to 3 days in advance and refrigerated, wrapped in plastic wrap, or frozen.

Mantecato di Funghi
Mashed Potatoes with *Porcini* Mushrooms

For reasons that I've never quite been able to understand, mashed potatoes are rarely featured in Tuscan kitchens. When they are, they are generally blended with rutabagas or sautéed shallots and herbs. I first tasted the following recipe at the wonderful Ristorante Lorenzo in Forte dei Marmi and was completely taken by the perfect harmony of flavors between mushrooms and potatoes. Here is my version which uses both dried and fresh funghi.

1 ounce dried *porcini* mushrooms
¼ pound button mushrooms, thinly sliced*
½ cup heavy cream
4 tablespoons unsalted butter

2 pounds boiling potatoes, cut into 1-inch cubes
Salt and freshly ground black pepper
8 sprigs fresh herbs for garnish

1. Soak the dried mushrooms in boiling water for 30 minutes. Squeeze dry and drain, reserving the liquid for another use. Rinse the mushrooms, squeeze again, and chop finely.

2. Add both dried and fresh mushrooms, the cream, and the butter to a small

saucepan and heat to boiling over low heat. Remove from heat, cover, and let sit for 15 minutes.

3. Meanwhile, cook the potatoes in boiling salted water for 15 minutes or until soft. Drain and return to the pot for 1 minute to dry. Transfer to a large bowl and, using a potato masher, mash to a somewhat chunky consistency.

4. Add the mushrooms to the potatoes and stir with a wooden spoon until creamy. Season with salt and pepper and serve, garnished with the fresh herbs.

SERVES 4   TIME: 30 minutes   LEVEL OF DIFFICULTY: Easy

*Do not substitute wild mushrooms of any kind, as they will cause the potatoes to turn an unappealing gray color.

Aldo Barsotti doesn't have a moment to lose as the vendemnia begins.

CHAPTER TEN

Broths, Oils, Dough, Sauces, and Pestos

Who Needs Artusi?

"At the age of ten, the orphaned Martino was taken in by Don Andrea, a local parish priest. One night, Don Andrea asked Martino to stand watch over a dead body as was the custom of the village. 'I will fill the larder with as much food as you can eat,' Don Andrea promised. 'But you must never leave the room wherein lies the casket. If you do, the Devil will claim the poor man's soul.' When everyone had gone to bed and the room was dark save for one small lamp, Martino filled his plate with bread and sausage and took his place beside the coffin. Possessed of a ravenous hunger, the boy finished the food in just four bites. As he was again raiding the larder for a hunk of cheese, the dead man came to life and began howling in a horrific manner. Martino looked at the man waving his arms and went placidly back to eating as if what was taking place was nothing out of the ordinary."

   —Excerpted from *Martino Senza Paura,* a book of short stories by Raffaele
     Lombardi Satriani

If literature is a window to the soul, then the Tuscan soul undoubtedly lies in its stomach. How else to explain the fact that the majority of its tales and legends revolve around the glorification of food? Take *Fiabe e Novelle* (Letterio di Francia, 1929), a classic collection of fables whose characters are frequently granted magical powers. In Disney, Grimm, or Hans Christian Andersen, the characters might then use those powers to conjure up wealth, or possessions, or at the very least, a magnificent lover. But in *Fiabe*, the characters' first choice is always food. In one story, for example, a boy finds a talking chestnut that tells him he can have whatever his heart desires. His choice? A heaping plate of *tagliatelle con funghi* (tagliatelle with mushrooms). In another story, two children manage to find the magic red road which, when stepped on, grants them anything they can imagine. Their first wish? A cauldron of *minestrone di salsiccia e fagioli* (sausage and red bean soup).

Then there's Quaddarineju, the title character of "L'Eroe," a story featured in *Racconti Popolari*. Quaddarineju kills a dragon and liberates the daughter of the king, who has been imprisoned for seven years. "The dragon is dead," he tells her. "But before dying, he prepared a magnificent feast to celebrate the seventh anniversary of your capture. I can take you immediately home to your father, or if you prefer, you can sit down at the table and partake first of this great feast." She, naturally, opts for the feast.

As the Tuscan proverb says, *Corpo pieno, anima consolata.* Full stomach, placid heart.

But food is more than a virtue in and of itself; it is also the central cog around which the Tuscan family revolves. Throughout Tuscany, nothing preempts *il pranzo* and *la cena* which—more than being sumptuous opportunities to partake of freshly prepared multi-course meals—are times for families to come together around the table and talk about the day's events in a leisurely, uninterrupted manner (phone calls are not an issue, since everyone else is engaged in precisely the same ritual).

The atmosphere is celebratory and the food superb in a manner befitting an event of great importance. There are no recycled leftovers at the typical Tuscan table, no shortcuts or quick-and-easy efforts. Every meal is a feast, the participants united in a tradition that is as unique as it is commonplace. "Mealtimes are like foundation stones," a Tuscan friend once told me. "Our lives are built around them, and our security depends on their existence. Whatever strength we have as individuals comes from the fact that, no matter what happens, we will, every day, sit down at the table with a group of people who love us unconditionally and will always be there. And then, of course, there's the food!"

As central to everyday life as is the daily meal, however, the ritual of eating together reaches its apex in the tradition of picnics—a tradition that, come springtime, supplants even politics in popularity. There are few things as certain in life as that the Sunday after the first wild asparagus sprouts from the earth, families from every part of Tuscany will pack into the car and head for their favorite outdoor spot.

Tuscans plain and simply love to eat outdoors. "Food is better when perfumed with the fragrance of a fresh open field," my aunt Emma used to say.

However, lest you conjure up images of sandwiches wrapped in foil and paper plates tossed onto hastily spread plastic cloths, let me be clear that Tuscan picnics sacrifice neither comfort nor gastronomic opulence. When Tuscans embark on a picnic, they do so complete with linen tablecloths, china place settings, and a dazzling array of foods, including appetizers, first courses, entrées, cheeses, fruits, desserts, thermos-packed espresso, and, of course, copious amounts of wine. And, unlike the Romans who ate lying down in all manner of swaddling undress, Tuscans sit at proper tables with proper chairs and in proper clothes.

Today is the last Sunday of April, the first Sunday when the weather is warm enough to spend the entire afternoon outdoors without a sweater. It is obviously a perfect day for a picnic, and a picnic is exactly what we have planned— 16 of us: aunts, uncles, nephews, nieces, and even two little Russian boys from Chernobyl who are living with my cousins Mauro and Renza for six weeks as part of a host program for victims of radiation. The picnic took two days to coordinate, two days of intense telephone discussion as to whether, in addition to the appetizer and entrée, we should have two first courses or only the fresh fava bean soup I agreed to make.

"Soup is not enough," said my aunt Elisa when she learned there was to be no pasta. My mother agreed with her sister. "Let's also have *taglierini con asparagi*," she suggested. My flamboyant cousin Mauro said maybe it would be good to add a fish entrée, and my Buddhist cousin, Reno, said that the argument highlighted one of the basic problems of our time: people's inability to be happy with little. The issue was ultimately resolved by my uncle Piero, who, as cousin Mauro later recounted, insisted the soup stand alone by virtue of the fact that my "American delicacies" might otherwise be offended.

The site for our event is slightly out of the ordinary and a bit disheveled in appearance, although with stunning views of the surrounding hills. The property belongs to my cousin Reno and his girlfriend, Allesandra, who are, together, restructuring the old stone house that stands at its center. Most of the actual grunt work falls to three young Poles who Reno met while walking on the beach a few months back. Apparently, Poland's rate of unemployment has recently reached an all-time high, and the men decided finally to seek their fortune elsewhere.

The land itself encompasses ten acres of woods and open fields and snuggles into the countryside surrounding Camaiore. Finding it is a fairly impossible task, as I discovered after the person driving the car in front of me (who I assumed to be Mauro, since he had offered to serve as my guide) turned out to be the village baker who was slightly puzzled when I, too, pulled into his driveway. In trying to retrace my steps, I stopped two different men to ask the way to Marignane and, each time, was greeted with what I have come to realize is a standard Tuscan preview to the actual giving of the directions. *"O Mamma!"* they say with great drama. "You have made a terrible mistake." No matter whether you are ten miles off track or simply a block away.

Mauro eventually came back for me, and we got to Marignane just as Reno was finishing up his guided tour of the property's borders. *"Ringrazia Dio!"* my mother said when she saw me coming through the open field. Thank God. Apparently there had been a great deal of worry over the fact that I was lost and it was almost time for lunch.

Allesandra takes me on my own private tour of the land, pointing out grape vines, the fig and hazelnut trees, and—her crowning achievement—the beginnings of a vegetable garden. Returning to the house, she and I place the table under a pergola covered with newly sprouting wisteria vines. *"Guarda di preparare una bella tavola,"* my aunt Elisa warns as Allesandra and I commence setting the table. Make sure you make it look good. As it turns out, the arrangement does not pass muster, neither of us having had the foresight to bring a tablecloth large enough for the oversize table. "We'll put these two white ones together, and no one will ever know," Allesandra ventures. But she is wrong. And except for

Marco, my cousin Daniela's boyfriend, who is so besotted with his *innamorata* that he wouldn't notice if we ate on bare stone, everyone subsequently comments on the *grande pasticcio.*

Our idyllic lunch begins with a wonderful platter of marinated vegetables — eggplant batons, cauliflower florets, sliced *porcini* mushrooms, julienned carrots, baby fennel, tiny white onions — and leisurely moves to the soup course, served over garlic-rubbed bread and topped with a sprinkling of lemon and parsley *gremolata.* "*Chi la fatta questa zuppa?*" (Who made this soup?) teases my cousin Mauro who maintains that, as the owner of a cooking school, I no longer cook; I merely crack my whip and my cooking school students do all the work.

From there we move on to grilled chicken breasts served with perfectly sautéed broccoli rabe and gorgeous oven-roasted beets. Then we take a little respite with some fruit and cheese before embarking on the dessert course which is, even by Tuscan standards, an embarrassment of riches. Despite the aforementioned surfeit of telephone planning, everyone, it seems, has brought their own favorite *dolce.* There is my aunt Elisa's famous yogurt cake, Daniela's chocolate-and-rice tarts, Mauro's *zuppa inglese* (pastry layered with cream), and some incredible marzipan cookies which Allesandra attributes to a recipe in Pellegrino Artusi's *The Science of Cooking.*

"I just bought the new version," she announces, referring to the fact that the book, considered to be Italy's cooking bible, was recently updated after 95 years of continuous publication in its original form.

She reaches under the table and pulls two large volumes from her bag. "I bought one for you, too," she says, handing my copy across the table. "It's written in Italian, but some of your students might enjoy looking through it."

The Science of Cooking — or simply Artusi, as it is more popularly known — was first published in 1891. Its fame was so immediate and so widespread that, by the time Artusi died twenty years later, the book had sold almost 60,000 copies, and he and all his relatives had become very rich people. A collection of 781 recipes written in highly specific — and personal — detail, the book established Artusi as Italy's Julia Child and, like Child's *Mastering the Art of French Cooking,* codified the basic rules of Italian cooking.

"Thank you," I say, opening the book to its introductory chapter which gives Artusi's views on the importance of food.

"There are two principal functions in life," I begin reading out loud. "Eating and propagating. And while human beings can certainly live blind and deaf, unless they satisfy their senses of taste and touch, the human race will die out. But in spite of this fact, we seem to place more importance on the things that satisfy sight and hearing—art and music, for example—than we do on eating. Why is he who appreciates a beautiful painting or a perfectly conducted symphony considered superior to he who appreciates a wonderful meal? Unfortunately for us, we live in a time when intellect exerts a tyrannical reign over the body. Perhaps we should return in spirit to the era of Menenius Agrippa, when the stomach dominated all other considerations. Let us, hence, no longer be ashamed of eating well, and let us move hastily towards a time when a discussion on the merits of cooking eel garners the same praise as a dissertation on Beatrice's smile."

When I have finished my reading, Reno lifts his glass in a celebratory *cin cin*. *"Detto benissimo,"* he toasts. Wisely spoken. He pours a healthy dollop of wine into everyone's glass, and we laugh over the wisdom of Artusi's pronouncements while adding our own individual thoughts on the joy of eating well. But out of the corner of my eye, I see Mauro ruminating darkly. *"Che c'e?"* I query. What's going on?

"Niente," he replies, but in the next minute he is jumping up from the table and striding around to where my book lies next to the dwindling plate of cookies. "Who *needs* Artusi?" he poses in an accusatory voice. "Certainly no one at this table." He taps his finger on the book's cover. "Frankly, I've never understood why *anybody* would spend money on a book like that."

We fall momentarily silent, wondering what will come next.

"A cookbook with unusual recipes, *si*," he continues. "But this is the way everybody cooks. Why do we need a book to tell us how to do it?"

"Well, perhaps everybody doesn't cook as *well* as you do," I submit in a coy, teasing voice.

"It's not whether they cook well or don't cook well," he retorts. "It's the point of having our cuisine codified in a book whose very popularity lies in the fact of its codification. People buy that book because Artusi is supposedly the undisputed arbiter of what precise ingredients go into a tomato *ragu*. It doesn't matter that everybody makes tomato *ragu* differently and each person loves the way they make it above all."

"So what are you saying?" I ask. "That you object to people buying cookbooks unless they're really going to cook something from them?" He is obviously not yet aware of cookbooks as simply entertaining reading. "You may not know this," I offer, "but a great many people buy cookbooks—mine included—knowing in advance that they might only make one or two of the recipes. It doesn't matter. They just like reading them." I needn't have wasted my breath; he isn't even listening.

"You know," he propounds, "in France, the best food is in restaurants. Here, it's in the home. Do you know why?

"Because we don't restrict ourselves to set recipes," he answers before I have even had time to formulate a thought. "There is a certain passion that underlies Italian cooking, a passion whose foundation rests on individual initiative. No one here says, 'I must consult Artusi before making tomato *ragu*,' the way the French consult Escoffier or Americans consult Julia Child. We are, each of us, the best cook in the world."

"We are also the only people who spend so much time arguing over whose *ragu* is better," adds Allesandra, reentering the discussion she so innocently instigated.

"But that's precisely why we don't need Artusi," counters Mauro. "In France, there can be no argument. The best is Escoffier, or Careme, or Bocuse, or any of the other chefs elevated because of their ability to perfectly recreate the recipe as codified a hundred years ago."

"Like classical music," says Reno, coming to his brother's defense. "The best is the person who performs the symphony exactly as Beethoven wrote it. Our strength as Italians is that we are all a nation of individual John Coltranes."

"Exactly!" Mauro crows. "We don't need someone saying, 'This is the way you do it.' We all do it our own way, and our own way is best."

Allesandra is not conceding. "And what about those poor, unfortunate few who aren't as talented as you two obviously think yourselves to be?" she says smugly. "What about people who don't know how to cook? Is it all right for them to buy Artusi?"

"Like who?" says Reno with cocky certitude. "Tuscans have cooking in their genes."

"Like you," she replies, cuffing him playfully before turning back to Mauro. "I think you're creating fires out of flames," she tenders. "Furthermore, you should be ecstatic at the international attention focused on an Italian. Artusi may not be Garibaldi, but his book has certainly advanced the impression of Italy as a unified country with unified methodology."

"And that's good?" Mauro is now on his feet.

"Yes, it's good. It's also good that we have distinct regional differences, but, at a certain point, we need things that help define us first and foremost as Italian. Artusi's strength lies in having given us a nationally defined cuisine to complement our range of regional dishes."

"We are in perfect agreement that Artusi codified the Italian kitchen. Where we differ is in the value of that accomplishment. To you, national codification is a good thing; to me, it not only robs us of our individuality, but destroys the creative spark that infuses everyone's personal approach to a certain dish. Take my mother and my aunt as examples." He points to our two mothers, sitting side by side at one end of the table. "They grew up in the same house and have lived 5 kilometers apart for most of their adult lives. But *Zia's* recipe for *cacciucco di funghi* is completely different from my mother's. Although just as good." He sneaks a sideways glance at the two women to make sure his comments have not offended in any way. "Thank God they don't go by Artusi; for one thing, we wouldn't have the *cacciucco* in the first place, since it's a regionally created recipe."

Having been lured into the conversational arena, my aunt Elisa now moves front and center. *"Basta!"* she says, waving her arms. "You two have bickered enough and it is not good for the digestion." She cuts the two Russian boys another piece of yogurt cake. "I am reminded of Mussolini," she says, sitting back down with her own little slice. "The man would attend state dinners, sit down before great platters of food, and spend the entire time arguing instead of eating."

Her friend, Rita, latches on to this unexpected shift in topic. *"Un buongustaio Mussolini non era"* (A gourmet Mussolini was not), she says with great certainty. "The newspapers said he had liver problems and could only eat plain grilled meat. *Beh,* my daughter has liver problems, too, but she nonetheless manages to eat her daily plate of pasta. *No no no.* The truth is Il Duce was simply not a gourmet."

"Now the king . . . ," adds Elisa's husband, Piero, "the king is another story altogether." A painful expression crosses his face, and I can see we have moved definitively into a new topical realm. *"Povero* Vittorio Emanuele. What did he do that was so wrong he had to be exiled to Switzerland? Nothing!"

My mother shakes her head in shared sorrow. *"Povero* Vittorio Emanuele," she repeated with great feeling. *"There* was a man who appreciated good food. I remember once reading that his favorite meal consisted of *polenta con coniglio e rapini* (polenta with rabbit and broccoli rabe). A man of the people, our king." Her face darkens. "But in the end, he was outmaneuvered by Mussolini, as were we all."

"La sapete questa," says Piero, recalling a joke. Do you know this one? Without

Rita Selvamini: "The truth is, Il Duce was simply not a gourmet."

waiting for a reply, he launches into the story of the time Vittorio Emanuele and Queen Elena were dressing for an important ball. "As they were just about to descend the great staircase in Palazzo Chigi, the Queen noticed that the King's handkerchief was missing from his breast pocket. 'Where is your handkerchief?' Elena asked him. *Be*, Vittorio Emanuele looked at the front of his jacket and was about to start rummaging through the pocket in case the handkerchief had been somehow pushed to the bottom. Then he suddenly remembered. 'Ah, Mussolini had a cold, and I gave it to him,' he answered. The Queen threw up her hands in disgust. 'Cretino!' she cried. 'It was the only thing you had left in which you could still stick you nose!'"

We all laugh as Piero folds his hands in prayer and raises them up over his head. "Oh dear God, why did you take away our King and saddle us with these rogues?"

But now it is Daniela stepping in to change the conversational drift. "Enough talking about the King," she orders. "Right now Vittorio and his entire family are stretched out on the deck of their luxury yacht and floating around Lake Geneva. And I can guarantee you they are not thinking about us." She throws her arms around Marco's waist and nuzzles her lips into the crook of his neck. "Why don't you get out your guitar, and we'll put an end to this discussion of Artusi and Mussolini and our poor, sainted king? Let's sing!" And with that, Marco walks over to the pile of terra-cotta roof tiles against which he has laid his guitar and returns to the table, music books in hand.

"I brought these for you," he says, handing me the librettos. "So you don't have to scat your way through *Azzurro*." It is a popular joke in my family that I can never remember the words to anything.

We pass the rest of the afternoon huddled into a semicircle around Marco, crooning everything from *"Tu Voi Fa L'Americano"* (a wonderfully funny old Neapolitan song about a street boy who pretends to be an American) to "Hey Jude" (Marco's favorite music book is the *Antologia delle Canzone dei Beatles*). The best singer of the group is definitely Mauro (who is also the best dancer), although I am surprised by how good Reno is, Reno always having been darker and more brooding than the rest of the family. The two little Russians even wind up knowing one of the Beatles songs—"I Want To Hold Your Hand"—and sing it in their own language.

There is much laughing and teasing and arms around each other's shoulders, and, inevitably, I wonder why there seem to be more occasions like this in Tuscany than in New York. Is it just that families are more intact here? Is it the weather? The food? The sense that there is nothing more important than being with those who are close to you and having a good time—not even one's career?

When it is time to go, I nudge Mauro in the ribs and ask if he would like to borrow my copy of Artusi. His wife, Renza—who missed our earlier discussion because she was off showing the two Russian boys how to graft a fig tree—overhears my question but misses the accompanying tone of sarcasm.

"Thanks," she says pleasantly, "but we have our own."

"Oh *really?*" I say, hurrying after Mauro who is suddenly hustling the boys off to the car.

"Renza bought it last year," he throws back over his shoulder.

But his luck has apparently run out, because Renza fails to pick up anything amiss. "No, Mauro, you bought it yourself, remember? You picked it up at that book fair in Lucca."

And with that, Mauro clamps his hand over Renza's mouth and hurries her off to the car, singing in a loud voice, *"Tu voi fa l'Ameri-caaa-no, l'Ameri-caaa-no, L'Ameri-caaa-no. Ma tu vien da Napoli."*

About Broths, Oils, Dough, Sauces, and Pestos

Ninety percent of Tuscan cuisine revolves around a few basic preparations. Creating a broth. Preparing green sauce. Making pasta. Concocting a pesto. Infusing your own oils. No matter how innovative the dish or distinct the ingredients, the basics—and a cook's understanding of them—are the most important factors in making a dish turn out well. A full repertoire of basic variations also gives you the ability to alter or enhance a recipe at will. Roasted root vegetables can easily be transformed into linguine with roasted root vegetables; boiled cranberry beans become cranberry bean soup with lemon *gremolata*.

This chapter deals with the basic preparations underlying many of the recipes in this book. Placing it here at the end reflects my belief that the best way to learn anything is to ease into it effortlessly. By now you have made your way through leaves and stalks and roots and bulbs, and are presumably a master at not only making *fettucine con funghi* but at making the *fettucine* from scratch. Opening the book to the first chapter and finding a long narrative explaining how to make pasta might have seemed too daunting; now, it is an affirmation of how far you've come.

Broths

As mentioned in the opening chapter, I make broths in large quantities, freeze them in ice cube trays, and empty into bags labeled "Root Broth," "Tomato Broth," "Mushroom Broth," and so on. Whenever I need a tablespoon of broth, I simply reach into the right bag and pull out a cube.

Broths can be made from one strong-flavored vegetable, such as leeks, or a medley of ingredients, such as root vegetables and herbs. They can be very light, or reduced by boiling to a more concentrated flavor. They can serve as a soup all unto themselves (it is very wonderful to come home on a cold winter night and, before dinner, pop a few cubes into a saucepan to create an instant cup of soup) or create the underlying flavor in a sauté or risotto.

Do not limit yourself to the recipes that follow. Experiment with different possibilities. I almost always have a pot of broth on the stove into which I throw all my vegetable peelings—onion skins, tomato tops, carrot scrapings. I let it cook over low heat for a few hours, strain it through a sieve, cool, and into the ice cube trays it goes. Leftover broth can be reheated indefinitely as well as infinitely recombined with other vegetables to make new broth. Don't worry about peeling, coring, or seeding the vegetables. All broths are sieved in the end anyway, and the more you put in, the more flavor you get. For best results, use organic vegetables and filtered water.

Brodo di Verdura
Basic Vegetable Broth

3 tablespoons extra-virgin olive oil
1 medium onion
1 carrot
1 stalk celery
2 onions
2 leeks, cleaned and halved
1 turnip, chopped

1 cup fresh chopped parsley leaves
  (discard stems)
1 bay leaf
8 whole peppercorns
1 teaspoon salt
2 quarts water

1. Place the oil in a large, heavy-gauge soup pot. Sauté the onion, carrot, and celery for 7 minutes over low heat or until soft. Add the remainder of the ingredients and bring to a boil over medium-high heat.

2. Reduce the heat to low, cover, and simmer for 2 hours. Taste for salt, adding more if necessary.

3. Remove from heat and strain through a fine-mesh sieve. Cool to room temperature and store in the refrigerator or freeze.

MAKES ABOUT 1½ QUARTS

VARIATIONS: For a lighter taste, eliminate the initial sauté, place all the ingredients into the pot cold, and proceed from Step 2.

Brodo Invernale
Basic Root Vegetable Broth

3 tablespoons extra-virgin olive oil
1 medium onion
1 carrot
1 stalk celery
2 rutabagas, chopped
1 parsnip, chopped
2 beets, chopped
10 leaves kale, roughly chopped

2 carrots, cut into 3 sections
2 large onions, halved
1 cup fresh chopped parsley, stems
  discarded
½ cup chopped fennel fronds
2 quarts water
1 bay leaf
1 teaspoon salt
8 whole peppercorns

1. Heat the oil in a large, heavy-gauge soup pot. Sauté the onion, carrot, and celery for 7 minutes over low heat or until soft.

2. Add the other ingredients. Cover and bring to a boil over medium-high heat. Reduce the heat to low and simmer for 2 hours. Remove from heat, strain through a fine-mesh sieve. Cool to room temperature and store in the refrigerator or freezer.

MAKES ABOUT 1½ QUARTS

VARIATIONS: Can also be made without the initial sauté. Add all ingredients to the soup pot and proceed as per Step 2.

Allesandra takes me on my own private tour of the land.

Brodo di Funghi
Basic Mushroom Broth

2 ounces dried *porcini* mushrooms
½ pound fresh wild mushrooms (*porcini*, chanterelles, *shiitake*, morels), coarsely chopped
3 carrots, cut into chunks
2 onions, halved

1 large celery stalk, cut into thirds
1 bay leaf
2 cloves
2 quarts water
1 teaspoon salt
10 whole peppercorns

1. Place all ingredients in a large, heavy-gauge soup pot. Cover and bring to a boil over medium-high heat. Reduce the heat to low and simmer for 2 hours.

2. Strain through a fine-mesh sieve, cool to room temperature, and store in refrigerator or freeze.

MAKES ABOUT 1½ QUARTS

Brodo di Pomodori
Basic Tomato Broth

3 tablespoons extra-virgin olive oil
1 medium onion, chopped
5 cloves garlic, minced
4 pounds very ripe tomatoes,
    coarsely chopped

8 leaves fresh basil
1 teaspoon salt
5 whole peppercorns
1½ quarts water

1. Heat the oil in a heavy-gauge soup pot. Sauté the onion and garlic over low heat for 7 minutes or until soft.

2. Meanwhile, force the tomatoes through a food mill and add the puree to the pot. Add the remaining ingredients, cover, and bring to a boil over medium-high heat. Reduce the heat to low and simmer for 1 hour.

3. Strain through a fine-mesh sieve, cool to room temperature, and store in the refrigerator or freeze.

MAKES ABOUT 1 QUART

A view of Corsanico from Aldo's vineyard: "Where have you ever seen a piece of land more spectacular than mine?"

Oils

In addition to oils made from olives, nuts, seeds, and vegetables (discussed at length in Chapter 1, pages 11 to 14), you can also make a series of aromatically infused oils to use for seasoning various types of food. Flavored oil can be infused with herbs, citrus peels, peppers, and spices. Generally, I use virgin olive oil as my base—extra-virgin has too strong a taste and overwhelms the infusion.

One caution: when making aromatic oils, avoid adding fresh elements (sprigs of herbs, chili peppers) at the end for decoration. They add little to an already infused liquid, and you run the risk of either contaminating the oil or hastening its rancidity. In any case, infused oils have a very short life and should be used within 2 or 3 weeks.

Olio Aromatico
Infused Oil

The preparation for each of the following oils is the same:

1. Warm 2 cups oil over low heat.

2. Place the aromatic agent in a glass jar. Pour in the oil, seal, and steep for 2 weeks in a warm spot (the kind of warm spot you might use for raising bread).

3. Strain through a fine-mesh sieve, place in a bottle, and seal.

VARIATIONS:

Olio di Rosmarino (Rosemary Oil): Use 6 tablespoons fresh rosemary leaves, thoroughly washed and completely dried.

Olio Piccante (Chili Oil): Use 16 fresh or dried chilis, rinsed and thoroughly dried.

Olio di Basilico (Basil Oil): Use 1 cup fresh basil leaves, rinsed, thoroughly dried, and chopped.

Olio di Cedro (Citrus Oil): Use 8 whole peppercorns and 1 cup mixed lemon, orange, and lime peels, rinsed and thoroughly dried.

Olio di Pomodori Secchi (Sun-Dried Tomato Oil): Use 1 cup sun-dried tomatoes, 4 whole peppercorns, and 1 sprig fresh thyme, thoroughly washed and dried.

Dough

Let's start with an affirmation: pasta-making is easy and fun. Say it three times, and you'll be ready to go. By the time you've finished making your first batch, you'll realize I was right and that the only thing you were fearing was fear itself.

There are two basic kinds of fresh pasta: the northern Italian version made with all-purpose flour and eggs, and the southern Italian kind made with semolina and water. Both can be made completely by hand, but I generally use an old hand-cranked pasta machine (see Chapter 1, page 9 for more information on pasta machines).

The most important ingredient is, obviously, flour—in this case, wheat flour, whose character is classified as either soft or hard depending on the texture of the wheat kernel. Harder wheats have more gluten and are used for sturdy yeast breads; softer wheats, for cakes and biscuits. All-purpose unbleached flour is a compromise between hard and soft and, as such, a perfect choice for pasta-making, with just enough gluten but still retaining its tender, soft texture. Make sure to always choose "unbleached" flour which retains more of a wheaty flavor than its bleached cousin, not to mention more vitamins and a higher level of gluten.

All-purpose flour alone is a little too weak to stand up to boiling, however, so, in addition to two parts all-purpose, I always add one part semolina which is a coarse flour made from durum wheat, the hardest of all wheats with the highest amount of gluten (*durum* is a Latin word for "hard").

Basic Pasta Dough

1 cup semolina	4 eggs
2 cups all-purpose unbleached flour	1 teaspoon extra-virgin olive oil
	½ teaspoon salt

1. Blend the two flours in a bowl and place in a heap on a flat surface. Using your fingers, make a well in the center. Beat the eggs, oil, and salt in a bowl and pour them into the well. With a fork, slowly incorporate small portions of the wall, being careful not to break through. Once you have incorporated all of the wall and formed a thick paste, roll it into a ball and place on a floured surface for kneading.

2. Knead the ball for about a minute or until you have a smooth, elastic dough. Divide the ball into four pieces and wrap each in plastic.

3. Set your pasta machine on the widest opening (generally 1). Unwrap one of the four balls and flatten with your hand. This makes it easier to fit into the pasta machine. Dust it with flour and sprinkle additional flour on the rollers.

4. Pass the dough through the rollers, feeding it with one hand and cranking with the other. The first pass will produce a very rough dough that is somewhat uneven in color.

5. Fold the dough into thirds and pass again through the rollers, lengthwise. Repeat once more.

6. Now set the rollers to the next-thinner size and roll again. Make sure to support the pasta with one hand as you feed it through the machine with the other. At this point, the pasta will be smoother and more velvety, with a homogenized color and texture.

7. Keep setting the rollers to the next-thinner size and passing the dough through. With one hand cranking and one gently pulling, extrude the dough (this is where friends come in handy) until it becomes too long to handle. Cut into about 1-foot lengths and keep rolling each piece until you are down to the thinnest setting (generally 5 or 6).

8. Now you are ready to cut. Pasta machines generally offer two alternatives: spaghetti or fettucine. If you want any other cut or if you're making ravioli or *tortelli*, you can either do it by hand or buy a special attachment. Feed each piece through the cutting rollers, dust lightly with flour, and place in loosely twirled "nests." Leave the nests uncovered to dry for about 5 minutes. This allows the flour to absorb some of the moisture and the pasta to firm up sightly before cooking.

9. If you are not cooking the pasta within the next two hours, store the dried nests in plastic bags and refrigerate for up to 48 hours. Past that, plan on freezing.

SERVES 4

Colored Pasta

Once you have mastered the basics of plain pasta, you can inject some color by simply adding a coloring agent to the eggs and mixing as you would normally. Coloring agents add a great deal of visual interest, although they change the basic flavor very little. The amount of coloring you add is based on the number of eggs used.

For a rich orange pasta, add 1 tablespoon tomato paste per egg.

For a speckled green color, add 4 ounces pureed fresh spinach per egg (2 ounces pureed frozen).

For pasta that is deep red, add 1 tablespoon mashed beet per egg.

For a deep yellow color, add 4 threads of saffron to the eggs and let sit for 10 minutes.

Basic Pizza Dough

I have never been able to understand why so many people think making pizza is difficult. The dough takes about 10 minutes of actual work, an hour or two to rise, and 10 minutes to cook in a 500-degree oven. And there is no comparison between homemade pizza and store-bought; for one thing, you can add whatever topping you like.

The best way to cook pizza (apart from owning your own stone oven) is on a stone specially made for that purpose and in an oven preheated to 500 degrees. Make sure to drizzle the top of the pizza with abundant olive oil and, if you're adding cheese, do so during the last 5 minutes of cooking.

1 teaspoon active dry yeast	2 tablespoons extra-virgin olive oil
4 cups unbleached all-purpose flour	½ teaspoon salt

1. Dissolve the yeast in ½ cup of warm water. Place the cup in a larger bowl of hot water and let sit for 10 minutes or until the yeast is foamy.

2. Pour the flour into a large bowl and add the yeast, oil, salt, and ¾ cup warm water. Stir with a fork until you have a thick dough that does not stick to the sides of the bowl.

3. Turn the dough out onto a floured surface and, with floured hands, knead energetically for 7 to 8 minutes. If necessary, add more flour. When done, the dough should be smooth and dry. Grease a bowl with olive oil and add the dough. Cover with a damp cloth and let rise until doubled, about 1 hour.

MAKES A 16-INCH-DIAMETER PIZZA

Picnicking in Marignane, food is better when perfumed with the fragrance of a fresh open field.

Sauces

Sauces are the backbone of an effective and innovative kitchen. Basic herb polenta, an appealing dish in its own right, becomes an entree worthy of gushing praise when drizzled with rosemary oil and topped with smoked tomato sauce; a simple dish of baked zucchini and tomatoes achieves masterpiece status when served with savory *acciugata* (anchovy, caper, and parsley sauce).

Although Tuscan cuisine encompasses literally hundreds of sauce variations, I have included only those that pair well with vegetables. All can be prepared in advance, and, except for *agliata* and *besciamella*, all can be frozen. I have deliberately avoided a discussion of which sauce goes best with which vegetables; each of the sauces listed work well with a myriad of vegetables.

Acciugata
Anchovy, Caper, and Parsley Sauce

½ cup extra-virgin olive oil

2 cloves garlic, crushed

3 tablespoons anchovy paste, or 6 anchovy filets, minced

3 tablespoons capers, drained and minced

2 tablespoons fresh chopped parsley (stems discarded)

1. Heat the oil in a skillet. Sauté the garlic over low heat for 3 minutes. Remove and discard.

2. Whisk in the anchovy paste and cook 3 minutes, whisking constantly. Stir in the capers and parsley and mix well. Remove from heat and serve hot.

MAKES ABOUT 1 CUP

Salsa di Funghi con Vino Rosso
Red Wine and Wild Mushroom Sauce

3 tablespoons extra-virgin olive oil
1 clove garlic, minced
1½ pounds assorted wild
    mushrooms (*porcini*,
    chanterelles, morels, black
    trumpets), cleaned and thinly
sliced (stems reserved for
    another use)
1 cup dry red wine
1 teaspoon chopped fresh thyme
Salt and freshly ground black
    pepper

1. Heat the oil in a skillet. Sauté the garlic over low heat for 3 minutes. Increase the heat to high. Add the mushrooms and cook, stirring constantly, for 3–5 minutes or until the mushrooms are just beginning to give up their liquid.

2. Pour the wine over the mushrooms and evaporate. Reduce the heat to medium. Add the thyme and cook for 5 minutes, stirring occasionally. Season with salt and pepper.

MAKES ABOUT 1½ CUPS

Salsa Cruda
Raw Tomato Sauce

1 pound very ripe tomatoes (not
    plum), peeled and seeded
3 shallots, peeled and minced
Salt to taste
3 tablespoons extra-virgin olive oil

1. Using a sharp knife, chop the tomatoes very fine. Add the shallots and salt and oil to taste. Mix well.

MAKES ABOUT 2 CUPS

VARIATIONS: Add additional ingredients—crushed garlic, chopped basil or other fresh herbs, lemon zest, or vinegar—as determined by the dish to be sauced.

Pomarola
Fresh Tomato Sauce

2 pounds very ripe Italian plum
    tomatoes, peeled, seeded, and
    roughly chopped
5 leaves fresh basil

4 tablespoons extra-virgin olive oil
Salt and freshly ground black
    pepper

1. Place the tomatoes and basil in a nonreactive pot. Cook over low heat for 30 minutes or until the juices have evaporated and the sauce is somewhat thickened.

2. Add the oil and mix well. Season with salt and pepper.

MAKES ABOUT 1½ CUPS

Pomarola Affumicata
Smoked Tomato Sauce

Wood chips soaked in water
2 tablespoons extra-virgin olive oil,
    plus oil for brushing the grill
2 pounds Italian plum tomatoes

2 cloves garlic, crushed
4 basil leaves, chopped
Salt and freshly ground black
    pepper

1. Prepare the fire at least 1½ hours before smoking the tomatoes. When the fire has died down to white ash, sprinkle the chips over the coals. Brush the grill with oil and set over the coals. At this point, the fire should not be hot enough to cook but merely to smoke.

2. Set the tomatoes on the grill. If you are using a commercial smoker, cover the smoker, leaving the vent just slightly open. If you are smoking on a covered barbecue, close the cover as well as any side vents. Smoke the tomatoes for 1 hour. When done, they will be slightly shrivelled, and the skins will be split. Transfer the tomatoes to a bowl and cool to room temperature.

3. Remove and discard the skins, cores, and seeds but reserve any juices. Pass the pulp and juices through a food mill.

4. Heat the oil in a skillet. Sauté the garlic for 3 minutes over low heat. Add the tomatoes and basil and simmer for 15 minutes. Season with salt and pepper.

MAKES ABOUT 2 CUPS

Agliata
Garlic and Bread Sauce

4 slices day-old peasant bread,
   roughly chopped
¼ cup red wine vinegar
2 tablespoons dry red wine

4 cloves garlic, peeled
½ teaspoon salt
1½ cups extra-virgin olive oil

1. Soak the bread in a mixture of vinegar and wine until soft, about 5 minutes. Squeeze dry and place in the bowl of a food processor with the garlic and salt.

2. With the motor running, pour the olive oil through the feeder tube in a steady stream. Continue adding oil until the mixture is dense and creamy.

MAKES ABOUT 2 CUPS

Salsa Verde
Basic Green Sauce

1 tablespoon fresh chopped parsley
   (stems discarded)
2 tablespoons capers, drained and
   chopped
3 gherkin pickles, chopped
1 small dried chili pepper, crushed
1 very small boiled potato, peeled
   and mashed

¼ clove garlic, minced
¼ small onion, grated
2 tablespoons extra-virgin olive oil
Salt and freshly ground black
   pepper
1 tablespoon red wine vinegar

1. Combine all ingredients except the vinegar in a large bowl and beat by hand for 5 minutes. Stir in the vinegar and mix well.

MAKES ABOUT ¾ CUP

Besciamella per Verdura
Basic White Sauce for Vegetables

½ cup unsalted butter
2 tablespoons unbleached
   all-purpose flour
1 cup milk

½ cup white wine vinegar
4 whole peppercorns
2 tablespoons heavy cream

1. Melt half the butter in a small saucepan. Whisk in the flour, slowly add the milk, and cook over low heat, whisking constantly until slightly thickened. Remove from heat and keep warm.

2. Place the vinegar and peppercorns in another small saucepan and boil gently until reduced by half. Strain through a sieve and add to the white sauce. Add the remaining butter a little at a time, whisking constantly.

3. Add the cream and whisk until all ingredients are well blended.

MAKES ABOUT 1½ CUPS

Salsa di Limone
Lemon and Garlic Sauce

3 tablespoons extra-virgin olive oil
3 cloves garlic, crushed
1 cup Basic Vegetable Broth (see page 308)
¼ cup fresh lemon juice

Zest of 1 lemon
¼ teaspoon salt
¼ teaspoon freshly ground white pepper
1 cup fresh chopped parsley (stems discarded)

1. Place the oil in a small skillet. Sauté the garlic over low heat for 10 minutes, stirring frequently. Increase the heat to medium, add the broth, and reduce by half.

2. Add the lemon juice, zest, salt, and pepper. Cook for 3 minutes, stirring constantly.

3. Meanwhile, place the parsley in the bowl of a food processor and puree until smooth. Stir the puree into the lemon sauce and cook for 3 minutes, until well blended.

MAKES ABOUT 1 CUP

The best singer in the group is definitely Mauro, although I am surprised by how good Reno is.

Pestos

Pesto means "pounded," which was how all pestos were once made: by hand, the leaves crushed in a mortar and pestle or pounded with a cleaver on a cutting board, a little at a time, until the herb or vegetable was reduced to a thick paste. The best pestos are still made this way, but most are pureed in a food processor.

This chapter presents a variety of pestos, by which I intend the term's original definition of mixtures pounded or chopped by hand. In general, Tuscans divide these chopped mixtures into three categories:

Battuto: A raw blend of finely chopped vegetables sautéed in extra-virgin olive oil over low heat until the flavors meld into an aromatic foundation. This foundation then flavors whatever ingredients are subsequently added—a process known as *insaporire* or "giving flavor to." *Battutos* always include at least onions, carrots, and celery; in many cases, parsley and/or leeks and/or garlic are also added. But whatever the initial blend, the ingredients are isolated in an initial sauté so that their melded flavor can permeate the rest of the dish.

Pesto: A finely chopped blend of raw vegetables, finely minced garlic, extra-virgin oil, sometimes nuts, and sometimes grated cheese. Pestos are generally used as toppings for pasta, pizza, polenta, and raw or cooked vegetables. They can also be stirred into soups or added to a vinaigrette. The most famous pesto is made from basil, garlic, pine nuts, and Parmesan cheese. The following pages present a number of equally delicious variations.

Gremolatas: A type of pesto but with lemon zest and sometimes lemon juice added. Like pestos, *gremolatas* can be used as a topping for pasta, pizza, polenta, or vegetables or as a savory addition to soups and salads.

Piero Selvamini: "Povero Vittorio Emanuele, what did he do that was so wrong he had to be exiled to Switzerland?"

Gremolata di Prezzemolo e Noce
Parsley, Walnut, and Lemon Zest Gremolata

Perfect stirred into soups or sprinkled over steamed vegetables. To use as a topping for pizza or pasta, blend with 5 tablespoons extra-virgin oil.

1 cup packed parsley leaves (discard stems)	Juice of ½ lemon
¼ cup walnut pieces, finely minced	¼ teaspoon salt
½ teaspoon lemon zest	⅛ teaspoon freshly ground black pepper

1. Mince the parsley until paste-like. Add the remainder of the ingredients and stir until well blended. The *gremolata* will be quite dry and have the consistency of finely chopped herbs.

MAKES ABOUT ¼ CUP

Gremolata di Aglio, Noce e Crema
Garlic, Pine Nut, and Cream Gremolata

This creamy gremolata makes a perfect last-minute addition to lentil soups or root vegetable stews. Try it as a topping for fried polenta wedges or on hot focaccia.

1 clove garlic, peeled	¼ teaspoon lemon zest
¼ cup pine nuts, toasted	½ cup heavy cream
¼ teaspoon coarse salt	

1. Place the garlic, nuts, and salt in a mortar. Crush with the pestle into a grainy paste. Add the zest and cream and continue to mash until thick and smooth.

MAKES ABOUT ¾ CUP

Pesto di Piscialetto
Dandelion Pesto

½ pound dandelion leaves, washed
and with stems discarded
½ pound cream cheese at room
temperature
1 clove garlic

¼ teaspoon freshly ground white
pepper
1 teaspoon anchovy paste, or
1 anchovy filet, minced

1. Place all ingredients in a food processor and puree until smooth.

MAKES ABOUT 1 CUP

Pesto di Prezzemolo
Parsley Pesto

1 cup fresh parsley leaves, stems
discarded

½ teaspoon coarse salt
½ cup extra-virgin oil

1. Place the parsley and salt in the bowl of a food processor. With the motor running, gradually add oil through the feeder tube. Puree until smooth.

MAKES ABOUT ¾ CUP

*Mauro: "Who needs Artusi? Certainly
no one at this table!"*

Pesto di Olive Nere
Black Olive Pesto

1 cup pitted Gaeta or other black
   olives
½ cup basil leaves

1 garlic clove, peeled
1 tablespoon fresh rosemary leaves
½ cup extra-virgin olive oil

1. Place the olives, basil, garlic, and rosemary in the bowl of a food processor. With the motor running, gradually add oil through the feeder tube. Puree until smooth.

MAKES ABOUT 1½ CUPS

Pesto di Arugula e Crescione
Arugula and Watercress Pesto

1 cup arugula leaves, stems
   discarded
1 cup watercress leaves, stems
   discarded
2 cloves garlic, peeled

½ teaspoon coarse salt
⅛ teaspoon freshly ground black
   pepper
½ cup roasted red peppers packed
   in oil, drained
½ cup extra-virgin olive oil

1. Place the arugula, watercress, garlic, salt, pepper, and roasted peppers in a food processor. With the motor running, gradually add oil through the feeder tube. Puree until smooth.

MAKES ABOUT 1 CUP

Index

About the Author

ANNE BIANCHI is a food writer who divides her time between New York and the Tuscan province of Lucca, where she also runs a cooking school called Toscana Saporita. She has written a number of books, most recently *Zuppa! Soups from the Italian Countryside* and *From the Tables of Tuscan Women,* also published by Ecco.